CURRENT RESEARCH IN FILM:
Audiences, Economics, and Law

Volume 5

COMMUNICATION AND INFORMATION SCIENCE

Edited by
BRENDA DERVIN
The Ohio State University

Recent Titles

Laurien Alexandre • The Voice of America: From Detente to the Reagan Doctrine
Bruce Austin • Current Research in Film Volume 4
Barbara Bate & Anita Taylor • Women Communicating: Studies of Women's Talk
Donal Carbaugh • Talking American: Cultural Discourses on Donahue
Kathryn Carter & Carole Spitzack • Doing Research on Women's Communication: Perspectives on Theory and Method
Fred L. Casmir • Communication in Development
Gladys Ganley & Oswald Ganley • To Inform or to Control Revised Edition
Robert Goldman & Arvind Rajagopal • Mapping Hegemony: Television News Coverage of Industrial Conflict
Enrique Gonzalez-Manet • The Hidden War of Information
Karen Joy Greenberg • Conversations on Communications Ethics
Gary Gumpert & Sandra Fish • Talking to Strangers: Mediated Therapeutic Communication
Robert Jacobson • An "Open" Approach to Information Policymaking
Manfred Kochen • The Small World
John Lawrence and Bernard Timberg • Fair Use and Free Inquiry Second Edition
Sven B. Lundstedt • Telecommunications, Values, and the Public Interest
Thomas Mandeville • Understanding Novelty: Information Technological Changes and the Patent System
Richard Morris & Peter Ehrenhaus • Cultural Legacies of Vietnam: Uses of the Past in the Present
Susan B. Neuman • Literacy in the Television Age
Eli M. Noam, & Joel C. Millonzi • The International Market in Film and Television Programs
Eli M. Noam & Gerald Pogorel • Asymmetric Deregulation: The Dynamics of Telecommunication Policy
Gerald M. Phillips • Teaching How to Work in Groups
Carl Erik Rosengren & Sven Windahl • Media Matter: TV Use in Childhood and Adolescence
Michael Rogers Rubin • Private Rights, Public Wrongs: The Computer and Personal Privacy
Ramona R. Rush & Donna Allen • Communications at the Crossroads. The Gender Gap Connection
Majid Tehranian • Technologies of Power: Information Machines and Democratic Processes
Sari Thomas • Studies in Mass Media and Technology, Volumes 1–4
J. M. Wober • Fission and Diffusion: The Possibility of Public Power Over and Through the Machine

CURRENT RESEARCH IN FILM: Audiences, Economics, and Law

Volume 5

Bruce A. Austin, *Editor*
Rochester Institute of Technology

Ablex Publishing Corporation
Norwood, New Jersey 07648

Printed in the United States of America.

ISBN: 0-89391-552-1 ISSN: 0748-8580

Ablex Publishing Corporation
355 Chestnut Street
Norwood, New Jersey 07648

Contents

About the Contributors

Geoffrey H. Blowers, PhD, is Senior Lecturer in the Department of Psychology at the University of Hong Kong. His interests include the philosophical and historical bases of psychology and he has written on the history of psychology in Hong Kong. He has taught courses on psychology and the cinema and his recent research interests are in the perception of images, including film, using repertory grid for the analysis of viewer perception.

Leslie Midkiff DeBauche is an Assistant Professor in the Communications Division at the University of Wisconsin-Stevens Point. Her work has appeared in *Film Reader*, *Wide Angle*, and *The Velvet Light Trap*. She is currently at work on a history of film distribution.

Emily D. Edwards is a professor of Broadcasting/Cinema at the University of North Carolina, Greensboro, where she teaches introduction to graduate studies, television directing, media theory, broadcast news reporting, television programming, and production. She has a professional background in television news reporting and production with ABC and NBC affiliates in Alabama and Tennessee. She was formerly the Director of the Broadcasting Sequence for the Department of Communications at the University of Alabama at Birmingham. She received her PhD from the University of Tennessee, Knoxville in 1984.

Thomas Guback is Research Professor of Communications, Institute of Communications Research, University of Illinois, Urbana-Champaign. He has published numerous articles on the economic structure and policy of the filmed entertainment business. He also has been a consultant and expert witness for antitrust litigation in the motion picture industry.

Ian Jarvie was educated at London School of Economics in the 1950s, and teaches philosophy and the social study of film at York University in Toronto. His most recent books are *Thinking About Society: Theory and Practice*

(Reidel, 1986); *Philosophy of the Film: Epistemology, Ontology, Esthetics* (Routledge, 1987).

Robert E. Kapsis is Associate Professor in the Department of Sociology and in the Film Studies Program at Queens College of the City University of New York where he teaches courses in the sociology of film and mass communications. He is currently completing a study of how organizational and institutional factors shape both the production of Hollywood genre films and the reputations of filmmakers. His articles on film have appeared in *American Film*, *Cineaste*, *Journal of Popular Film and Television*, and in a recent anthology on the mass media.

Patricia A. Lawrence is a visiting instructor in the Department of Communication Studies at the University of Nevada, Las Vegas. She is currently investigating the links between psychophysiological arousal needs and motives for theatrical film consumption.

Philip Palmgreen is a Professor in the Department of Communication, University of Kentucky. He received his PhD in mass communication at the University of Michigan. He is primarily interested in audience uses of the mass media and theories of mass media consumption. He is author of "Uses and Gratifications: A Theoretical Perspective" in *Communication Yearbook 8*, and is coeditor, with Karl Erik Rosengren and Lawrence A. Wenner, of *Media Gratifications Research: Current Perspectives*.

Richard A. Parker is Associate Professor of Speech Communication in the School of Communication at Northern Arizona University. He holds a PhD in Speech from the University of Pittsburgh. He specializes in critical analysis of contemporary judicial opinions and of revisionist histories of the First Amendment.

Lorraine A. Vachon is a doctoral candidate in the Department of Communication Studies at the University of Iowa.

James B. Weaver, III (PhD, Indiana University, 1987) is an Associate Professor of Mass Communication in the Department of Speech Communication at Auburn University, AL, 36849-5211. His research interests include the social and psychological effects of mass communications, entertainment theory, and the uses of media messages.

Justin Wyatt completed his PhD in Film and Television Studies at UCLA. The majority of his work involves a critical examination of the economics and aesthetics of high concept, and a theorization of "post"-classical Hollywood style. Most recently he has published articles in *Wide Angle* and *The Southern Quarterly*.

Patricia R. Zimmermann is Associate Professor of Cinema and Photography, School of Communications, Ithaca College, Ithaca, NY. Her research on the social history of mass culture has appeared in *Screen*, *Wide Angle*, *Journal of Film and Video*, *Afterimage*, *Cinema Journal*, *Motion Picture*, and *Current Research in Film*.

Foreword

Publication of the fifth volume of Current Research in Film is for me a rewarding event. When I first proposed the series to Ablex I was, of course, convinced there was important and sufficient research on the three dimensions of motion pictures *CRF* selected as its editorial niche to warrant such a forum. While it is nice to have one's armchair speculation confirmed, the reward is much greater than that.

Volume Five demonstrates that scholarly research on movie audiences, economics, and law is a vital and necessary component of cinema studies/mass communications. Including the studies published in the present volume, *CRF* has offered 61 research reports authored by a total of 85 scholars. Especially pleasing is that over the course of five volumes a number of contributors have returned to *CRF* to offer readers continued and extended analyses of their specific subject matter.

The essays published in the present volume, once again, display the diversity of interests, theoretical and methodological approaches, and subject matter that typify the energy and enthusiasm of previous issues of *CRF*. In the Foreword to Volume One, I promised that *CRF* would offer innovative and important research on film audiences, economics, and law on an annual basis. Slight publication delays aside, I believe this promise has been kept. And there is every indication that this is only the beginning.

Bruce A. Austin
Rochester, New York
September, 1988

1

The Impact of Exposure to Horror Film Violence on Perceptions of Women: Is it the Violence or an Artifact?*

James B. Weaver, III

A considerable debate has evolved over the question of exactly what effects exposure to mass media depictions of human sexuality, and especially those presented as forms of entertainment (i.e., erotica and pornography), has on individuals and society. Initial reviews (e.g., 9) concluded that consumption of such materials had little, if any, impact on an individual's social or sexual perceptions and behaviors. Critics of such "all effects are trivial" conclusions were quite vocal (e.g., 3, 4, 10, 14, 16), however, and stimulated an active debate over the possible consequences of exposure to contemporary sexually explicit media images (cf. 51). For example, some advocates (cf. 41), echoing the predominant sentiment of the *Commission on Obscenity and Pornography* (9), contend that such materials perform a positive function serving as important educational and/or therapeutic tools that "celebrate sexual pleasure and sexual abandon" and help eradicate "puritanical attitudes about sex that have long dominated our society" (17, p. 32). Many analysts, however, have rejected the idea that viewing sexually explicit media depictions produces no discernible negative effects. Indeed, advocates representing a wide variety of social and political orientations (e.g., feminists, family, and community organizations) have condemned such materials, charging that they foster detrimental perceptions of female sexuality, a misogynous cultural climate, and promote inter-

* Partial funding for this project was provided by a University of Kentucky Summer Faculty Research Fellowship. An earlier version of this work was presented at the May 1988 meeting of the International Communication Association in New Orleans, LA. The comments of Dolf Zillmann on a preliminary draft of this chapter are greatly appreciated.

gender violence (e.g., 1, 22, 33). Additionally, the intensity of this debate has been amplified substantially by the recent broad diffusion of new entertainment technologies (such as, cable television and videocassettes) which has permitted the prolific distribution of sexually explicit materials throughout American society (cf. 51).

Against this backdrop several recent investigations examining the content features of contemporary sexually explicit materials have documented that the most consistently and persistently presented theme involves depictions of women as panting-playthings, actively soliciting participation in, and responding with hysterical euphoria to, any of a variety of sexual encounters. Palys (30; also see 31), for example, conducted an extensive content analysis of sexually explicit feature films available on videocassette and found that women were most often portrayed engaging in, and expressing "positive affect" toward, a variety of abusive, demeaning, and/or degrading (i.e., incest, anal intercourse, etc.) sexual activities. On the other hand, the expression of love or affection was evident in only a small proportion (3 percent) of the depictions. Presentations of sexual violence were even less frequent. Other research examining the content of the "hard-core" sexually explicit films (34) and magazines (40) reveals essentially the same pattern. As these findings illustrate, the "standard-fare" of contemporary sexually explicit materials typically portrays women as tolerating and/or enjoying abusive, demeaning, and degrading treatment as part of otherwise "normal" sexual activities; a portrayal that clearly could serve to compose a "dangerously distorted picture of female sexuality" (5, p. 34).

Consistent with other research and theorizing on mass media effects (e.g., 2, 6), the findings of a growing volume of research highlight the fact that exposure to such characterizations of human sexual behavior can occasion adverse perceptual, dispositional, and behavioral consequences. Zillmann and Bryant (45, 46), for example, recorded a variety of perceptual changes concerning female sexuality after subjects were repeatedly exposed to nonviolent pornography. These included the trivialization of rape as a criminal offense and increased sexual callousness toward women. Weaver (36) found that even brief exposure to sexually explicit materials strongly influenced perceptions of the "sexual receptivity" of otherwise sexually nonpermissive females. Weaver, Masland, and Zillmann (39; also see 20) found that subjects briefly exposed to sexually explicit pictures of beautiful nude females—such as those presented as "centerfold" models in *Playboy* and *Penthouse* magazines—indicated that their mates were less sexually attractive. Zillmann and Bryant (48, 50) reported that subjects who viewed nonviolent pornography in six consecutive weekly one-hour sessions, when compared to a control group, reported greater acceptance of sexual promiscuity and sexual infidelity and elevated discontent and distrust for several other sexual matters. Additionally, other research (e.g., 8, 23, 27, 35) indicates that exposure to "standard-fare" sexually explicit materials can promote a manipulative and, in some instances, aggressive orientation toward women. In sum, evidence from numerous investigations illustrates that even brief exposure to nonviolent, sexually explicit media presentations can yield pronounced adverse effects (cf. 1, 36, 51).

Despite the growing volume of empirical evidence, some advocates have argued that concern over the negative consequences of exposure to sexually explicit materials is ill-founded. In particular, Donnerstein and his associates contend that "standard-fare" sexually explicit materials do not foster negative attitudes or behavior unless they involve images of violence (cf. 13). Specifically, in what has been characterized as an attempt at "shifting blame" (49, p. 190), Donnerstein and Linz maintain that "the single most important problem in the media today, as clearly indicated by social science research, is not pornography but violence" (12, p. 56) and that "it must be concluded that violent images, rather than sexual ones, are most responsible for people's attitudes about women and rape" (12, p. 59).

From this perspective, Donnerstein and his associates have focused their attention on the possible deleterious consequences occasioned by exposure to contemporary "teen-age slasher" horror films (11, 13, 21, 24, 26). They propose that consumption of the graphic, gory portrayals of violence presented in modern horror—and, in particular, those depictions which involve the victimization of women—may foster and/or reinforce detrimental, malicious perceptions of women and encourage physically and sexually abusive treatment of women in daily life. Specifically, it has been hypothesized that generalized affective insensitivity or desensitization induced by repeated exposure to graphic horror films may "spill-over" into higher-order cognitions adversely influencing numerous perceptions of women and, in particular, perceptions of sexual assault victims (11, 13, 24, 26).

In order to test this "desensitization spill-over" proposition, Linz et al. (24, 26) exposed a small group of male subjects to a contemporary horror movie[1] daily for five consecutive days. Each day after viewing a film, subjects completed the Multiple Affect Adjective Checklist (MAAC; 53) and responded to a 16-item questionnaire on which they rated the sexual and violent content of the movie and their enjoyment. On the fifth day, immediately after viewing the film and completing the MAAC and film evaluation questionnaire items, the exposure treatment subjects were joined by another group of men who had experienced no other experimental treatment, viewed a videotaped mock-jury rape trial, and complete a questionnaire indicating their perceptions of the defendant and vic-

[1] Unfortunately, there is considerable confusion over the exact content attributes of films used in this research (see 1, pp. 1020–1021). In studies reported by Linz (24, 26), for example, commercially released "teen-age slasher" movies—including *Maniac* and *Texas Chainsaw Massacre*—were described as "R-rated, sexually violent films" (11, p. 14). In fact, however, *Maniac* was released with a "self-imposed" X-rating. *Texas Chainsaw Massacre*, on the other hand, is essentially devoid of any sexual content (38). Further, two films described by Linz (24) as sexually violent (i.e., *Toolbox Murders* and *Vice Squad*) were used elsewhere (21) to operationalize "violent" films. Clearly, the theoretical implications of these conceptual ambiguities must be considered.

tim. The findings revealed that the exposure treatment reduced self-perceptions of anxiety and depression. Some perceptions of the films were also altered between the first and fifth day exposure treatments. For example, subjects reported perceiving less violence and degradation of women. However, there were no differences in the reported level of sexual violence in the films or enjoyment. More important, subjects who participated in the five-day exposure treatment, compared with the no-treatment control group, perceived the rape victim as significantly less injured and less worthy. It should be recognized, however, that these between condition effects must be quite fragile since the authors found it necessary to employ pooled error terms derived from two additional exposure conditions that were otherwise disregarded as inconsistent with the "theoretical focus" of the study (24, 26; also see 25, 36, 49). Furthermore, the observed pattern of intercorrelations between the affective reactions to (i.e., anxiety and depression) and perceptions of the film content and dispositions toward the rape victim did not provide direct support to the proposed "desensitization spill-over" process. Thus, although significant differences in perceptions of the rape victim were evident between the exposure treatment and no-treatment control conditions, it is not clear which factors mediated this effect.

In a second study, Linz (24) modified the above protocol slightly to further explore the hypothesized process. Male subjects received essentially the same exposure treatment (that is, viewing a film and completing the MAAC and film evaluation questionnaires) in either two or five sessions held every other day. Two days after the final exposure treatment, subjects completed an extensive questionnaire involving numerous self-perceptions and viewed and responded to a mock-trial rape case. Surprisingly, no significant direct effects were found as a result of viewing the horror films. There was evidence, however, that the men involved in the more extensive exposure treatment tended to express less compassion for the rape victim. But, these subjects also expressed greater anxiety about their own personal vulnerability to criminal victimization (28). This latter consideration is, of course, quite inconsistent with the "desensitization spill-over" hypothesis.

Other recent research findings also appear contradictory to the proposed "desensitization spill-over" process. Krafka (21) found that female subjects failed to report reduced sensitivity to the violent content of contemporary horror films after repeated exposure. However, compared to a no exposure control group, women repeatedly exposed to horror did report significantly less concern and sympathy for a rape victim. Furthermore, adverse perceptions of sexual assault victims have been observed in circumstances where the exposure treatment would appear insufficient to induce affective desensitization (cf. 32). Weaver (36) found, for example, that even brief exposure (i.e., about 10–12 minutes) to scenes of eroticized violence taken from modern horror movies was, compared to viewing neutral materials, sufficient to significantly lower punitive judgments against a convicted rapist reported by both male and female subjects. Similarly, Wyer, Bodenhausen, and Gorman (42) found that extremely brief exposure to negative outcomes of aggression involving the victimization of males (for example, pictures showing a dead soldier and a lynching victim), compared with a neutral materials exposure condition, produced significantly greater attribution of responsibility to the female victims of rape among both male and female subjects. These and other findings (e.g., 19) suggest that cognitive mediators—in particular, cognitive biases resulting from the sensitization of individuals to the consequences of violence—may best account for the observed adverse perceptions of rape victims occasioned by exposure to contemporary horror films.

In sum, the range of evidence offers essentially no empirical support for the contention that exposure to horror films induces affective insensitivity that "spills-over" to adversely influence subsequent perceptions of women. Indeed, the findings of Linz et al. (24, 26) appear to present the only exception to this conclusion, raising serious questions about how the reported pattern of effects might best be explained.

Although a number of conditional explanations have been advanced (13, 24, 25, 26), one unexplored possibility is that the findings represent an experimental artifact (cf. 44, 49). Specifically, careful consideration of the procedures employed by Linz et al. (24, 26) suggests that experimenter demand characteristics (29)—initiated through repeated administration of reactive film evaluation measures that cued constructs associated with the sexual abuse and degradation of women—may offer a more parsimonious account for the initial findings. Indeed, even a cursory examination of the film evaluation questionnaire leaves little doubt of the experimenter's interest in the sexually violent aspects of the exposure materials. For example, in five of the sixteen film evaluation items subjects were asked: (a) "Overall to what extent did sex and violence occur together in this film?"; (b) "Of the violent scenes (if any), how many also contained sexual content? (This may include intercourse, rape, simple nudity, or other suggestive scenes.)"; (c) "How many scenes involved the rape (sexual assault) of a woman?"; (d) "Did this film portray violence toward women in a sexual context?"; and (e) "How degrading is this film to women?" Equally important, it must be recognized that the potential effect of this female-degradation cue demand characteristic was further exaggerated by the use of a static control group—an elementary experimental-design flaw that confounds the demand characteristic with the investigation's single independent variable (i.e., film exposure)—which jeopardizes both the internal and external validity of the findings (7).

Taken together, these considerations suggest that the findings reported by Linz et al. (24, 26), rather than reflecting the impact of viewing horror films on perceptions of a rape victim, may represent, instead, the impact of repeated administration of the reactive film evaluation measures. However, since the available data prohibit further consideration of this demand characteristic effect, the question remains: Is it the violence or an artifact?

In order to address this question, the investigation reported here employed a 2

X 2 X 2 factorial design with film content (neutral, eroticized-violence), female degradation cue (cued, not cued), and subject gender (male, female) as independent-measure factors. The study was conducted in two phases. First, subjects were randomly assigned to view three brief scenes representative of one of the two film content conditions. After viewing each scene, the subjects reported their reactions to the stimulus materials. Approximately half of the subjects responded to questions designed to cue constructs associated with female degradation (such as, "how degrading to women was this scene?"). The remaining subjects answered neutrally worded questions (such as, "how well produced was this scene?").

The second phase of the study was conducted immediately following the exposure treatment. In an ostensibly unrelated project, subjects read summaries of three legal proceedings in which men were said to have been convicted of physical and/or sexual assaults against women. After reading each summary the subjects reported both punitive judgments for and perceptual dispositions toward the men and women involved in each case. In order to provide a range of circumstances under which the proposed effects might materialize, three substantially difference scenarios were employed. The first case described an incident of nonsexual "domestic" violence and was included to see whether effects would prove specific to sexual transgressions. The second scenario was adapted from previous research (e.g., 36, 45) and unambiguously described the brutal rape of a woman by a stranger. The third case involved a guilt-ambiguous scenario that was designed to parallel those employed in some previous studies (e.g., 21, 24, 26). Specifically, case three summarized the events of a sexual assault in which the perpetrator "enjoyed some mitigating circumstances" (44, p. 112) surrounding the assault and subsequent interactions that induced substantial ambiguity in attribution of guilt to him.

METHOD

Subjects

Forty-nine male and 34 female undergraduates were recruited from an introductory communications class at Indiana University in Spring, 1985. Subjects were told that the study was one of several dealing with the psychology of entertainment. They received course credit for participation.

Procedure

Within gender, subjects were randomly assigned to experimental conditions. They were tested by a same gender experimenter in small groups of six to 10 persons.

After greeting the subjects, the experimenter explained that they would be participating in two small, unrelated projects that had been combined for convenience and asked the subjects to listen carefully to tape-recorded descriptions of both projects. The recording disclosed that, in the first study, subjects were to evaluate three segments taken from contemporary movies and television programs. Subjects were informed that some of the segments had been taken from "R-rated" movies and that anyone who might be offended by such material was free to discontinue participation without penalty. The experimenter stopped the tape to ascertain if anyone objected to seeing the material. None of the subjects did at this or any later time. It was further explained that, in the second study, subjects would read summaries of the facts presented in three legal proceedings. The subjects were told that they would be asked to consider each case carefully and then, in a fashion similar to a judge, provide a punitive judgment for each defendant. They were also told that they would be asked to report their impressions of the individuals involved in each case.

Following these instructions, the subjects were asked to read and complete an informed consent form. The consent form restated the subjects' right to withdraw from the experiment at any time. The experimenter then distributed the film evaluation questionnaire, pointed out that it contained three identical pages (i.e., one for each segment), and noted that the videotape would be stopped after each segment so that they could complete the questionnaire. Dependent on the experimental condition, this questionnaire did or did not contain degradation items. After answering questions for clarification, the experimenter exposed the subjects to the stimulus materials and allowed time for evaluation.

Upon completion, subjects received detailed instructions for the second study. They were given the written documentation of three criminal cases and asked to read these cases along with the identical spoken text presented from tape. It was explained that they would be asked to render a punitive judgment for the defendant immediately after reviewing each case. Then, they would be shown slides of both the victim and the assailant and asked to indicate their impressions of each.

Following completion of both studies, the subjects were debriefed and thanked for participating.

Manipulations

Film content. In both film conditions, the stimulus material consisted of three segments from different sources. The *neutral* condition featured nonsexual and noncoercive intergender interactions. One segment explained the use of the Braille system. The other segments showed men and women conversing about nonsexual and nonviolent topics. The *eroticized-violence* condition featured segments from the kind of teen-age horror movie in which graphically violent acts were frequently depicted in an erotic context. In a segment from the movie *The Toolbox Murders*, for instance, a young woman is shown taking a bath. A man forcefully enters her apartment. The nude woman tries to escape. Being unsuccessful, she attempts to seduce her attacker. But the attacker is sexually disinterested and sadistically murders the woman. He shoots her repeatedly with a nail gun. Eventually he slaughters her with a nail into the brain. The other segments, taken from the movies *Friday the 13th, Part III* and *Ten to Midnight*, were similarly gruesome. They also featured the terrorization of nude women by men without apparent sexual interest. In both the neutral and the eroticized-violence conditions, the segments totaled about 12 minutes in duration.

Degradation cues. Female degradation was cued by incorporating sensitizing questions in the film evaluation questionnaire. Specifically, two versions of the questionnaire were created. *Degradation was cued* by a set of eight items adapted from Linz et al. (24, 26). In the order presented, the items were: (a) How explicitly violent was this segment?, (b) How explicitly sexual was it?, (c) How degrading to women was this segment?, (d) How degrading to men?, (e) How entertaining was it?, (f) How offensive was it?, (g) Did this segment feature men as triumphantly dominant?, and (h) Did this segment feature women as suffering from submission? Subjects reported their responses to each item on 11-point unipolar scales. For questions (a) through (f), the extremes of each scale were labeled "not at all" [0] and "extremely" [10].The scales for questions (g) and (h) ranged from "not at all" [0] to "very much so" [10]. *Degradation was not cued* by the alternative questionnaire that excluded all references to violence, sex, degradation, male dominance, and female suffering. Instead, subjects evaluated six aspects of the stimulus materials: exciting, boring, entertaining, aesthetically pleasing, well produced, and offensive. Ratings were made on 11-point unipolar scales labeled "not at all" [0] and "extremely" [10]. Subjects were additionally asked to indicate the minimal age (in years) of viewers for whom they thought the materials suited.

Dependent Measures

Legal cases. The proceedings of three criminal trials were summarized. In all cases, a man had committed a crime against a woman and was found guilty of the offense. In the last case, the female victim eventually retaliated against her male assailant and also was found guilty of this offense. The summaries provided information suggesting that the assaults had recently occurred in the community where the research was conducted. After reading each case, subjects were asked to render a punitive judgment against the assailant. The judgments were expressed in damages (dollars) or incarceration (years, months). Subjects were then shown slides of victim and assailant in each case and asked to report their perceptions of them. They responded on 11-point unipolar scales that, unless otherwise noted, ranged from "not at all" [0] to "extremely" [10].

Case one featured *a man's violent assault on a woman*. It described the attack on a young woman by her intoxicated live-in boyfriend. The woman was said to have sustained substantial physical injuries (i.e., fractured ribs, broken teeth, and a large facial cut) and to have suffered financial loss. The man was described as having been found guilty of wrongfully hurting the woman and was liable for damages to her. Subjects were first asked to recommend a monetary award on a scale ranging from zero to 60,000 dollars. Next, perceptions of the victim were reported by responding to five questions. The questions, in the order of presentation, were: (a) In your judgment, how likable is she?; (b) To what extent did she provoke the violence perpetrated against her?; (c) How intense was her suffering during and immediately following the violence?; (d) Do you feel that her emotional suffering lasted for months after the violent incident?; and (e) Upon learning about the victim's suffering, how sorry did you feel for her? For question (b), the extremes were labeled "did not provoke" [0] and "clearly did provoke" [10]. The scale for question (d) ranged from "not at all" [0] to "very much so" [10]. Finally, the subjects responded to three questions about the assailant: (a) How impulsive a person do you think he is?; (b) Do you feel that he was upset to a point where he did things he did not mean to do?; and (c) Upon learning about his losing his temper, how sorry did you feel for him? The extremes for question (b) were labeled "not at all"[0] and "very much so" [10].

Case two concerned *a violent sexual assault* committed by a stranger. It detailed the brutal knife-point rape of a woman in the laundry room of an apartment complex. Subjects were asked to recommend a sentence on a scale ranging from zero to 100 years. They then responded to nine questions about the rape victim: (a) How likable is she?; (b) To what extent did her conduct invite rape?; (c) To what extent did her character invite rape?; (d) Do you feel that she could and should have done more to prevent the rape?; (e) Do you feel that she should have fought, even at the risk of physical injury to herself?; (f) How intense was her suffering during and immediately following the rape?; (g) Do you feel that her emotional suffering lasted for months after the rape?; (h) Do you feel that her traumatic experience will alter her sexuality for years, if not forever?; and (i) Do you feel that the rape makes the victim a lesser woman? The extremes of the scales for questions (b) and (c) were labeled "did not invite" [0] and "clearly did invite" [10]. For questions (d), (e), (g), (h), and (i) the scales ranged from "not at all" [0] to "very much so" [10]. Five questions were used to ascertain the perception of the rapist: (a) How impulsive a person do you think he is?; (b) Do you feel that he was sexually deprived and aroused to a point where he did things he did not mean to do?; (c) Given that he could not control his sexual urges, how sorry did you feel for him?; (d) Do you feel that this rape was premeditated to attain sexual gratification and performed in total disregard for the welfare of the victim?; and (e) Do you feel that this rape was motivated by a desire to brutalize a woman? The extremes of the scales for questions (b), (d), and (e) were labeled "not at all" and "very much so."

Case three dealt with the somewhat ambiguous *sexual assault on a female by two male conspirators*. It described an incident in which a young woman, deceitfully tied to the bed by her boyfriend, was forced into coition with another man while her boyfriend was watching. The woman was said to have responded in terror and to have immediately terminated her relationship with the boyfriend.

She did not file any charges. However, when the boyfriend attempted to re-establish the relationship, she responded with violent rage to his advances, attacked him, and caused significant injury to his face that left lasting scars. Subjects were first asked to recommend a monetary award against the boyfriend for the emotional duress suffered by the young woman. They made ratings on a scale ranging from zero to 800,000 dollars. Using the same scale, the subjects were also asked to recommend a monetary award against the young woman for the physical damages to the boyfriend's face. Perceptions of the young woman were ascertained by nine questions: (a) How likable is she?; (b) How impulsive a person do you think she is?; (c) Do you feel that she was upset to a point where she did things she did not mean to do?; (d) Upon learning about her temper and resorting to violence, how sorry did you feel for her?; (e) Upon learning about her sexual abuse, how sorry did you feel for her?; (f) How intense was her suffering during and immediately following her being sexually abused?; (g) Do you feel that her emotional suffering lasted for months after the abuse?; (h) Do you feel that her traumatic experience will alter her sexuality for years, if not forever?; and (i) Do you feel that it makes the victim a lesser woman? The extremes of the scales for the (c), (g), (h), and (i) items were labeled "not at all" and "very much so." Four questions were used for reactions to the boyfriend: (a) How likable is he?; (b) To what extent did he invite and provoke the violence perpetrated against him?; (c) How intense was his suffering during and immediately following the violent act?; and (d) Upon learning about the violence perpetrated against the boyfriend, how sorry did you feel for him? The extremes of the scale for question (b) were "did not provoke" and "clearly did provoke."

Affective responses to films. The two different versions of the film-evaluation questionnaire, required in order to implement the manipulation of degradation cues, had two items in common: entertaining and offensive. These ratings of the three segments were averaged within each film condition for subsequent analyses.

Data reduction. In order to reduce the person perception data to a more workable number of measures, principal components factor analyses with oblique rotation to simple structures were performed. These analyses were conducted independently for the female victims and the male assailants across the three cases.

Seven *female-victim* factors, accounting for 69.9 percent of the total variance, were produced by the factor analysis. The first three factors reflected concern for the female victim in each case. Factor one was defined by high loadings (i.e., coefficients between -0.60 and 0.60, with no more than half of this loading on any other factor) on the questions (d) through (h) which asked abut the young woman in the third case. The second factor derived from high loadings on questions (f) through (h) which asked about the rape victim (case two). Responses to questions (a), (c), and (e) about case one loaded on the third factor.

These factors were labeled, in order, *Concern for Victim of Sexual Assault*, *Concern for Rape Victim*, and *Concern for Victim of Violent Assault*. The fourth factor proved sensitive to the worthiness of the two victims of sexual assault. It was defined by high loadings on question (i) which asked about both case two and case three females and was labeled *Lesser Womanhood*. The fifth and sixth factors pertained to perceptions of the rape victims' responsibility for the occurrence of rape. Factor five was defined by questions (b) and (c) of case two and was labeled *Victim-Provoked Rape*. Responses to questions (d) and (e) of case two defined factor six. It was labeled *Victim-Conceded Rape*. The seventh factor was not defined.

The factor analysis of the perpetrator perceptions yielded five *male-assailant* factors that accounted for 61.8 percent of the total variance. Factor one proved sensitive to judgments of sympathy for the men involved in the first two scenarios with high loadings on question (c) of both cases. It was labeled *Sympathy for Male Assailant*. Similarly, factor two was derived from high loadings on questions (c) and (d) which asked about the case three male and was labeled *Sympathy for Male Assailant-Victim*. The third factor was labeled *Justification* of assailants' actions. It was defined by high loadings on question (b) about the case one male and question (e) for the case two male. Factor four reflected perceptions that the males involved in the first and second scenarios acted impulsively—question (a) of both cases—and was labeled *Impulsiveness* of assailants' actions. The fifth factor was defined by a single high loading on question (b) of case three and was labeled *Counterviolence*. Composite factor measures were computed by averaging the unweighted scores of the most salient variables on each factor. These measures were used in subsequent analyses.

RESULTS

Punitive Judgments

The three judgments that involved punishment of the male assailants were subjected to multivariate analysis of variance (MANOVA) with film content condition (neutral, eroticized-violence), female degradation cue (cued, not cued), and subject gender (male, female) as independent-measure factors. Using the Hotelling-Lawley algorithm, this analysis yielded a significant film content main effect [$F(3, 73) = 2.786$, $p < .05$]. Additionally, both the female degradation cue by subject gender [$F(3, 73) = 2.66$, $p = .05$] and the film content by degradation cue by subject gender [$F(3, 73) = 2.197$, $p = .09$] interactions approached significance.

Inspection of the subsequent univariate analyses of variance revealed a significant film content main effect [$F(1, 75) = 7.83$, $p < .01$] for the monetary award to the violent assault victim (case one). The means associated with this effect show that subjects in the neutral film content condition (M = $12,272.1) recommended a substantially smaller punitive award than those in the eroticized-violence condition (M = \$22,835.0). The univariate analyses also produced a significant female degradation cue by subject gender interaction [$F(1, 75) = 5.05, p < .05$] for the case one award. As can be seen in Table 1, the degradation manipulation significantly lowered the monetary award recommended by female subjects for the violent assault victim. Male subjects who were cued, on the other hand, tended to suggest a larger award.

A film content by female degradation cue by subject gender interaction [$F(1, 75) = 4.55, p < .05$] was also evident for the punitive judgment against the convicted rapist. The means for this effect are presented in Table 1. As can be seen, among female subjects in the eroticized-violence condition, those who completed the degradation cue questionnaire recommended a significantly longer period of incarceration for the rapist than those did who were not cued. On the other hand, the means for male subjects exposed to the eroticized-violence stimuli display the opposite pattern, but do not differ significantly.

Interestingly, the univariate tests of the punitive judgments for the individuals involved in the somewhat ambiguous sexual assault of the third case failed to yield effects that reached the conventional level of significance. Specifically, the degradation cue by subject gender interaction for the monetary award to the female sexual assault victim only approached significance [$F(1, 75) = 3.57, p = .06$] and the punitive judgment against the female yielded trivial ($F \leq 1$) variation on all main effects and interactions.

Perceptions of Female Victims

The six composite measures generated for the female victims factors were also subjected to a MANOVA. This analysis yielded significance for both the female degradation cue [$F(6, 70) = 2.78, p < .05$] and subject gender [$F(6, 70) = 3.39, p < .005$] main effects. The film content main effect and the interactions produced trivial variation, however.

Table 1. Punitive Judgments Against Male Assailants as a Function of Degradation Cueing, Film Content, and Subject Gender

			Degradation	
Case	Subject gender	Film content	Not cued	Cued
Violent assault[a] (case #1)	Male	Combined	$16.0^{a,b}$	21.1^{b}
	Female	Combined	21.5^{b}	9.6^{a}
Rape[b] (case #2)	Male	Neutral	395.5	400.2
		Erotic violence	$409.7^{a,b}$	270.6^{a}
	Female	Neutral	596.0	426.7
		Erotic violence	287.2^{a}	654.7^{b}

Note. Means having no letter in their superscripts in common differ at $p < .05$ by two-tailed t test.
[a]Means are in thousands of dollars.
[b]Means are in months of incarceration.

Subsequent analyses of variance for each variant revealed significant female degradation cue main effects for the Concern for Victim of Violent Assault [$F(1, 75) = 8.39$, $p < .005$] and Lesser Womanhood [$F(1, 75) = 7.41$, $p < .01$] measures. As can be seen in Table 2, subjects who were initially made sensitive to constructs associated with female degradation and humiliation, compared with those who were not cued, responded with substantially less compassion to the plight of the female assault victims.

The follow-up analyses also produced significant subject gender main effects for the Concern for Rape Victim [$F(1, 75) = 19.84$, $p < .001$] and Lesser Womanhood [$F(1, 75) = 5.71$, $p < .05$] measures. On both measures, male subjects (Concern for Rape Victim, $M = 7.40$; Lesser Womanhood, $M = 2.26$) expressed more calloused perceptions than did female subjects (Concern for Rape Victim, $M = 8.96$; Lesser Womanhood, $M = 1.24$).

Perceptions of Male Assailants

The multivariate analysis of variance on the five male assailant factor composite measures failed to produce any significant main effects or interactions. Similarly, the univariate tests did not yield effects within the conventional ($p < .05$) significance level.

Affective Responses to Films

A MANOVA performed on the entertaining and offensive ratings of the experimental stimuli yielded significant main effects for both female degradation [$F(2, 74) = 5.47$, $p < .01$], and film content [$F(2, 74) = 49.98$, $p < .001$]. The subject gender by film content interaction also was significant [$F(2, 74) = 3.862$, $p < .05$]. The subject gender main effect and the other interactions were not significant, however.

Examination of the follow-up univariate tests revealed that the female degradation cue main effect was significant for the entertaining measure only [$F(1, 75) = 10.89$, $p < .001$]. The means associated with this effect show that the female degradation cued subjects ($M = 2.84$) reported that the exposure materials were substantially less entertaining than did the degradation not cued ($M = 4.08$)

Table 2. Perception of Female Assault Victims as a Function of Degradation Cueing and Film Content

Factor indices	Film content	Degradation: Not cued	Degradation: Cued
Concern for Victim of Violent Assault	Combined	7.12[b]	6.43[a]
Lesser Womanhood from Sexual Assault	Combined	1.27[a]	2.39[b]

Note. Means having no letter in their superscripts in common differ at $p < .05$ by two-tailed t test.

subjects. These analyses also produced a significant film content main effect for both the entertaining [$F(1, 75) = 9.63, p < .01$] and offensive [$F(1, 75) = 101.23, p < .001$] variates. Compared with subjects who viewed the neutral film content (entertaining, $M = 3.95$; offensive, $M = 0.72$), those exposed to the eroticized-violence content reported the exposure materials to be less entertaining ($M = 2.93$) and more offensive ($M = 5.57$). Additionally, the subject gender by film content interaction proved significant [$F(1, 75) = 6.86, p < .01$]. Subsequent two-tailed t tests showed that this effect resulted from the fact that female subjects who viewed the eroticized-violence film content ($M = 2.10$) found the materials less entertaining than those who viewed the neutral film content ($M = 4.24$). All other main effects and interactions failed to reach conventional levels of significance.

DISCUSSION

The findings of this investigation strongly suggest that adverse dispositional and perceptual consequences occasioned by exposure to the fictional violence of contemporary horror films may not be as pervasive as some have asserted (12, 13, 25). Indeed, the data show that previous findings (24, 26), which were attributed to the "spill-over" of affective insensitivity induced by viewing graphic violence, can be more parsimoniously explained as experimental artifact. More specifically, the findings demonstrate that, independent of both the exposure treatment content and subject gender, the use of reactive film evaluation measures—which cue constructs associated with the abusive and humiliating treatment of women—can result in subsequent judgments that reflect the disparagement of and a loss of compassion for female victims of physical and/or sexual assaults. Equally important, the strength of these effects is quite surprising given the rather mild female-degradation cue manipulation that was employed (e.g., no specific reference to sexual-violence). Further, it highlights the prudence of the experimental artifact interpretation of previous research—especially those studies that compared cued treatment groups with a static control group (24, 26).

The data also show that the female degradation cue manipulation affected punitive judgments against men who assaulted women in a manner that differed significantly between male and female subjects. Among females, for example, those exposed to the degradation cue prescribed significantly lower punitive judgments against the perpetrator who physically assaulted his female cohabitant. Although not significantly different, male subjects tended to respond in the opposite manner. A different pattern emerged for judgments of the convicted rapist. Among female subjects who viewed the eroticized violence, those also exposed to the degradation cue recommended a significantly longer period of incarceration for the rapist. Again, male subject's judgments, while not significant, leaned in the opposite direction. Interestingly, no significant effects were evident for the punitive judgments reported for the guilt-ambiguous sexual assault. This fact, in light of the other significant findings of this study, suggests that the degree of guilt-ambiguity incorporated into an assault scenario is a quite plausible explanation (cf. 44) for similar null findings reported in previous research (e.g., 21, 24). Unfortunately, the factors that might mediate the observed pattern of punitive judgments are not clearly evident from the data at hand. One speculation is that the manipulations activated self-protective, image-management cognitions among the female subjects (19, 21, 36, 37). Further research is necessary to clarify this consideration, however.

Taken together, these data—in combination with the growing volume of research on sexually explicit materials—present a severe challenge to contentions asserting "that violent images, rather than sexual ones, are most responsible for people's attitudes about women and rape" (12, p. 59). They also suggest some puzzling questions. For example, one can only speculate about what considerations inspired Donnerstein and his colleagues to overlook such basic procedural shortcomings and convey almost unconditioned credence to their work (cf. 11, 13, 26). Such actions appear particularly surprising in view of the fact that these researchers have discussed in detail many factors that can jeopardize the validity and generalizability of experimental investigations (13) and, based on such factors, have been especially critical of research findings that are inconsistent with their "it is not sex, but violence" (12, p. 56; 13) philosophy. More basically, one must wonder why a perspective that has long been recognized as overly simplistic and unviable (10, 14) has been revived and advocated with such acclaim. Be this as it may, the findings of this investigation emphasize the fact that considerable care must be employed when evaluating previous research and theory on this topic (cf. 49).

Finally, the reader is cautioned not to interpret the results of this study as suggesting that affective reactions to media presentations have *no* effect on cognitions and behaviors. Indeed, a growing volume of research suggests there is considerable reason to suspect that exposure to either sexually explicit or graphically violent media depictions—portrayals that, by design, are intended to arouse, frighten, and/or disgust—can induce strong affective states that modify subsequent cognitive and behavioral responses (e.g., 15, 36, 44, 47). It is also evident (cf. 18, 43), however, that the linkages between affect, cognition, and social behavior are quite complex—especially when negative feeling states (i.e., those potentially induced by viewing sex or violence) are considered—and can be modified by a number of personality factors. For instance, recent evidence indicates that the display of mastery in response to horror (i.e., the exhibition of affective desensitization) can produce significant positive consequences for both enjoyment of such films and interpersonal attraction (52). Clearly, these considerations suggest that further exploration of the factors that might mediate both the apparent appeal and potential impact of viewing contemporary media portrayals of sex and/or violence would be most informative and that future research should be encouraged.

REFERENCES

1. Attorney General's Commission on Pornography. *Final Report*. Washington, DC: U.S. Department of Justice, U.S. Government Printing Office, 1986.
2. Bandura, A. *Social Foundations of Thought and Action: A Social Cognitive Theory*. Englewood Cliffs, NJ: Prentice-Hall, 1986.
3. Berkowitz, L. "Sex and Violence: We Can't Have it Both Ways." *Psychology Today*, December 1971, pp. 14, 18, 20, 22–23.
4. Brownmiller, S. *Against Our Will: Men, Women, and Rape*. New York: Simon and Schuster, 1975.
5. Brownmiller, S. "The Place of Pornography: Packaging Eros for a Violent Age" [Comments to a Forum held at the New School for Social Research in New York City moderated by L. H. Lapham]. *Harper's*, November 1984, pp. 31–39, 42–45.
6. Bryant, J. and Zillmann, D. (Eds.). *Perspectives on Media Effects*. Hillsdale, NJ: Erlbaum, 1985.
7. Campbell, D. T. and Stanley, J. C. *Experimental and Quasi-Experimental Designs for Research*. Boston: Houghton Mifflin, 1963.
8. Check, J. V. P. "The Effects of Violent and Nonviolent Pornography" (Contract No. 05SV 19200-3-0899). Ottawa, Ontario: Canadian Department of Justice, 1985.
9. Commission on Obscenity and Pornography. *Report of the Commission on Obscenity and Pornography*. Washington, DC: U.S. Government Printing Office, 1970.
10. Dienstbier, R. A. "Sex and Violence: Can Research Have it Both Ways?" *Journal of Communication* 27(3), Summer 1977, pp. 176–188.
11. Donnerstein, E. and Linz, D. "Sexual Violence in the Media: A Warning." *Psychology Today*, January 1984, pp. 14–15.
12. Donnerstein, E. and Linz, D. "The Question of Pornography." *Psychology Today*, December 1986, pp. 56–59.
13. Donnerstein, E., Linz, D. and Penrod, S. *The Question of Pornography: Research Findings and Policy Implications*. New York: The Free Press, 1987.
14. Eysenck, H. J. and Nias, D. K. B. *Sex, Violence, and the Media*. New York: Harper and Row, 1978.
15. Forgas, J. P., and Moylan, S. "After the Movies: Transient Mood and Social Judgments." *Personality and Social Psychology Bulletin* 13, 1987, pp. 467–477.
16. Garry, A. "Pornography and Respect for Women." *Social Theory and Practice* 4, 1978, pp. 395–422.
17. Goldstein, A. "The Place of Pornography: Packaging Eros for a Violent Age" [Comments to a Forum held at the New School for Social Research in New York City moderated by L. H. Lapham]. *Harper's*, November 1984, pp. 31–39, 42–45.
18. Isen, A. M. "Toward Understanding the Role of Affect in Cognition." In R. S. Wyer, Jr. and T. K. Srull (Eds.), *Handbook of Social Cognition* (Vol. 3). Hillsdale, NJ: Erlbaum, 1984, pp. 179–236.
19. Janoff-Bulman, R., Timko, C. and Carli, L. L. "Cognitive Biases in Blaming the Victim." *Journal of Experimental Social Psychology* 21, 1985, pp. 161–177.
20. Kenrick, D. T., Gutierres, S. E. and Goldberg, L. "Influence of Popular Erotica on Judgments of Strangers and Mates." *Journal of Experimental Social Psychology* 25, 1989, pp. 159–167.
21. Krafka, C. L. "Sexually Explicit, Sexually Violent, and Violent Media: Effects of Multiple Naturalistic Exposures and Debriefing on Female Viewers." Doctoral dissertation, University of Wisconsin, Madison, 1985.
22. Lederer, L. *Take Back the Night: Women on Pornography*. New York: William Morrow, 1980.
23. Leonard, K. E. and Taylor, S. P. "Exposure to Pornography, Permissive and Nonpermissive Cues, and Male Aggression Toward Females." *Motivation and Emotion* 7, 1983, pp. 291–299.
24. Linz, D. G. "Sexual Violence in the Media: Effects on Male Viewers and Implications for Society." Doctoral dissertation, University of Wisconsin, Madison, 1985.

25. Linz, D. and Donnerstein, E. "Colloquy: The Methods and Merits of Pornography Research." *Journal of Communication* 38(2), Spring 1988, pp. 180–184.
26. Linz, D., Donnerstein, E. and Penrod, S. "The Effects of Multiple Exposures to Filmed Violence Against Women." *Journal of Communication* 34(3), Summer 1984, pp. 130–147.
27. Mohr, D. and Zanna, M. P. "Treating Women as Sexual Objects: Look to the (Gender Schematic) Male who has Viewed Pornography." *Personality and Social Psychology Bulletin*, in press.
28. Ogles, R. M. and Hoffner, C. "Film Violence and Perceptions of Crime: The Cultivation Effect." In M. L. McLaughlin (Ed.), *Communication Yearbook 10*. Newbury Park, CA: Sage, 1987, pp. 384–394.
29. Orne, M. T. "Demand Characteristics and the Concept of Quasi-Controls." In R. Rosenthal and R. L. Rosnow (Eds.), *Artifact in Behavioral Research*. New York: Academic Press, 1969, pp. 143–179.
30. Palys, T. S. "A Content Analysis of Sexually Explicit Videos in British Columbia." *Working Papers on Pornography and Prostitution* (Research Report #15). Ottawa, Canada: Department of Justice, 1984.
31. Prince, S. "Power, Pain, and Pleasure in Pornography: A Content Analysis of Pornographic Feature Films, 1972–1985." Doctoral dissertation, University of Pennsylvania, 1987.
32. Redd, W. H., Porterfield, A. L. and Andersen, B. L. *Behavior Modification: Behavioral Approaches to Human Problems*. New York: Random House, 1979.
33. Scott, D. A. *Pornography: Its Effects on the Family, Community and Culture*. Washington, DC: The Child and Family Protection Institute, 1985.
34. Slade, J. W. "Violence in the Hard-Core Pornographic Film: A Historical Survey." *Journal of Communication* 34(3), Summer 1984, pp. 148–163.
35. Smeaton, G. and Byrne, D. "The Effects of R-rated Violence and Erotica, Individual Differences, and Victim Characteristics on Acquaintance Rape Proclivity." *Journal of Research in Personality* 21, 1987, pp. 171–184.
36. Weaver, J. B. "Effects of Portrayals of Female Sexuality and Violence Against Women on Perceptions of Women." Doctoral dissertation, Indiana University, Bloomington, 1987.
37. Weaver, J. B. "Effects of Portrayals of Female Sexuality and Violence Against Women on Self-Perceptions." Unpublished manuscript, University of Kentucky, 1988.
38. Weaver, J. B. "A Content Analysis of Ten Commercially Successful 'Teen-age Slasher' Horror Films." Paper presented at the Speech Communication Association conference in New Orleans, LA, November, 1988.
39. Weaver, J. B., Masland, J. L. and Zillmann, D. "Effect of Erotica on Young Men's Aesthetic Perception of Their Female Sexual Partners." *Perceptual and Motor Skills* 58, 1984, pp. 929–930.
40. Winick, C. "A Content Analysis of Sexually Explicit Magazines Sold in an Adult Bookstore." *Journal of Sex Research* 21, 1985, pp. 206–210.
41. Wilson, W. C. "Can Pornography Contribute to the Prevention of Sexual Problems?" In C. B. Qualls, J. P. Wincze and D. H. Barlow (Eds.), *The Prevention of Sexual Disorders: Issues and Approaches*. New York: Plenum, 1978, pp. 159–179.
42. Wyer, R. S., Jr., Bodenhausen, G. V. and Gorman, T. F. "Cognitive Mediators of Reactions to Rape." *Journal of Personality and Social Psychology* 48, 1985, pp. 324–348.
43. Zillmann, D. *Connections Between Sex and Aggression*. Hillsdale, NJ: Erlbaum, 1984.
44. Zillmann, D. "Effects of Prolonged Consumption of Pornography." In Zillmann, D. and Bryant, J. (Eds.). *Pornography: Research Advances and Policy Considerations*. Hillsdale, NJ: Erlbaum, 1989, pp. 127–157.
45. Zillmann, D. and Bryant, J. "Pornography, Sexual Callousness, and the Trivialization of Rape. *Journal of Communication* 32(4), Autumn 1982, pp. 10–21.
46. Zillmann, D. and Bryant, J. "Effects of Massive Exposure to Pornography." In N. M. Malamuth and E. Donnerstein (Eds.), *Pornography and Sexual Aggression*. Orlando, FL: Academic Press, 1984, pp. 115–138.

47. Zillmann, D. and Bryant, J. "Shifting Preferences in Pornography Consumption." *Communication Research* 13, 1986, pp. 560–578.
48. Zillmann, D. and Bryant, J. "Pornography's Impact on Sexual Satisfaction." *Journal of Applied Social Psychology* 18, 1988, pp. 438–453.
49. Zillmann, D. and Bryant, J. "Colloquy: The Methods and Merits of Pornography Research." *Journal of Communication* 38(2), Spring 1988, pp. 185–192.
50. Zillmann, D. and Bryant, J. "Effects of Pornography Consumption on Family Values." *Journal of Family Issues* 9, 1988, pp. 518–544.
51. Zillmann, D. and Bryant, J. (Eds.). *Pornography: Research Advances and Policy Considerations*. Hillsdale, NJ: Erlbaum, 1989.
52. Zillmann, D., Weaver, J. B., Mundorf, N. and Aust, C. F. "Effects of an Opposite-Gender Companion's Affect to Horror on Distress, Delight, and Attraction." *Journal of Personality and Social Psychology* 51, 1986, pp. 586–594.
53. Zuckerman, M. and Lubin, B. *Manual for the Multiple Affect Adjective Checklist*. San Diego, CA: Educational and Industrial Testing Service, 1965.

2

The Ecstasy of Horrible Expectations: Morbid Curiosity, Sensation Seeking, and Interest in Horror Movies

Emily D. Edwards

More than any other movie genre, horror movies have content which is noticeably pessimistic, tension-arousing, fear-inducing, threatening, and unpleasant, a prime example of what Haskins (23, pp. 4–10) called "hypernegative communication." Hypernegative communication is abundant in the mass media from the extremely bad news found in print and broadcast journalism, to the sometimes grotesque images in music television, to violent and vice-ridden novels, to the gruesome monsters of Saturday morning cartoons. But nowhere is hypernegative communication and the allure of morbid curiosity more evident than in the horror movie, which has been cashing in on human fascination for the fearful and the hideous since the beginnings of the movie industry.[1] On its face, this popularity of a genre seeped in the morbid is perplexing.

To better understand this phenomenon, it is helpful to employ the uses and gratifications approach, which considers the audience member as an active selector of media communications and not a passive receiver (27). The reasons behind media choices and the uses of messages are considered intervening variables in the process of the effects of communication. Unlike research concerned with reactions or emotional consequences of exposure to horror films, research using the uses and gratifications model investigates the social and psychological needs, which generate expectations of the mass media. These

[1] There are a number of interesting histories of the horror film, which document the birth and growth of the genre and its fascination for audiences (7, 25, 15, 11, 12, 20). Trade and popular press articles (11, 17, 9, 27, 24, 31) also suggest that because of its popularity with audiences, horror is good movie business.

needs are thought to lead audiences to different patterns of media exposure for the purpose of gratification.

Aesthetic theories also involve gratification, the search for and arousal of sensations through art, an idea not in opposition to Zuckerman's (44) belief that the need for stimulation of the limbic reward system of the brain drives individuals to seek out various sensations. Berlyne (3) related aesthetic preferences to psychobiology, noting that since aesthetic behavior is fundamental to human culture, it must stem from some characteristics of the human nervous system. An electrochemical reaction produced through the vicarious experience of pain without the actual painful experience may result in pleasurable feelings.

This study examines audience motives for exposure to horror movies, particularly the sensation-seeking motive, to see if a relationship exists between interest in horror movies (and its subgenres) and in sensation seeking (and its subfactors). If such a relationship exists, it would provide support for the contention that some audiences are motivated to view horror by a biologically based need for the stimulation.[2]

SPECULATIONS ABOUT THE ATTRACTION TO HORROR

Horror and Curiosity

The devils, madmen, and fantasy murder of the horror movies have obvious counterparts in myths and folklore, indicating that themes found in horror are not recent additions to the culture but have been an evolving part of it. A study of recurrent themes in myths identified culturally universal themes (28), many of which are common to the horror genre. The study found no culture without myths or tales relating to witchcraft, and most cultures had monster themes. Thus, attraction to the horrible is not new or unique to American life. However, interest in the morbid and the horrible may be on the rise. Research has concluded that even though art in general has never been very optimistic, recently the trend has been toward more and more pessimism and ugliness in the popular arts (10). Considering the marketing imperative among popular arts, this may indicate a rise in morbid curiosity among audiences (22).

---

[2] Recent research has shown a modest relationship between sensation seeking and attendance to horror movies among horror fans. A survey of audience members leaving the theatre after viewing *Halloween II* suggested that sensation seeking was not as important a determinant of the genre's appeal as other variables, particularly a just resolution to the movie. On its face these findings seem suspicious. A just resolution is not a consistent trait of horror movies and it is unlikely that audiences know how a movie will be resolved before attending. It is more likely that audiences attend horror for exposure to the terrible predators, the violence, or the atmosphere, more predictable genre traits. Also, the subjects in the study were members of an audience for one particular horror, the second of a series in which the predator was left lurking. The findings reflecting the appeal of a just resolution for these horror fans may reflect this audience's desire to see Michael Myers finally put out of his misery.

Morbid curiosity has been defined as "an enduring and unusually strong attraction to information about highly unpleasant events and objects that are irrelevant to the individual's life" (22, p. 8). Irrelevance to the person's life is the key here. Attention to the morbid by itself is not an indication of morbid curiosity if the unpleasant material might be useful in decision making or danger avoidance. For example, researchers discovered that general attendance at a film depicting murder increased markedly in a community following an incident of real murder in that community (5). Interest in a murder movie in this instance may not be an indication of morbid curiosity but indicate a need for a vicarious experience with what was viewed as an authentic threat. Individuals using a horror movie this way may be vicariously rehearsing for the possibility of such an awful event in their own future.

Berlyne (4) differentiated between curiosity and diversive exploration. Diversive exploration is motivated by boredom; curiosity is motivated by anxiety. Bored individuals want to increase arousal to a more pleasant level, which causes them to seek out external stimulation that might increase that arousal. Horror movies may provide the stimulation necessary to relieve boredom. Zillman and Bryant (41) proposed that individuals choose communication that either reduces unfavorable affective states or preserves and increases the intensity of pleasurable affective states. This is similar to Zuckerman's (44) suggestion that the brain's need for stimulation causes people to seek out novel, even unpleasant and dangerous stimuli. Curious individuals have the opposite situation; they hope to reduce arousal through a search for information which will solve a problem or lower their anxiety. In the example above, the individual who chooses to see a murder movie following an incident of real murder in her community may be vicariously preparing for horrible confrontations and that vicarious preparation reduces his or her anxiety.

Though morbid curiosity is differentiated from normal curiosity by its irrelevance to an individual's life, it may have evolved from a biological readiness to respond to dangerous situations, the distant echo of a period when constant alertness to the danger of predators had positive survival value for individuals. Lionel Tiger proposes that just as we must exercise our bodies in this contemporary period of sedentary employment, we may also have to exercise our behavioral structure in an age when predators are generally not the kind that we can physically run away from or turn to fight with tooth and nail. Tiger believes "we have to see ourselves as a very old animal in rather new circumstances, and it's not quite clear that the fit is that easy" (39, p. 187). This is related to Wilson's (44) suggestion that natural selection has caused the human brain to evolve through the years, producing a biological foundation for those behaviors with high survival value. Behaviors that had survival value for the hunting and gathering animal that we were, however, may be dysfunctional for the computer operators we have become.

Horror and the Sacred

Several critics have remarked that horror entertainment has religious aspects. For some audiences horror movies may reaffirm human faith in the supernatural. Dickstein (13, p. 37) claimed that the increasing secularization of society has given more and more mythical response to popular culture, which satisfies human needs for bonding and common experience. Too much of our sense of awe and evil has been exorcised by liberalism and secularism. Rosenbaum (33, p. 72) suggested that the sensations sought in horror movies are similar to the awe, enchantment, mystery, and dread the religious believer feels in the presence of his or her higher being. Otto (29) suggested the emotions of horror, feelings of dread and awe are the emotional material from which religious faith evolved. What separates modern horror from earlier myths and legends, which have similar traits, is the skepticism which was ushered in by the 18th century "Age of Reason." The classification of horror as a genre seems to have developed simultaneously with skepticism and the idea of fiction. Horace Walpole's *Castle of Otranto* and the horror novels that followed can be explained as a deliberate reaction to the realism of the 18-century belief that human beings can, through rational analysis, discover adequate explanations for everything. Skepticism about the supernatural had become prevalent—at least in academic circles. Under the influence of this new doubt, Aristotle's (32, p. 230) definition of art as an instinctive expression that should be "in accord with nature and its laws" took on new meaning. Fantasy and the supernatural, which were believed to be a part of natural law prior to the 18th century, were eliminated (or minimized) in the drama according to the neoclassical ideal. In addition, Church authority, anxious to rid the Church of the taint of superstition, tended to promote skepticism over mysticism (26).

The strict cultivation of reason was soon followed by a swing in the opposite direction. As the romanticism of the 19th century grew, faith in reason gave way to trust in instinct. The supernatural and the mysterious became accepted subjects for artistic exploration. Belief in the supernatural, however, remained clouded with doubt.

Charles Darwin's *Origin of the Species* may have had great impact on horror as a genre in the latter half of the 19th century. The implications of Darwin's theses became new grounds for artistic examination. Darwin's theories cast suspicion on the existence of God as traditionally viewed. A new belief in God as an impersonal force rather than a private deity became, if not popular, at least recognized. Humankind lost the status of a privileged creation cast in the divine image. Having evolved along with the rest of the cosmos, humankind became simply another subject for study and exploration. Spiritual aspects were depreciated. Macabre fantasy in the safe form of entertainment allowed people to consider ideas that were no longer scientifically accepted.

There is some evidence that a belief in magic and the unknown persists today, though not usually acknowledged. The use of horoscopes, yoga and meditation, and the widespread use of drugs and alcohol to achieve altered states have been cited as examples of contemporary interest in the occult and supernatural (18). Researchers have concluded that the current use of rabbit's feet, charms, oaths, and special jewelry to bring luck are evidence that a belief in magic and the supernatural probably persists beneath a level of awareness (19). Although there is no empirical evidence linking the often denied yet persistent beliefs in the mystical and mysterious with attraction to horror movies, the logic behind such a link is attractive. The horror movie opens a spiritual door, forcing audiences to glimpse in a symbolic way beyond the boundaries of daily life.

Horror and Eroticism

The horror movies of the 1970s and 1980s have become more and more openly erotic. Many critics have noticed that much of erotic fantasy seems to have an important dark side (6, 14). Even the violent death of horror movies may have erotic qualities for some audiences. Bataille defined eroticism as "assenting to life even in death" (2, p. 11) and asserted that there is a connection between death and sexual excitement that has nothing to do with a state of neurosis but has instead to do with the relationship between life ("discontinuity") and death ("continuity"). Bataille described three states of eroticism: physical eroticism (which is physical activity), emotional eroticism (which is detached from physical activity but is often derived from it and is expressed as emotional arousal, often love), and religious eroticism. All eroticism has a sacramental character, but the physical and emotional eroticisms are secular activities in which systematically seeking continuity of existence beyond the immediate world signifies essentially religious intentions. With each type of eroticism the concern is to substitute a "feeling of profound continuity" for "isolated discontinuity." In other words, through erotic behavior individuals seek to lose their individuality, to merge with others, or to merge with a higher sphere of existence. According to Bataille, elemental violence is vital to every manifestation of eroticism. (Bataille used the word "violence" in its broadest possible sense, encompassing not only force and injury, but also passion and excitement.) Violence is necessary to make the transition from discontinuity to continuity and continuity to discontinuity, "to keep things in a state of flux" (2, p. 16).

Horror and Death

The fear of death may be the major motivating principle in human behavior. The fundamental paradox of human existence and the constant burden with which we must all live is an awareness of ourselves as unique individuals and the knowledge that we will die. The horror story responds to the most abiding human concern, the prospect of personal annihilation and oblivion in death.[3] Death is the

[3] An interesting discussion of death in movies can be found in Sobchack's "The Violent Dance" (34).

single most important element in the horror movie, forcing audiences to vicariously face what they hope to avoid. According to Berlyne (4), this vicarious danger that audiences face in the horror movie may result in "sublime pleasure," an electrochemical response in the brain caused by the idea of unpleasantness without its actual experience. Audiences may be highly interested in subjects they find distasteful. A graphically gory sequence in a movie may seize the attention of an audience member even though she finds the scene repulsive, and afterwards she may experience addicting sensations of euphoria in knowing the ordeal is over and it didn't actually happen to begin with. What may be initially perceived as negative or frightening becomes pleasant (39). Haskins suggests that this phenomenon is causing hypernegative content in mass media to escalate (22, p. 37). Like a drug addict, the horror movie fan requires more and more graphic gore in order to achieve the same level of stimulation and corresponding euphoria.

BOUNDARIES OF HORROR

Genre Definitions

Producers of horror movies have avoided labeling their works "horror" in hopes of transcending the bias associated with the genre (30, p. 53). Horror movies have hidden under euphemisms such as "suspense thriller," "adventure fantasy," "intense psychological drama," and "science fiction," in order to escape association with low budget "B" productions that are conjured up when the term "horror" is applied. Movies such as *The Howling*, *The Thing*, *Poltergeist*, and *An American Werewolf in London* are major films with sizable budgets and dazzling special effects and they would like to lose the stigma associated with the horror label. Whether or not the horror label is used, any film which relies heavily on a serious predator/prey relationship, contains elements of the fantastic, a strong atmospheric setting, and suspense which rests heavily on the anticipation of the next victim's death is a likely candidate for the horror genre. Violence and unnatural death are important genre themes. If there is not at least one corpse in the work, it cannot be classified as horror.

Horror, however, does have subgenres which may have different appeals and provide different gratifications for audiences. Penzoldt (30) outlined the subcategories of the horror tale: the gothic tale, science fiction tale, and psychological horror story. Although these subcategories were used to describe fiction, they can be just as easily applied to film. In fact, Derry (14) in his psychological history of the modern horror film defined similar subcategories which he called: the Horror of the Demonic, the Horror of Armageddon, and the Horror of Personality. Although they may be referred to by different names, similar categories are recognized by other horror historians, indicating that fright films have various subgenres. These subgenres are distinguished by their atmosphere, the occult devices they employ (occult devices are mysterious, supernatural, or little understood elements which lend atmosphere to the film), and the type of predator depicted in the movie.

The science fiction horror, or Horror of Armageddon, is usually set in the present or future and features some type of chemistry or machinery as the occult device. Typically the predators of the science fiction film will be evil aliens from unknown planets, mutants created by science, creatures provoked by humankind and the new technology, or even technology that has developed an evil will. Often a "monsterous creation has transpired, but has gone masked as scientific advance" (12, p. 48). Derry uses the term "Armageddon" to describe this subgenre because of the ultimate and mythical struggle involved in these films and because of the strong relationship between these films and the stories from the Bible in which many plagues are sent to express the wrath of God. Bees, frogs, birds, man-eating fish, and snakes are examples of a vengeful nature commonly depicted in the Horror of Armageddon subgenre. These movies may also be set in the aftermath of an atomic explosion, which awakens sleeping dinosaurs or other monsters.

The Gothic horror, or the Horror of the Demonic, most often has its emphasis in the past and may feature ghosts, vampires, werewolves, witches, animal spooks, and magicians as predators. Occult devices used in the gothic horror include magic, sorcery, and metamorphosis.

The Psychological horror, or Horror of Personality, usually has a current setting and employs exaggerated portrayals of real predators. The psychotic killer is the principal predator in this type of movie. Kapsis (27) noted that this type of predator has spawned recent interest because of the popularity of films like *Halloween*, *Prom Night*, *Friday the 13th*, and *Terror Train*. The plot of these movies, called "slice-and-dice" films by the industry (8), involves a maniac terrorizing young women or whole towns. A popular occult device for this type of film involves the mystery of mental illness, the impetus for a special breed of monster.

SENSATION SEEKING AND ATTRACTION TO HORROR

Theorists believe a biological need for exposure to arousing stimuli may cause some people to seek out the dangerous and negative.[4] This preference for morbid, dangerous messages may be an acquired tendency to study potentially dangerous situations which historically had important survival value. "But," argues Haskins, "in the absence of real danger signals, the human may turn automatically to the substitute stimulation provided by . . . fictious media accounts" (22, p. 38).

---

[4] Several theorists believe interest in negative and dangerous stimuli has a biological determinant (4, 22, 23, 42, 43, 44, 45).

Zuckerman (44) defined sensation seeking as a need some people have for varied, novel, and complex stimulations and experiences, coupled with a willingness to take physical and social risks for the sake of those experiences. He explains:

> The high sensation-seeker is sensitive to his or her internal sensations and chooses external stimuli that maximizes them . . . Tastes in art and music, clothes, and friends may also depend on the capacity of sensory and social stimuli to produce novel sensations and experience. (44, p. 10)

The sensation-seeking scale (SSS) developed by Zuckerman to measure this trait yielded a measure of four subfactors of the trait as well as a measure of the general factor of sensation seeking (42, 43, 44). These subfactors were: Thrill and Adventure Seeking, Experience Seeking, Disinhibition, and Boredom Susceptibility. Thrill and Adventure Seeking is a measure of the desire to engage in dangerous sports, such as sky diving, or other elements involving elements of physical danger. Experience Seeking is an enjoyment of mystical or artistic kinds of thought, an emphasis on feeling and intuition as opposed to conventional rationality. Disinhibition measures an extraverted philosophy and hedonistic social life. Boredom Susceptibility measures a dislike of the repetitive, the routine, the predictable, and a restless reaction to monotony. The general sensation-seeking trait has been found to be related to age, gender, and interests.

The sensation-seeking variable is expected to be a predictor of horror movie interest and attendance, especially in the experience seeking category, since this subscale measures an inclination toward mystical thought. If it is true that people attend horror movies to obtain vicarious experience with the unknown and supernatural, then the correlation should be greater between horror movie interest and experience seeking than between horror movie interest and thrill and adventure seeking, which measures the desire not for vicarious experience but the desire to actually engage in dangerous physical activity.

METHODS

Hypotheses

The research reported here examined the relationship between the various dimensions of sensation seeking, interest in horror movies and subgenres of horror movies, and actual attendance at horror movies. The variables under study were: thematic and total interest in horror movies, sensation seeking, and interest in supernatural and occult subjects. The following are specific hypotheses under study:

H1: There will be a positive correlation between Zuckerman's general sensation-seeking trait and frequency of horror movie attendance.

H2: There will be a positive correlation between Zuckerman's general sensation-seeking trait and interest in horror movies.
- H2a: There will be a positive correlation between experience seeking and interest in horror movies.
- H2b: There will be a positive correlation between thrill and adventure seeking and interest in horror movies.
- H2c: There will be a positive correlation between disinhibition seeking and interest in horror movies.
- H2d: There will be a positive correlation between boredom susceptibility and interest in horror movies.

H3. There will be a positive correlation between religious orthodoxy and interest in horror movies.

MEASURES

The data gathering method was a mail questionnaire which included the primary measures of horror movie interest and sensation seeking.

The Horror Movie Interest Measure (HMIM) is a multiple-item additive scale composed of the titles, descriptions, and movie industry ratings (PG, R) of hypothetical horror movies. These titles, descriptions, and movie industry ratings were invented to represent the various subgenres of horror movies and written to read like the descriptions listed in cable guides and newspaper guides to movies. It was assumed that subjects would be accustomed to making viewing decisions based on information provided in these guides, since such guides are often the only information available about a movie. Names of actors and any indication of other production elements which might have an attraction of their own were omitted from item descriptions. No mention was made of studios, directors, authors, or special effects.

Twenty-eight items were composed with a range of response from 0 to 7 (0 signified no interest in viewing a movie of this description, 7 signified a high interest in viewing a movie of this description). Ten items represented gothic themes, 10 items represented science fiction themes, and eight items represented psychological themes. The hypothetical movies were given movie industry rating in the mid-ranges (PG-R). Movie industry ratings were distributed across the horror subgenres. Since horror movies by definition contain violence or the suggestion of violence and violent death, none of the hypothetical films was given a G movie industry rating (suitable for all audiences). The other extreme, the X rating, was also avoided.

In addition to the HMIM, subjects were asked to respond to Zuckerman's Sensation-seeking scale (SSS). Since high sensation seekers tend to have more actual experience with and seek out such things as risky sports, risky social encounters, sexual variety, drugs and alcohol, the sensation-seeking variable was expected to be a predictor of interest in horror movies and attendance to this type of entertainment. The 40-item SSS also measured subcategories of sensation seeking: Thrill and Adventure Seeking, Experience Seeking, Disinhibition, and Boredom Susceptibility (43).

Other variables which were measured included frequency of general movie attendance, cable and VCR use, frequency of attendance at horror movies, movie viewing preferences, religious orthodoxy, and demographic variables. Frequency of attendance at horror movies combined both cinema and television viewing.

Reliability, Validity, and Factor Analysis of HMIM

The HMIM was pretested by the SPSSX subprogram Reliability using the data gathered from a sample of participants of Deepsouthcon II, an annual convention of science fiction, fantasy, and horror fans ($N=94$). Results showed high reliability for the three subscales of the HMIM. Analysis for the science fiction subscale reported .85 (Cronbach's alpha). Analyses for both the gothic and psychological subscales were .93.

Factor analysis was performed on pretest data to determine if the patterns described by the critical literature as the horror subgenres gothic, science fiction, and psychological would be observed in the interest ratings of the respondents. The method chosen for factoring was Principal Factoring with iteration. Initial factor loadings using the general population sample showed all items from HMIM loading heavily on Factor I. When the program was asked to produce three factors, the subgenres did break apart on the rotated factor matrix, indicating that the pretest samples discriminated among the subgenres in their preferences (see Table 1).

Finally, the pretest of HMIM showed that it was a strong predictor of horror movie viewing. When HMIM scores and frequency of horror movie viewing were correlated, $r = .71$; $p < .001$.

Population

A cross-sectional survey was employed to make descriptive assertions about the distribution of the sensation-seeking trait, horror movie attendance, and the overall interest in horror movies in a general population and to determine if a relationship exists between these variables. The general population sample was a sample of Knoxville residents derived by a fixed interval sampling method of residents listed in the city directory ($N=250$). Six weeks after the questionnaire was mailed the response rate reached 39 percent or 92 cases out of 237. Thirteen questionnaires were returned because of an insufficient address. Although some consider this an adequate response (16), nonresponse bias hampers the generalizability of findings. However, the resulting sample did not differ significantly from the Knoxville census with regard to age and gender, and indication that the sample was representative regarding proportions of males, females, and age groups.

Table 1. Rotated Factors from HMIM Items

Loadings						
Convention Sample			General Population Sample			
Factor 1	Factor 2	Factor 3	Factor 1	Factor 2	Factor 3	Items Predefined as Having Gothic Horror Characteristics
.48	.27	.32	.69	.40	.18	H3 VAMPIRE SEDUCTION ''A murder shrouded in mystery brings a beautiful reporter to a quaint New England town and into danger.'' (R, violence, nudity)
.66	.32	.12	.67	.54	.17	H10 LUMINIOUS ''A deadly ghost haunts the buildings of an old college.'' (PG, violence)
.77	.14	.13	.75	.25	.44	H11 AZAZEL ''A monk succumbs to depravity and the evils of ultimate power, when a demon becomes his master.'' (R, violence)
.65	.24	.11	.73	.19	.47	H15 VLAD, THE VAMPYRE ''More evil than Caligula, this is the myth of Vlad Dracul, the first vampire.'' (R, violence, nudity)
.72	.24	.20	.74	.30	.39	H16 THE DEMON WITHIN ''The soul of an ancient devil is awakened when archelogists uncover the ruins of a lost city.'' (R, violence)
.73	.18	.26	.87	.31	.19	H21 THROUGH MISTY RAIN ''On a visit to the country two young girls discover the remains of an old chapel. Evil waits inside.'' (R, violence, nudity)
.75	.04	.13	.75	.28	.40	H22 THE TALISMAN ''An historian discovers an amulet that holds evil, destructive powers.'' (PG, violence)
.72	.34	.15	.79	.44	.18	H23 OMISSION ''The one thing a young woman's lover doesn't tell her, haunts her with horrible results.'' (PG, violence, adult situations)
.63	.33	.07	.85	.36	.12	H25 CLAUDETTE ''While subletting an old chalet, a young man discovers the erotic and terrible secret of its long dead mistress.'' (PG, violence, adult situations)
.82	.29	.09	.83	.28	.24	H28 ALLHALLOW'S FAIR ''A man and his wife hire a servant at the Allhallow's Fair, only to discover that she has an uncanny influence over their dead son.'' (PG, violence, adult situations)

Table 1. *(continued)*

Loadings						
Convention Sample			General Population Sample			
Factor 1	Factor 2	Factor 3	Factor 1	Factor 2	Factor 3	Items Predefined as Having Psychological Horror Characteristics
.23	.43	.51	.44	.48	.44	H2 A LIGHT IN THE CAVERN "Runaways find refuge with a strange family living in a cavern, only to learn that this is a family of cannibals." (PG, violence)
.14	.84	.22	.30	.63	.41	H4 SLAUGHTERED "Death lurks behind the doors of a meat-packing company." (R, violence)
.24	.75	.10	.24	.82	.27	H6 SKEWER'S "Four adventurous young people become lost in a wilderness nightmare, chased by psychopaths." (R, violence)
.29	.79	.10	.24	.82	.27	H8 CUTLERY "A lunatic killer plunges the jewelry industry into terror." (PG, violence)
.47	.63	.07	.30	.57	.56	H13 SEWER MEN "The sewer becomes a haven for murdering brothers." (R, violence)
.48	.57	.14	.43	.63	.34	H14 UNDER THE BASEMENT STEPS "A lunatic boy keeps an oozing, terrifying secret under the basement steps." (PG, violence)
.27	.85	.14	.25	.82	.13	H20 MAN WITH A KNIFE "A psychotic killer terrorizes the women of a resort town." (PG, violence)
.21	.72	.26	.38	.76	.01	H27 STALKED "Models for an advertising agency are murdered one by one. The name of the next victim inscribed on the body of the last." (R, violence, nudity)

						Items Predefined as Having Science Fiction Horror Characteristics
.04	.06	.60	.28	.32	.60	H1 THE CITIZENS "In a futuristic bureaucracy it is legislated who will live, who will die, and who will become 'the citizens.' " (PG, violence)
.25	.06	.62	.56	.24	.51	H5 GRIM INTRUDER "Astronauts on an alien planet discover seductive evil older than mankind." (PG violence, adult situations)
.16	.21	.61	.51	.43	.41	H7 NECROSIS "Something strange is happening to the personnel of a nuclear power station." (R, violence)
.47	.63	.07	.42	.46	.51	H12 HEIR APPARENT "An experimental drug creates a deviant race." (R, violence)
.59	.30	.26	.56	.43	.53	H17 THE MARRIAGE CONTRACT "When a young woman arrives a scientist, no lawyer can save her from the hidden 'claws' in her contract." (R, violence, nudity)
.23	.61	.10	.34	.57	.53	H18 TICKS "A remote southern town is beset with a blood sucking menance." (PG, violence)
.19	.35	.48	.57	.33	.37	H19 UNESSENTIAL PERSONNEL "A future government plans the systematic destruction of welfare recipients." (R, violence)
.51	.24	.31	.74	.19	.48	H24 FORBIDDEN FOUNTAIN "Scientists discover a youth elixir with unexpected side effects." (PG, violence, adult situations)
.70	.44	.08	.80	.34	.19	H26 AN ALIEN'S MOTHER "A young husband discovers the chilling secret behind the abduction of three women." (PG, violence, adult situations)

RESULTS

Interest in Horror Movies

Among the general population sample a significantly larger proportion avoided or seldom watched horror movies than frequently or always watched the genre (2 = 8.85; $p < .01$). Fourteen percent said they never watched movies of this genre, 26.3 percent seldom watched horror movies, 36.3 percent occasionally watched horror movies, 14.3 percent frequently watched horror movies, and 8.7 percent always watched horror movies when they were available. Regarding interest in viewing movies like the ones described by HMIM items, 34.8 percent had extremely little or no interest in viewing movies like the ones described, 30.4 percent had a small interest, 22.9 percent had moderate interest, and 10.9 percent had a high interest in viewing the movies described by HMIM.

Those who always or frequently watched horror movies indicated a more frequent movie attendance overall. Cable service subscribers were likely to be high or moderate in their attendance to horror movies. The most popular way to watch movies appeared to be with one other person, either a family member or a friend. Those who seldom or never watched horror movies picked this mode almost exclusively. Thirty percent of those who frequently watched horror enjoyed watching movies alone.

Relationship Between Interest in Horror Movies and Sensation Seeking

Sensation seeking proved to be correlated to both interest in horror movies and frequency of attendance at the genre. In the subcategories of Sensation seeking, Disinhibition (the measure of an extroverted philosophy and hedonistic social life) correlated most strongly with both interest and frequency of attendance at the genre. The next strongest correlation was with Experience seeking (the measure of enjoyment of mystical or artistic kinds of thought). The gothic subgenre seemed to have the strongest correlations with sensation seeking in all instances and psychological horrors had the weakest correlations in all instances. Table 2 summarizes the main findings, providing Pearson correlations for the variables discussed above.

Sensation Seeking, Horror, and Demographic Variables

Sensation seeking had a negative relationship with age ($r = -.44$; $p < .001$), which supports findings of earlier research (44). Younger respondents were more likely to score higher on the sensation-seeking trait than were older respondents. Interest in viewing horror movies also had a negative correlation to age ($r = -.28$; $p < .001$). Chi-square significance tests performed for the groups male and female showed no significant differences between men and women on these variables. Earlier studies reported differences between men and women on the sensation-seeking variable, with women scoring lower than men in all categories but experience seeking (48). There were no significant differences between men and women on either attendance to horror movies or interest in the genre.

Table 2. Pearson Correlations for the Variables Frequency of Attendance to Horror Movies, Interest in Horror Movies, and Sensation Seeking

	Frequency of Horror Movie Attendance	Total Horror Movie Interest	Gothic Interest	Sci-Fi Interest	Psycho Interest
Total SSS	.32***	.56***	.62***	.55***	.35***
Boredom	.19*	.44***	.46***	.42***	.35***
Disinhibition	.36***	.58***	.63***	.58***	.38***
Thrill Adventure	.22**	.35***	.38***	.33***	.22**
Experience Seeking	.28***	.47***	.53***	.44***	.19**

*$P < .05$
**$p < .01$
***$p < .001$

Partial Correlations

Partial correlation provides a means of describing the relationship between two variables, in this case sensation seeking and interest in viewing horror movies, while adjusting for the effects of one or more variables. Since age has been highly negatively correlated to both sensation seeking (44) and moviegoing in general (36), and was found in this study to be closely related to interest in horror movies, the effects of subjects' age needed to be controlled in order to better understand the relationship between sensation seeking and interest in the horror genre. The effects of age were assumed to be linear, making partial correlation possible.

The results of the partial correlation show that the relationship between sensation seeking and interest in horror movies is not a spurious one, $r = .51$; $p < .001$. Table 3 summarizes the main findings, showing a comparison of Pearson and partial correlations.

Table 3. A Comparison of Pearson Correlations and Partial Correlations for the Variables of Sensation Seeking and Interest in Horror Movies

	Pearson Correlations	Partial Correlations Controlling for Age
	Total Horror Interest	Total Horror Interest
Total Sensation–seeking score	.56***	.51***
Thrill and Adventure	.35***	.24**
Disinhibition	.58***	.54***
Boredom Susceptibility	.44***	.41***
Experience Seeking	.47***	.39***

*$p < .05$.
**$p < .01$.
***$p < .001$.

Religious Orthodoxy and Horror Movies

Fifty-two percent of the respondents agreed that an orthodox religion was important in their lives, and 54 percent said it was important to go to church. Forty-eight percent said orthodox religions did not provide satisfactory answers to spiritual questions. Younger respondents were more likely to be dissatisfied with orthodox religions. Age was negatively correlated with religious orthodoxy ($r = -.26$; $p < .001$).

A negative relationship was found between religious orthodoxy and interest in horror movies ($r = -.26$; $p < .001$). Religious orthodoxy had a significant negative correlation with frequency of attendance to horror movies ($r = -.36$; $p < .001$) and overall interest in the genre ($r = -.26$; $p < .001$). In addition, t-tests showed significant differences between those who rarely attended and those who frequently attended horror movies with regard to religious orthodoxy ($t = 4.03$; $p < .001$).

DISCUSSION

The hypothesis that a positive relationship exists between the sensation-seeking trait and interest in horror movies was supported in the findings of this research. Also supported was the hypothesis that a positive correlation would exist between sensation seeking and frequency of attendance at horror movies. These findings are high compared to those reported in other studies (37).

The positive relationship between sensation seeking and interest in horror movies was true not only for the overall genre and the total sensation-seeking scale, but was also true for subgenres and subscales. The strongest correlates of sensation-seeking were experience-seeking and disinhibition for all subgenres except the psychological horror subgenre. The sensation-seeking subfactor, thrill and adventure seeking, had the weakest correlation with interest in horror movies for all subgenres except, again, the psychological horror. Psychological horror also had a lower correlation with experience seeking. This might be explained by the tendency of the psychological horror to rely less on supernatural elements of its predators and more on knife-kill suspense. The stimulation audiences seek in psychological horrors may be slightly different, more physically arousing than those horrors that make use of predators which are truly mysterious. Real murderers rarely take on the superhuman (and subhuman) characteristics that are often given to the mad killers of the psychological horror movie, characteristics which include the uncanny knack of surviving against all odds to attack victims just when everyone presumed it was safe. Yet, mad killers are not as unfathomable as vampires, aliens, ghosts, and werewolves. It takes less effort for audiences to suspend disbelief for a psychological horror. The weaker correlation of thrill and adventure seeking with the other subgenres might be explained for similar reasons. Thrill and adventure seeking measures a subject's willingness to engage in physically dangerous activities, such as some outdoor sports. It is not a measure of a person's eagerness for vicarious experience. Science fiction and gothic horrors place more emphasis on supernatural and fantastic elements than the psychological horrors do, thus offering vicarious experiences which are not only undesirable in real life, but highly unlikely as well.

It was expected that experience seeking, as a measure of enjoyment of mystical thought and emphasis on intuition as opposed to conventional rationality, would have a strong relationship with interest in horror movies. A stronger relationship existed between disinhibition and interest in horror movies for all subgenres. A doctrine that places personal pleasure or happiness as the chief good in life seems on its face far removed from interest in horror. So why would a subscale designed to measure an extroverted philosophy and hedonistic social life correlate more strongly with horror movie interest than other sensation-seeking measures? The answer to this may be found in the willingness of disinhibition seekers to search out new and exciting experiences and sensations even if they are frightening, unconventional, or illegal. Horror movies, perhaps more than any other genre, allow a person to go beyond social boundaries and experience the wildest parties, the ugliest hallucinations, the ultimate power trip, the worst atrocity. In the horror movie nothing need be repressed; any taboo can be explored.

The correlations with religious orthodoxy were negative for both interest in horror movies and sensation seeking. In addition, those who were highly orthodox in their religious beliefs were not likely to be high sensation seekers. This might be explained by the observation that orthodox religions tend to promote skepticism over mysticism in order to be cleared of the taint of superstition. In addition, horror movies often deal with social taboos and the mystically evil things which the orthodox are often taught to shun.

The discrepancy between earlier findings and the findings of this study regarding differences between men and women on the sensation-seeking variable may indicate a problem with the representativeness of this sample. More likely, however, is that the effects of the women's movement and changing attitudes regarding appropriate behavior for women encouraged the expression of sensation-seeking aspects of female personalities in this later study. Dangerous sports and hedonistic pleasures are no longer reserved for men only.

The results of this research lend support to the idea that some people purposefully seek out hypernegative entertainment in order to gratify needs for stimulation. The sensation seeker's fascination for unconventional, uncharted territories, and a macho willingness to venture into scary waters, causes him or her to run the risk of being traumatized for the sake of excitement. That risk may in fact give audiences what Berlyne (4) described as a divine pleasure, mental but not physical involvement with danger.

But, horror movie audiences may also consciously or unconsciously be using the genre to help them develop inner resources. Although sensation seeking is not equated with cognitive curiosity, it is not incompatible with intellectual questing. The implication is strong that the desire to know about subjects with which it is impossible or undesirable to have direct experience brings some people to the horror film. Although the relationship between sensation seeking and interest in horror movies is clear, whether the motive for most audience members is curiosity or diversive exploration is yet to be discovered.

This study suggests a relationship exists between attraction to horror entertainment and sensation seeking, however, this does not support the larger assertion that curiosity about morbid things and the biological readiness to respond to dangerous situations, which may have had positive survival value for our ancestors, is in present day becoming a dysfunctional, morbid curiosity, an interest in irrelevant, morbid material because it is biologically stimulating. The question of whether there is an inherited biological foundation for behavior, and the question of perceived relevance of morbid material remain unanswered. In addition, other speculative explanations for the attraction horror movies hold for some audiences need to be empirically explored. These include: the idea that audiences are attracted to horror because of religious or supernatural aspects of the genre, that horror is attractive because of its dark eroticism, that people use horror as a rehearsal for bad death, and that the violence of these movies may be addicting, even for those audience members who may not be initially attracted to violent content.

Horror movies offer a distinct visual presentation in which the supernatural predator is clearly established, easily identified, easily observed. A person may even experience violent death through watching a horror film and live to tell of it. For some audiences the horror film may make the supernatural understood on an elementary level, satisfying a curiosity about those things that are primary, universal, and beyond the reach of science. The genre provides a tangible field for the brain's restless need to explore those subjects that may be the most stimulating and the most elusive: sex, violence, death, and the supernatural.

REFERENCES

1. Ansen, D. "The Beauty of Horror." *Newsweek*, March 8, 1981, pp. 73–77.
2. Bataille, G. *Death and Sensuality: A Study of Eroticism and the Taboo*. New York: Walker Company, 1962.
3. Berlyne, D. E. *Aesthetics and Psychobiology*. New York: McGraw Hill, 1971.
4. Berlyne, D. and Madsen, K. B. *Pleasure, Reward and Preference*. New York: Academic Press, 1973.
5. Boyanowsky, E., Newston, D., and Walster, E. "Film Preferences Following a Murder." *Communication Research 1*, 1974, pp. 32–43.
6. Brain, J. *The Last Taboo: Sex and the Fear of Death*. Garden City, New York: Ancho Press, 1979.
7. Butler, I. *Horror in the Cinema*. New York: Paperback Library, 1971.
8. Cain, S. "Woe is the Fan of Horror." *Atlanta Journal and Constitutional Weekend*, February 4, 1984, pp. 14.
9. Carroll, N. "Nightmare and the Horror Film: the Symbolic Biology of Fantastic Beings." *Film Quarterly 34*, 1981, pp. 16–26.
10. Clark, J. R. and Motto, A. L. "A Bevy of Negations Invades the Popular Arts." *Studies in Popular Culture* 3 Spring, 1980, pp. 20–34.

11. Daniels, L. *Living in Fear: A History of Horror in the Mass Media*. New York: Scribner, 1975.
12. Derry, C. *Dark Dreams: A Psychological History of Modern Horror Films*. London: Thomas Yosleff, 1977.
13. Dickstein, M. "The Aesthetics of Fright." *American Film*, September 1980, pp. 32–41.
14. Dunn, A. F. "The Dark Side of Erotic Fantasy." *Human Behavior*, November 1979, pp. 18–23.
15. Everson, W. K. *Classics of the Horror Film*. Secaucus, NJ: Citadel Press, 1974.
16. Fletcher, A. and Bowers, T. *Fundamentals of Advertising Research*. Columbus, OH: Grid Publishing, 1979.
17. Frederick, R. "Fantasy and Horror Genres Clicked at 1981 Pay Window." *Variety*, January 13, 1982, pp. 15.
18. Freedland, N. *The Occult Explosion*. New York: G. P. Putnam's Sons, 1972.
19. Gmelch, G. and Felson, R. "Can a Lucky Charm Get You Through Organic Chemistry?" *Psychology Today*, 1980, pp. 75–78.
20. Goldsmith, Williams. "Beloved Monsters: A Psychodynamic Appraisal of Horror." *Journal of Contemporary Psychotherapy* 7, 1975, pp. 17–22.
21. Haskins, J. B. "Toward a Psychobiological Theory of Motivations for Human Communication Behavior." Paper presented at the International Communication Association Conference, Boston, 1982.
22. Haskins, J. B. "Morbid Curiosity and the Mass Media: a Synergistic Relationship." In J. A. Crook, J. B. Haskins and P. G. Ashdown (Eds.), *Morbid Curiosity and the Mass Media: Proceedings of a Symposium*. Knoxville, TN: School of Journalism, University of Tennessee, Knoxville and the Gannett Foundation, 1984, pp. 1–44.
23. Haskins, J. B. "Morbid Curiosity and Mass Media." Keynote speech presented at the Morbid Curiosity and Media Culture Symposium. The University of Alabama at Birmingham, Department of Communication Studies. 31 October 1984.
24. Horwitz, J. "The Scare Movies." *Cosmopolitan*, July 1980, pp. 289–364.
25. Huss, R. and Ross, J. *Focus on the Horror Film*. Englewood Cliffs, NJ: Prentice-Hall, 1972.
26. Ingills, B. *Natural and Supernatural: A History of the Paranormal from Earliest Times to 1914*. London: Hodder and Stroughton, 1977.
27. Kapsis, R. "Dressed to Kill." *American Film*, March 1982, pp. 53–56.
28. Katz, E., Gurevitch, M. and Hass, H. "On the Use of Mass Media for Important Things." *American Sociological Review 38*, 1973, pp. 164–181.
29. Kluckhohn, C. "Recurrent Themes in Myths and Mythmaking." In *Myths and Mythmaking*. New York: George Braziller, 1960, pp. 46–59.
30. Otto, R. *The Idea of the Holy: An Inquiry into the Nontraditional Factor in the Idea of the Divine and its Relation to the Rational*, London: Oxford University Press, 1950.
31. Penzoldt, P. *The Supernatural in Fiction*. New York: Columbia University Press, 1965.
32. Rickey, C. "Hooked on Horror: Why We Like Scary Movies." *Mademoiselle*, November 1982, pp. 168–170.
33. Roberts, W. R. and Bywater, I. *Rhetoric and poetics of Aristotle*. New York: Random House, 1954, trans. (Reprinted from the Oxford Translation of Aristotle, Oxford: Clarendon Press.)
34. Rosenbaum, R. "Gooseflesh." *Harpers*, September 1979, pp. 86–75.
35. Sobchack, V. "The Violent Dance: A Personal Memoir of Death in the Movies." *Journal of Popular Film 3*, 1974, pp. 2–14.
36. Solomon, R. "The Opponent Process Theory of Behavioral Motivation." *American Psychologist*, *35*(8), 1982, pp. 691–712.
37. Steinberg, C. *Film Facts*. New York: Facts on File Inc., 1980.
38. Tamborini, R. and Stiff, J. "Predictors of Horror Film: Attendance and Appeal." *Communication Research 14*, 1987, pp. 415–436.
39. Tellote, J. P. "Human Artifice and the Science Fiction Film." *Film Quarterly 36*, 1983, pp. 44–51.
40. Tiger, L. "The Danger Vitamin." In J. A. Crook, J. B. Haskins and P. G. Ashdown (Eds.),

Morbid Curiosity and the Mass Media: Proceedings of a Symposium. Knoxville, TN: School of Journalism, The University of Tennessee and the Gannett Foundation, 1984, pp. 182–200.

41. Wilson, E. *On Human Nature*. Cambridge, MA: Harvard University Press, 1978.
42. Zillman, D. and Bryant, J. "Affect, Mood and Emotion as Determinants of Selective Exposure." In D. Zillman and J. Bryant (Eds.), *Selective Exposure to Communication* Hillsdale, NJ: Lawrence Erlbaum Associates, 1985, pp. 157–190.
43. Zuckerman, M. and Link, K. "Construct Validity for the Sensation Seeking Scale." *Journal of Consulting and Clinical Psychology 32*, 1968, pp. 420–426.
44. Zuckerman, M. "Dimensions of Sensation-seeking." *Journal of Consulting and Clinical Psychology 36*, 1971, pp. 45–52.
45. Zuckerman, M. *Sensation seeking: Beyond the optimal level of arousal*. New York: John Wiley, 1979.
46. Zuckerman, M. and Little, P. "Personality and Curiosity about Morbid and Sexual Events." *Personality and Individual Differences 7*, 1986, pp. 49–56.

3

Avoidances, Gratifications, and Consumption of Theatrical Films: The Rest of the Story

Philip Palmgreen
Patricia A. Lawrence

Research on uses and gratifications has amply demonstrated that media consumption is activated and guided by a wide range of motives, including surveillance, entertainment, social utility, personal identity, and parasocial interaction (7, 30). Moreover, rarely is consumption behavior dominated by a single motive. Instead, the typical consumption experience results from a number of motives acting in concert in ways that are as yet not well understood. For example, exposure to television news may be guided principally by a surveillance motive, but may be influenced simultaneously by the desire to escape from one's own personal cares, to interact parasocially with correspondents and anchorpersons, and to obtain information to use in social contexts (28, 36). Precisely which motivational pattern will predominate will vary according to the individual, the situation, the medium, and the type of content involved.

Understanding the dynamics of this motivational mix is a serious challenge to media gratification researchers. Perhaps what they need least at this point is evidence indicating that this already formidable endeavor is even more daunting than widely believed. But this is indeed the case for, despite the broad gamut of motivations which have been examined, researchers so far have focused almost exclusively on one general class of motivations—those activated by various gratifications sought from consumption experiences. Almost no attention has been given to motives for *avoiding* contact with the media. This is a peculiarly one-sided view of audience behavior, for psychologists long have understood that the motivation to avoid a person, object, situation, and so on, often may outweigh the pull of attracting forces. For example, the drug-induced pleasures of smoking may be counterbalanced by the threat of cancer, or the potential exhilaration of skydiving by fear for life and limb.

An understanding of such approach-avoidance conflicts is basic to the understanding of much human behavior, and may be no less crucial to an appreciation of the motivational forces underlying mass media consumption. For example, negative affective reactions engendered by television game shows may cause individuals to avoid that genre altogether. Theatrical movies, the medium which is the topic of this investigation, possess a host of features (e.g., high ticket prices, crowded seating, objectionable movie themes) which might motivate one to avoid going to a movie theater. The same might be said about other media and content types, yet only a few uses and gratifications studies have distinguished between "positive" motives (gratifications sought from media consumption) and "negative" gratifications or avoidances (reasons for avoiding such consumption), and these have focused exclusively on political media content (see 6, 8, 22). In the Becker (6) study, gratifications sought (GS) and avoidances emerged as separate factors, providing evidence that GS and avoidances are distinct conceptual entities and not merely mirror images. Also, McLeod and Becker (22) showed that GS and avoidances contributed separately and about equally to variance in a number of political effects variables.

Much work, however, remains to be done in identifying the dimensions of avoidance motivations for other content types across different media. How important a role avoidance motivations play, in comparison to gratifications sought in media consumption and effects processes, needs to be determined. Are the negative attributes of many media consumption situations so unpalatable that avoidance behavior frequently results, or are they relatively trivial "irritations" easily brushed aside? McLeod and Becker's (22) study is the only investigation to date which contrasted (in a multiple regression framework) the predictive capabilities of GS and avoidances, and their finding of relative parity may not hold in other contexts. In addition, the dependent variables in their study were various "political effects" measures, and the precise nature of the theoretical connection between effects measures and avoidances is unclear. Before such "avoidances and effects" studies are pursued seriously, investigations are needed which link avoidances to media consumption indices (e.g., exposure and medium and content choice) and to measures of psychological dependency on various media. This study explored gratifications sought and avoidance motivations related to a mass medium which has received very little attention from media gratifications researchers—theatrical films.

THE MOTIVATIONAL FRAMEWORK OF MOVIE GOING

Most uses and gratifications research has focused on the dominant medium of television, with a modicum of attention to newspapers and much less to radio and magazines. Curiously, though, very little research has been devoted exclusively to the investigation of motives for movie attendance. This is surprising, considering the social significance and level of popularity of the medium. As Austin (3) has observed, much of what little we know about the public's motives for movie attendance comes to us from comparative uses and gratifications studies which happened to include movies (12, 16, 18, 21). These studies appear to show that movies are superior to other media in fulfilling diversionary needs, such as escape and entertainment, but are less successful in gratifying more "important" or "meaningful" needs, such as surveillance (3).

Useful as these studies may be in placing movie use within the context of other mass media consumption, they do not represent in-depth investigations of the movie medium itself. In addition, they often suffer from the disadvantage of assuming that gratification categories developed for other media are directly relevant to, and inclusive of, audience motivations for movie going. These assumptions may not be warranted, given the many differences between theatrical movies and other mass media in terms of content, technical and structural characteristics, and context of consumption.

The few studies which have focused solely on theatrical films shed additional light on the diversity of audience uses of this unique medium. We will give only a brief summary of these studies here, which have been reviewed in detail in Austin (4) and Palmgreen et al. (26). Collectively, these scattered European and American studies on movie uses indicate that movie-going motives include entertainment, passing time, learning, relaxation, escape, social utility, and aesthetic experience (11, 19, 20, 23, 24, 39).

A more recent study of the move attendance motives of U.S. audience members was carried out by Austin (2, 3). In addition to many of the factors mentioned above, Austin's study found several dimensions (social activity, communication resources, relieve loneliness, social conformity) which emphasize the strong social character of movie attendance. Furthermore, three factors revealed the ability of movies to enhance or reduce positive and negative affective states (arousal/excitement, positive mood enhancement, relaxation).

Past research, therefore, despite its relative scarcity and limited scope, has yielded some important insights into the many different types of motives which may lead individuals to attend theatrical movies. The past research has many shortcomings, however. Only one of the investigations cited (2, 3) was guided by a theoretical framework (in this case, uses and gratifications). Also, either the researchers employed only a few open-ended questions (without accompanying closed-ended scales with their greater measurement precision) or they utilized closed-ended scales which had not been developed systematically from earlier more qualitative investigations directed specifically at movies. In addition, none of these studies examined movie avoidance motives.

Finally, only one study (2, 3) investigated the impact of various movie-going motives on actual theater attendance. In the 1985 paper, nine of twelve gratifications sought factors correlated significantly and positively with frequency of movie attendance. In the 1986 article, which utilized the same data set with more stringent factoring criteria, four of seven GS factors were found to be positively related to movie attendance. The four factors were enjoyment, escape, a general learning factor, and learning about one's self.

There is a need for additional research, therefore, on the motives for attendance and avoidance of theatrical films. In particular, studies are needed which explore the impact of gratifications sought and avoidances on movie attendance and related psychological constructs, such as movie dependency.

THE PRESENT STUDY

Respondents

A total of 486 college students (226 males and 260 females), enrolled in lower and upper division undergraduate communication classes at the University of Kentucky, responded in class to a 14-page questionnaire which had been pretested and modified before its administration. Students were awarded extra course credit for their participation.

Variables

The primary variables measured were gratifications sought from movie going and theatrical movie avoidances. Data also were gathered on frequency of movie attendance, movie dependency, frequency of discussing movies with others (by role relationship), and gender.

Measurement of Gratifications and Avoidances

In a preliminary investigation, 205 undergraduate students, enrolled in lower and upper division communication classes at the University of Kentucky, were asked to write separate essays on, not only their reasons *for* attending movies at theaters, but also on things they *disliked* about attending theatrical films.

For the present study, 50 gratifications sought items were developed from the essay responses. These were randomly ordered and described to respondents as "a list of reasons others have given for going to the movies in a movie theater." Respondents replied to each statement (e.g., "I go to movies to see the films everyone is talking about") using a seven-point "strongly agree" (scored as "7") to "strongly disagree" (scored as "1") scale.

Avoidances were conceptualized and measured according to the expectancy-value typology of consumption motivations developed by Palmgreen (25; see also 27). According to this conceptualization, "true avoidance" involves the belief that a media object in question (for example, political content) possesses a negatively valued attribute. From the preliminary essays, 20 attributes of theatrical films which were evaluated negatively by many of the essay writers were identified (e.g., "movie prices," "explicit sex or nudity in movies," "sticky floors in movie theaters"). To tap the avoidance motives connected with these attributes, two 20-item scales were constructed. One, which we shall label

Avoidance Attitude, sought to measure respondents' affective evaluations of each of the avoidance attributes. Respondents replied to the randomly ordered items (e.g., "movies contain too much sex and nudity") using a seven-point "strongly agree" (scored as "7") to "strongly disagree" (scored as "1") scale.

Since a negative attitude toward an attribute does not necessarily mean that this characteristic is an *important* reason for avoiding theatrical films, a second scale was constructed, termed Avoidance Importance. This scale tapped the importance of each of the above attributes as a cause for avoiding going to the movies in the future. Respondents indicated importance using a seven-point scale ("extremely important" = "7"; "not important at all" = "1").

A multiplicative avoidance index was then created for each attribute by multiplying each attitude measure by its corresponding importance measure. This weighted scale was employed as the measure of movie avoidance in the analyses which follow (range = 1–49).

Frequency of Attendance

Respondents were asked how often they attended movies (on the average). Choices included six foils ranging from "hardly ever" (scored as "1") to "once a week" (scored as "6").

Movie Dependency

Media dependency, which ordinarily is conceptualized in uses and gratifications studies as a psychological attachment to a media source, has been the focus of considerable attention in recent years (25). The prominence of the media dependency concept (also called "attachment" and "affinity") probably stems from its connections with the concept of functional alternatives (31) and with media dependency theory (5; see also 35). It has been found that dependency is related to a number of motives for attending to the media (10, 14, 32, 33, 34, 36, 37, 38). The more motivated that persons are in seeking gratifications from a particular medium, or the more they perceive they are obtaining gratifications, the more they will come to depend on that medium (35).

The movie dependency scale in this study was adapted from Rubin and Rubin's (34) television affinity index. Respondents were asked to indicate on a seven-point scale ("strongly agree" = "7"; "strongly disagree" = "1") the extent to which they agreed with five statements related to going to movies at a movie theater: (1) I would rather spend my leisure time at the movies than some place else; (2) I could easily do without going to a movie for several months; (3) I would feel lost without the movies to go to; (4) If for some reason I couldn't go to the movies at a movie theater, I would really miss it; and (5) Going to the movies is an important part of my lifestyle. Item number 2 was recoded to correspond directionally with the other dependency items. Reliability analysis yielded a coefficient alpha of .82 and indicated that all five items contributed to the strength of the scale. Movie dependency was moderately to strongly correlated with frequency of attendance ($r = .55$, $p < .001$).

Interpersonal Utility

Since movie going has been shown by previous research to have a strong social dimension, a scale indicating the frequency of discussion of movies with others was created and employed as a predictor of frequency of attendance and movie dependency. Using a seven-point scale ("very frequently" = "7"; "not at all frequently" = "1"), respondents indicated how frequently they talked about movies with friends, dates, family members, and co-workers. Responses to the four scales were averaged to create a movie discussion index.

GS and Avoidance Factor Scales

Gratifications sought and the multiplicative avoidance measures were factor analyzed separately using SPSSX with orthogonal rotation. These analyses employed the principal factors method with iteration and R^2 communality estimates in the diagonal and varimax rotation. Factor criteria were a minimum eigenvalue of 1.0 and at least two items with loadings ≥.40 per factor.[1]

Gratifications sought. Ten factors which met the above criteria emerged in this analysis, which together accounted for 61 percent of the total variance. Table 1 lists the items for each factor and the factor loadings. The factor structure is relatively pure, as indicated by the fact that only one item had loadings ≥.40 on more than one factor. Six of the 50 items did not load on any factor at ≥.40.

Table 2 lists the percent of total variance explained by each GS factor and the means, standard deviations, and reliabilities (coefficient alpha) of the factor scores, which were calculated by summing the scores for all items with loadings ≥.40 on a particular factor and dividing by the number of items.[2]

The factors which emerged were labeled:

1. *General Learning*—to learn about other cultures, people, and lifestyles;
2. *Mood Control/Enhancement*—using movies to change moods, especially to escape from distressing situations;

---

[1] The decision to employ this factoring procedure was based on extensive comparative analyses of the same data set reported in Palmgreen et al. (26). In these analyses both GS items and the Avoidance Importance items (the measure of avoidance employed in that study) were factor analyzed using both SPSSX and SAS, and employing orthogonal and oblique rotations. In general, the orthogonal solutions were more clearly interpretable and conformed to conceptual expectations more closely than the oblique solutions. The SAS-SPSSX comparison yielded general agreement for the GS orthogonal solutions; for example, the same number of factors emerged and the same items loaded on each factor with almost identical rank-ordering. For the avoidance items, however, SAS yielded three orthogonal factors which were difficult to interpret, while SPSSX yielded five factors which were conceptually meaningful. For comparison's sake, therefore, the SPSSX orthogonal solutions were employed for both GS and avoidances in that study, and they are employed here to maintain both within and across study comparability.

[2] The evidence from a number of investigations indicates that no one method of computing factor index scores is superior, and that all methods yield scores that are highly correlated (1, 9, 13, 15, 17). The unweighted sum method employed here has the advantage of yielding an index that may be interpreted in terms of the original 7-point scale.

Table 1. Factor Loadings* for Movies Gratifications Sought (GS) Questionnaire Format: "I GO TO MOVIES. . . ."

Factor 1: General Learning	**Loadings**
to learn more about other cultures	.81
to learn about other people, places, and things	.79
to learn about historical periods and events	.69
to see the beautiful scenes and places	.65
to learn more about other lifestyles	.62
to enjoy the movie photography	.46
because movies are thought-provoking	.43
Factor 2: Mood Control/Enhancement	
to change my mood	.62
to put myself in a better frame of mind	.57
to get away from my problems	.57
to get away from a boring routine	.56
because I can usually find one to fit the mood I want	.48
to relax	.48
to get away from people I live/work with	.43
Factor 3: Social Utility	
because it's a good thing to do socially	.68
to see films everyone is talking about	.66
to give me something to do with others	.59
because it's a good place to go (or take) a date	.57
because it gives me something to talk about with others	.46**
because it's a fun thing to do with friends	.42
Factor 4: Medium Characteristics	
because the good sound system helps me get involved with the film	.75
because the big screen helps me get involved with the film	.71
because the darkness helps me get involved with the film	.71
because I like the theater atmosphere	.47
to enjoy the special effects	.40
Factor 5: Personal Identity	
because I can often identify with the characters' personal problems	.69
to compare my life with those of the characters in the film	.69
because I can identify with certain characters	.61
because I can learn things which help me deal with my own problems	.56
because I like to fantasize about the film	.42
Factor 6: Entertainment	
for enjoyment	.81
to have a good time	.73
to be entertained	.63
Factor 7: Social facilitation	
because . . .	
I like to compare my reactions to the film with the audience's	.68
I like to watch other people's reactions to the film	.66
the audience reactions increase my enjoyment of the film	.48

Table 1. (*Continued*)

Factor 8: Communication Avoidance	
because I don't have to talk to anyone during the film	.60
because it lets me avoid talking for a while on a first date	.51
to be "alone in a crowd"	.50
Factor 9: Communication Utility	
because my friends like to talk about the latest films	.62
because I sometimes feel "out of it" with my friends if I haven't seen any of the recent films	.52
because it gives me something to talk about with others	.48**
because movies give me something to talk about on a date	.40
Factor 10: Great Expectations	
to see certain actors and actresses	.57
to compare a film with the book on which it is based	.54

*All loadings ≥ .40 are reported.
**Loaded on two factors.

3. *Social Utility*—going to movies with others as a social event;
4. *Medium Characteristics*—attributes of the medium itself, including sound, big screen, and darkness;
5. *Personal Identity*—identification with movie characters and their problems;
6. *Entertainment*—going for enjoyment and a good time;
7. *Social Facilitation*—crowd reactions facilitate enjoyment;
8. *Communication Avoidance*—avoiding talking with others, especially in initial stages of a relationship;
9. *Communication Utility*—using movies as topic of discussion;

Table 2. Factor Statistics for Movie Gratifications Sought (GS)

Factor Label	Variance Explained	Mean*	Standard Deviation	Coefficient Alpha
1. General Learning	23.8	3.98	1.29	.87
2. Mood Control/Enhancement	7.9	4.45	1.21	.81
3. Social Utility	5.3	4.97	1.14	.81
4. Medium Characteristics	4.9	3.89	1.34	.81
5. Personal Identity	4.0	3.55	1.32	.83
6. Entertainment	3.3	6.47	0.83	.85
7. Social Facilitation	2.8	2.66	1.27	.71
8. Communication Avoidance	2.5	2.40	1.24	.62
9. Communication Utility	2.3	3.27	1.25	.78
10. Great Expectations	2.2	4.56	1.43	.50

*Range: 1 to 7 with "1" = "low" to "7" = high"

10. *Great Expectations*—movie expectations based on a book or on the reputation/image of the actors.[3]

Avoidances. Analysis of the multiplicative avoidance measures yielded five factors which accounted for 42 percent of the total variance. Table 3 lists the items for each factor and the factor loadings. Again, the factor structure is relatively pure, with only one item double-loading at ≥.40. Only three items failed to load on any of the five factors at ≥.40. One of these, "inappropriate crowd reactions," did have a loading of .39 on the Social Environmental Constraints factor.

Table 3. Factor Loadings* for Avoidance Factors

Factor 1: Specific Content	Loadings
obscene language in movies	.88
explicit sex and nudity in movies	.85
violence in movies	.78
Factor 2: General Environmental Constraints	
movie theaters that are too hot or cold	.64
having to crawl over other people	.60
other people blocking my view of the movie	.53**
having to fight traffic to get to the movie	.46
sticky floors in movie theaters	.44
sound tracks that are too loud or too soft	.43
Factor 3: Physical Environmental Constraints	
having to sit close to strangers in theaters	.55
having to sit still for long periods of time	.55
uncomfortable theater seats	.44
Factor 4: Social Environmental Constraints	
other people in the audience talking too much	.62
crying babies and noisy kids at movies	.54
other people blocking my view of the moive	.40**
(inappropriate crowd reactions to the movie	.39)
Factor 5: General Content	
the themes of today's movies	.65
movies that don't live up to my expectations	.59
movies that lack good taste	.53

*All loadings ≥ .40 are reported.
**Loaded on two factors.

[3] For an in-depth discussion of these factors and their implications, the reader is referred to Palmgreen et al. (26).

Table 4. Factor Statistics for Avoidance Factors

Factor Label	Variance Explained	Mean*	Standard Deviation	Standard Mean**	Coefficient Alpha
1. Specific Content	19.3	13.43	11.05	4.48	.68
2. General Constraints	12.5	21.18	8.44	3.53	.88
3. Physical Constraints	4.3	14.57	7.83	4.86	.66
4. Social Constraints	3.2	24.36	9.69	6.09	.68
5. General Content	2.7	17.81	8.19	5.93	.66

*Range: 1 to 49 with "1" = "low" to "49" = "high"

**Mean multiplicative product divided by the number of items per factor to yield a standardized index for comparison.

Table 4 lists the percent of total variance explained by each avoidance factor, and the means, standard deviations, and reliabilities (coefficient alpha) of the factor scores (calculated in the same manner as the GS factor scores).

The factors which emerged were:

1. *Specific Content*—obscene language, explicit sex, violence;
2. *General Environmental Constraints*—certain features of the sensory/physical environment, such as theaters being too hot or cold, having to crawl over other people, or fight traffic;
3. *Physical Environmental Constraints*—physical factors relating to seating and viewing comfort, such as sitting close to strangers, sitting still, uncomfortable seats;
4. *Social Environmental Constraints*—various irritating social factors, including other people talking and babies crying;
5. *General Content*—objectionable thematic characteristics of movies as a whole.[4]

The avoidance item "movie prices" failed to emerge clearly on any of the factors. By contrast, the high cost of movie tickets was almost a universal complaint in the pre-survey essays, and the movie prices item had a mean of 5.55 on the Avoidance Importance scale (highest of the 20 items) and a mean of 6.10 on the Avoidance Attitude scale (second highest among the 20 items). This suggests the need for refinement of the measuring instrument to include other costs related to movies (e.g., the price of concession items) which might allow economics/cost to emerge as a separate factor, as one might expect. In any case,

[4] An in-depth discussion of movie avoidances is provided in Palmgreen et al. (26). That study, employing the same data set, factor analyzed what we have termed here the Avoidance Importance items, rather than the Attitude-Importance product, using the same factoring procedures employed here. That analysis also yielded five avoidance factors which were very similar to the five which emerged here. Correlating the factor scores of conceptually similar factors yielded Pearson *r*'s ranging from .68 to .91.

the movie prices item is included in the avoidance block in subsequent analyses here.

RESULTS

Correlates of Movie Attendance and Dependency on Movies

The zero-order Pearson correlations between frequency of movie attendance, psychological dependency on movies, and their various predictors are displayed in Table 5.

All but one of the gratifications sought factors display significant positive correlations with frequency of attendance. Mood Control/Enhancement is the strongest predictor among these factors ($r = .28$), indicating that there is an important affective component in the motivational structure of movie going. The second strongest GS predictor is Social Utility ($r = .22$). This, when coupled with the fact that the strongest correlate of attendance is the frequency of

Table 5. Pearson Correlations Between Frequency of Movie Attendance, Movie Dependency and Various Predictors

	Frequency of Movie Attendance		Movie Dependency	
Predictor	***r***	**Sig. Level**	***r***	**Sig. Level**
Antecedents				
Gender*	.07	.076	−.08	.046
Movie Discussion	.30	.001	.30	.001
Gratifications Sought				
General Learning	.11	.006	.21	.001
Mood Control	.28	.001	.40	.001
Social Utility	.22	.001	.36	.001
Medium Characteristics	.16	.001	.27	.001
Personal Identity	.15	.001	.34	.001
Entertainment	.25	.001	.27	.001
Social Facilitation	.03	.237 (n.s.)	.16	.001
Communication Avoidance	.07	.053	.20	.001
Communication Utility	.16	.001	.28	.001
Great Expectations	.11	.007	.08	.048
Avoidances				
Movie Prices	−.10	.011	−.14	.001
Specific Content	−.09	.024	.03	.227 (n.s.)
General Environment	−.10	.014	−.08	.043
Physical Environment	−.08	.048	−.09	.030
Social Environment	.05	.120 (n.s.)	.10	.017
General Content	−.19	.001	−.18	.001

*dummy coded: 0 = female; 1 = male

discussing movies with others ($r = .30$), underscores the strong social nature of movie going discussed earlier.

All but one of the avoidance factors show significant negative correlations with movie attendance, although the magnitude of the coefficients is lower than that for the GS factors as a group. General Content is the strongest of the avoidance predictors ($r = -.19$).

All of the gratifications sought factors are significant predictors of movie dependency, and in all 10 instances the correlation between a GS factor and dependency is stronger (sometimes considerably so) than the corresponding correlation between that particular factor and frequency of attendance. The average correlation between the GS factors and frequency of movie attendance is .15, while the corresponding GS/dependency average is .26.This is to be expected,since availability factors (e.g., work schedule, amount of leisure time, proximity to movie theaters, theater offerings) can be expected to reduce the influence of gratifications sought on frequency of movie attendance, while an individual's psychological and affective attachment to theatrical films should be less affected by such factors.

As with frequency of attendance, Mood Control/Enhancement is the strongest GS correlate of dependency ($r = .40$), followed again by Social Utility ($r = .36$). The highly social character of movie going again is emphasized by the relatively strong correlations between dependency and movie discussion ($r = .30$) and Communication Utility ($r = .28$). Personal Identity, however, also is a strong predictor of dependency ($r = .34$), indicating that the ability to associate one's own problems and situations with those of movie characters promotes feelings of attachment to the medium.

Four of the avoidance factors display the expected significant negative correlations with dependency on movies, with General Content again the strongest negative correlate ($r = -.18$). Social Environmental Constraints, however, has a significant positive relationship with dependency ($r = .10$). This variable also had shown a positive (though nonsignificant) correlation with attendance. This is surprising, since this factor had the highest standardized mean (see Table 4) among the five-factor analytically derived avoidance dimensions. No convincing explanation readily presents itself for this apparent anomaly.

Hierarchical Regression Analysis

Examination, therefore, of the zero-order correlations yields some indication of the relative strengths of various individual variables as predictors of movie attendance and dependency. Unfortunately, the relatively strong intercorrelations among the 10 GS factors (25 of the 45 nonredundant correlations ranged from .30 to .64), and among the avoidance measures (5 of the 15 nonredundant correlations ranged from .33 to .49), meant that multicollinearity would have caused problems with the stability of Beta coefficients in multiple regression analyses aimed at examining the relative contributions of individual factors.

However, the fact that the GS factors were essentially uncorrelated with the avoidances (as Becker's (6) findings led us to expect) made it possible to enter the GS factors and the avoidance measures as separate blocks of variables in hierarchical regression analyses directed at examining the relative contributions of these two types of motivational factors to variance in movie attendance and dependency. The analyses followed the transactional approach suggested by McLeod and Becker (22) and Wenner (36, 37), in which more stable transituational variables are entered prior to gratification indices. In this particular case, gender and frequency of movie discussion were entered as a block first, followed by the GS factors. The avoidance block was entered last in the equations. It was reasoned that if avoidance motivations are in fact conceptually and empirically distinct from gratifications sought, and if they add to our understanding of media consumption, they should account for significant additional variance in the dependent variables after the inclusion of the GS block. The results of these analyses are shown in Tables 6 and 7.

Table 6 clearly demonstrates that gratifications sought are relatively strong predictors of movie dependency, accounting as a block for an additional 16.9 percent of the variance after the entry of the gender/movie discussion control block ($p<.001$). Avoidances, too, explain significant additional variance after both GS and the control variables are entered, though their contribution (4.1 percent; $p<.001$) in comparison to gratifications sought is relatively small.

As might have been anticipated on the basis of the correlational findings and discussion, gratifications sought do less well as predictors of movie attendance, though they do explain an additional 7.8 percent of the variance after the control block is entered ($p<.001$). In an absolute sense, avoidances explain approximately the same amount of additional variance in attendance (3.8 percent; $p<.001$) as they do for dependency (4.1 percent). Relative to gratifications sought, however, avoidances appear to be a much more important motivational factor in explaining attendance than they do in accounting for variance in dependency. With dependency, the GS block explains over four times as much additional variance as the avoidance block (16.9 percent to 4.1 percent). With attendance, this ratio falls to approximately two to one (7.8 percent to 3.8 percent).The explanation may lie in the fact that the avoidance importance component (i.e., the importance of reasons "to avoid going to movies in the

Table 6. Hierarchical Regression: GS and Avoidance Blocks as Predictors of Movie Dependency

Factors Entered	Multiple *R*	*R* Square	*R* Square Change	Sig. Level of Change
Gender/Discussion	.302	.091	.091	.001
Gratifications Sought	.510	.260	.169	.001
Avoidances	.548	.301	.041	.001

Table 7. Hierarchical Regression: GS and Avoidance Blocks as Predictors of Movie Attendance

Factors Entered	Multiple *R*	*R* Square	*R* Square Change	Sig. Level of Change
Gender/Discussion	.302	.091	.091	.001
Gratifications Sought	.411	.169	.078	.001
Avoidances	.455	.207	.038	.001

future") of the multiplicative avoidance index deals specifically with movie attendance. Avoidance as a concept, in fact, is concerned directly with exposure, in this case, attendance of films. It should, therefore, be more strongly correlated with exposure measures than with dependency. Gratifications sought, however, as we argued previously, should be more strongly related to dependency than to exposure because of the influence of availability factors. This latter finding is consistent with Wenner's (37) findings for both network television news and "60 Minutes."

Hierarchical regression analyses (not shown here) also were run which reversed the order of entry of the gratifications sought and avoidance blocks. This resulted in only minor changes in the variance increments discussed above, although the avoidance block did perform slightly better when entered before gratifications sought.[5]

DISCUSSION

The results of this study strongly suggest that avoidances constitute a distinct and important type of media consumption motivation. In the context of movie going, they provide at least preliminary evidence that avoidance motives play a more important role, relative to gratifications sought, in influencing actual behavior (i.e., movie attendance) than they do in affecting related psychological constructs, such as dependency on movies.

While it is clear that gratifications sought are more powerful predictors of theatrical film consumption measures than are avoidances, the perceived negative attributes of film cannot be considered only minor irritations. It would seem that the motion picture and theater industries can ill-afford to neglect the avoidance motives spawned by such factors as high ticket prices, objectionable movie themes and content, theater seating arrangements, and even the ubiquitous sticky

[5] The predictive abilities of the multiplicative avoidance index were compared to those of the importance and attitude indices considered separately by substituting one then the other of these measures for the multiplicative index in the hierarchical regression analyses. The multiplicative index was consistently superior as a predictor of attendance and dependency in these comparisons, though the differences usually were not large.

floors. It should be noted, too, that this study concerned a sample of college students. These are young, especially avid members of the movie audience who may be more emotionally and psychologically resilient than older individuals, and whose psyches may be particularly impervious to dealing with heavy traffic, faulty sound tracks, and sexual or violent movie content. Movie audience attendance figures and some comments in the pre-survey essays from this study indicate that, in fact, sex and violence serve as powerful attractants, rather than repellents, for many college-age students. Older audiences, however, may find many of the avoidance factors identified here less easy to ignore. Studies conducted with older populations are called for; they may find that avoidances are relatively more powerful predictors of movie consumption measures, and may constitute major reasons why older individuals attend movies much less frequently. Among the elderly and infirm, even the sheer physical rigors of going to the cinema may prove too much to overcome except on an infrequent basis.

Therefore, we are far from being able to state convincing generalizations about the place occupied by avoidance factors in the motivational framework of media consumption. It is likely that distinctive media and content types, which have been shown to be differentiated on a number of dimensions of gratifications sought (29), are probably equally differentiated in regard to their avoidance characteristics. In addition, the strength of avoidance motives may vary with different audience subgroups, as we have noted. Finally, the context of media consumption may be an important factor. Just how and why most media gratifications research has managed to avoid the study of avoidances are questions which perhaps should be explored. Whatever the reasons for this exclusion, however, it is time to begin redressing the balance by paying more attention to audience motives for *not* engaging in mass media consumption.

REFERENCES

1. Alwin, D. F. "The Use of Factor Analysis in Constructing Linear Composites in Social Research." *Sociological Methods and Research* 2, 1973, pp. 191–214.
2. Austin, B. A. "Motivations for Movie Attendance." Paper presented to the conference of the Eastern Communication Association, Providence, RI, 1985.
3. Austin, B. A. "Motivations for Movie Attendance." *Communication Quarterly* 34(2), 1986, pp. 115–126.
4. Austin, B. A., *Immediate Seating: A Look at Movie Audiences*. Belmont, CA: Wadsworth Pub. Co., 1989.
5. Ball-Rokeach, S. J. and DeFleur, M. L. "A Dependency Model of Mass Media Effects." *Communication Research* 3, 1976, pp. 3–21.
6. Becker, L. B. "Measurement of Gratifications." *Communication Research* 6(1), 1979, pp. 54–73.
7. Blumler, J. G. and Katz, E. *The Uses of Mass Communications: Current Perspectives on Gratifications Research*. Beverly Hills: Sage, 1974.
8. Blumler, J. G. and McQuail, D. *Television in Politics*. Chicago: University of Chicago Press, 1969.
9. Dagenais, F. and Marascuilo, L. A. "The Effect of Factor Scores, Guttman Scores, and Simple

Sum Scores on the Size of F ratios in an Analysis of Variance Design." *Multivariate Behavior Research* 8, 1973, pp. 491–502.

10. de Bock, H. "Gratification During a Newspaper Strike and TV Blackout." *Journalism Quarterly* 57, 1980, pp. 61–66, 78.
11. DeMaday, A. "An Enquiry Respecting the Cinematography Made in the Schools of Neuchatel, Lausanne and Geneva." *International Review of Educational Cinematography*, November 1929, pp. 531–552; December 1929, pp. 638–667.
12. Elliott, W. A. and Quattlebaum, C. P. "Similarities and Patterns of Media Use: A Cluster Analysis of Media Gratifications." *Western Journal of Speech Communication* 43, 1979, pp. 61–72.
13. Gorsuch, R. L. *Factor Analysis*. Philadelphia: Saunders, 1974.
14. Greenberg, B. S. "Gratifications of Television Viewing and Their Correlates for British Children." In J. G. Blumler and E. Katz (Eds.), *The Uses of Mass Communications: Current Perspectives on Gratifications Research*. Beverly Hills: Sage, 1974, pp. 71–92.
15. Horn, J. L. "An Empirical Comparison of Methods for Estimating Factor Scores." *Educational and Psychological Measurements* 25, 1965, pp. 313–322.
16. Katz, E., Gurevitch, M. and Haas, H. "On the Use of the Mass Media for Important Things." *American Sociological Review* 38, 1973, pp. 164–181.
17. Kim, J. and Mueller, C. W. *Introduction to Factor Analysis: What it is and How to Do It*. Beverly Hills: Sage, 1978.
18. Kippax, S. and Murray, J. P. "Using the Mass Media: Need Gratification and Perceived Utility." *Communication Research* 7(3), 1980, pp. 335–360.
19. Krasilov, A. F. Study cited in Gaer, F. D. "The Soviet Film Audience: A Confidential View." *Problems of Communism* 23, 1974, pp. 56–70.
20. Lassner, R. "Sex and Age Determinants of Theatre and Movie Interests." *Journal of General Psychology* 31, 1944, pp. 241–271.
21. Lichtenstein, A. and Rosenfeld, L. B. "Uses and Misuses of Gratifications Research: An Explication of Media Functions." *Communication Research* 10(1), 1983, pp. 97–109.
22. McLeod, J. M. and Becker, L. B. "Testing the Validity of Gratification Measures Through Political Effects Analysis." In J. G. Blumler and E. Katz (Eds.), *The Uses of Mass Communications: Current Perspectives on Gratifications Research*. Beverly Hills: Sage, 1974, pp. 137–164.
23. O'Brien, J. M. *Experiencing the Popular Film: An Audience Gratifications Study*. Unpublished Ph.D. dissertation, Northwestern University, 1977.
24. Opinion Research Corporation. *The Public Appraises Movies: Survey for Motion Picture Association of America*. In National Association of Theatre Owners File, Department of Archives and Manuscripts, Brigham Young University, Box 9, Folder 10, 1957.
25. Palmgreen, P. "Uses and Gratifications: A Theoretical Perspective." In R. N. Bostrom (Ed.), *Communication Yearbook*. Beverly Hills: Sage, 1984, pp. 20–55.
26. Palmgreen, P., Cook, P. L., Harvill, J. and Helm, D. "The Motivational Framework of Movie Going: Uses and Avoidances of Theatrical Films." In B. Austin (Ed.), *Current Research in Film* (Vol. 4). Norwood, NJ: Ablex, 1988, pp. 1–23.
27. Palmgreen, P. and Rayburn, J. D. "An Expectancy-Value Approach to Media Gratifications." In K. E. Rosengren, L. A. Wenner and P. Palmgreen (Eds.), *Media Gratifications Research: Current Perspectives*. Beverly Hills: Sage, 1985, pp. 61–72.
28. Palmgreen, P., Wenner, L. A. and Rayburn, J. D. "Relations Between Gratifications Sought and Obtained: A Study of Television News." *Communication research* 7, 1980, pp. 161–192.
29. Palmgreen, P., Wenner, L.A. and Rosengren, K. E. "Uses and Gratifications Research: The Past Ten Years." In K. E. Rosengren, L. A. Wenner and P. Palmgreen (Eds.), *Media Gratifications Research: Current Perspectives*. Beverly Hills: Sage, 1985, pp. 11–37.
30. Rosengren, K. E., Wenner, L. A. and Palmgreen, P. *Media Gratifications Research: Current Perspectives*. Beverly Hills: Sage, 1985.

31. Rosengren, K. E. and Windahl, S. "Mass Media Consumption as a Functional Alternative." In D. McQuail (Ed.), *Sociology of Mass Communications*. Harmondsworth: Penguin, 1972.
32. Rubin, A. M. "An Examination of Television Viewing Motivations." *Communications Research* 8, 1981, pp. 141–165.
33. Rubin, A. M. "Television Uses and Gratifications: The Interaction of Viewing Patterns and Motivations." *Journal of Broadcasting* 27, 1983, pp. 37–51.
34. Rubin, A. M. and Rubin, R. B. "Older Persons' TV Viewing Patterns and Motivations." *Communication Research* 9, 1982, pp. 287–313.
35. Rubin, A. M. and Windahl, S. "The Uses and Dependency Model of Mass Communication." *Critical Studies in Mass Communication* 3, 1986, pp. 184–199.
36. Wenner, L. A. "Gratifications Sought and Obtained in Program Dependency: A Study of Network Evening News Programs and '60 Minutes'." *Communication Research* 9, 1982, pp. 539–560.
37. Wenner, L. A. "Model Specification and Theoretical Development in Gratifications Sought and Obtained Research: A Comparison of Discrepancy and Transactional Approaches." *Communication Monographs* 53, 1986, pp. 160–179.
38. Windahl, S., Hojerback, I. and Hedinsson, E. "Adolescents Without Television: A Study in Media Deprivation." *Journal of Broadcasting and Electronic Media* 30, 1986, pp. 47–63.
39. Wozniacki, J. "Kino i teatr a uczestnictwo w kulturze." *Kultura: Spoleczenstwo* 21, 1977, pp. 163–173.

4

Psychological Approaches to Film Audience Research: A Critique*

Geoffrey H. Blowers

INTRODUCTION

Historically, research into the audiences for film, as opposed to that for television or radio, has proceeded at a snail's pace. This is an unusual state of affairs as the film industry has made and continues to make vast fortunes (as well as some spectacular losses) and accounts in the U.S. for over 50 percent of all expenditures on "spectator amusements."[1] In spite of the fact that in absolute terms film audiences (in the conventional context of the movie theatre) are diminishing universally, returns can still be enormously high on a fraction of the films produced and distributed annually. Yet the world's film industries have been seemingly reluctant or simply uninterested in fostering audience research except on occasion in purely marketing terms. The questions of interest to producers spring from the marketplace ("who" and "how many" go to see a film) not the psychological laboratory ("why" or "for what purpose").

Yet psychology is implicated in nearly all questions posed about film audiences. Since the viewing process, indeed the institution of cinema, would not be possible were it not for the visual illusion of apparent movement (the *phi phenomenon*), and the fusion of light at high frequencies of flashing, perception can be taken as fundamental. The psychology of perception not only tries to

---

* This article is based upon an invited paper given in a symposium on Philippine Film and Television Culture at the Psikolohiyang Pilipino National Conference held in the Bulacan Convention Center, Malolos, Bulacan on October 25, 1986. Supported by grant no: 335/014/0019 made available by the Research Grants Committee of the University of Hong Hong.

[1] Taken from "The Motion Picture Audience: A Neglected Aspect of Film Research" in Austin (5).

account for *phi* activity (see for example, Anderson & Anderson, 1) and flicker fusion (27), but also the visual "momentum" a viewer experiences when watching a film crafted according to conventional editing techniques (17, 18), and the way successive scenes of a film are integrated (19). At this level it is a matter of trying to understand how basic elements of film lead phenomenally to simple forms and movements (although their explanations are by no means simple).

Beyond this are questions of the way meaning is imputed to such forms. Here the answers, such as they are, are couched in terms of the qualities of percepts (e.g., Arnheim, 2) or, from other theoretical perspectives, past experiences (memory) or unconscious processes (psychoanalysis). Questions about the nature of perception underlie not only the problems of how the film viewer comprehends film but also how the viewer *qua* experimental subject understands the psychological task set him or her in the research study in which he or she partakes. For the psychological task, the researcher's assessment is as much a part of the subject's phenomenal field as is the object of that assessment (the viewing experience). This latter point is often overlooked by many audience researchers who implicitly believe that the methods they employ somehow transparently reveal the psychic phenomena they study. But many methods, far from achieving this, actually constrain the researcher's accessibility to knowing what his experimental subjects know. Since much film audience research is concerned with fathoming viewing experience, its findings are likely to be severely limited until or unless alternative modes of enquiry are found.[2]

In support of this position I review a few selected examples of studies from the film audience literature. Specifically I have chosen a cross section of studies which have conceptualized film audiences in psychological terms in order to review the psychological questions posed about such audiences, and concomitantly the methods invoked to answer those questions. In doing so I propose some criteria which must be met if the study of individual filmic perception is to advance, and suggest a method which meets such criteria and may yet bear fruit.

Austin's recent bibliography (5) and update (4) of film audience research studies have made the start of this task considerably easier. Austin's project has raised our awareness of the need for rigorous systematic research in this area (as opposed to what he sees as "armchair philosophizing") by the application of social science methods. Such methods will be of interest to those with a stake in the psychology of film, particularly where that psychology extends to national and cultural boundaries. But I want to argue that while there have been some gains using them, these methods are themselves subject to criticisms which need to be examined before further work in this area should be undertaken.

[2] This chapter is not a critique of all possible approaches; rather it focuses upon those methods which have been employed in the investigation of *psychological* questions of film audiences. For a critique of some alternative approaches to film audience research I refer the reader to the eloquent article by Gina Marchetti (26).

CONVENTIONAL APPROACHES

Motivations and Attitudes

After detailing a number of reasons for why there has been a dearth of film audience research, Austin highlights a number of possible areas for research by way of analyses of research-to-date. One of these is what he terms "antecedent conditions to movie-going" in which he points to several studies, including his own, which have purportedly shown that "respondents evaluate subject matter as an important factor in determining whether or not to see a movie . . . behind-the-screen production personnel as the least important" (5, p. xxviii) and that decision making is inevitably directed towards a particular film (as opposed to film in general). Little is known of individual "motivations" for attending particular films and it is to this aim that future research should be directed.

Austin's research, like that of many others in this area, makes use of a conventional research tool: the questionnaire and the rating scale in which typically respondents (already a self-selected group of volunteers) reply to written questions, either prior to or immediately after viewing a film, or are recruited from universities in answer to advertisements seeking regular movie goers. Subjects are then categorized into "heavy" and "light" viewers. Questions are pre-selected by an experimenter. Answers can be correlated with a variety of variables of interest, such as the type of film generally preferred, the rating of the film,[3] type of theatre in which film is viewed, and so forth. The criticisms of this approach in general have been made before but we should be reminded that the answers people give in questionnaires do not necessarily reflect what they feel, think or do in a situation which any particular question addresses (see, for example, 20).

Also the questions presuppose certain answers. For example, the researcher may wish to assess the extent to which a "word-of-mouth" operation is likely to take effect with a particular audience. In the prepared questionnaire, respondents are usually asked—"Would you recommend the film you have just seen to your friends?" Word-of-mouth advertising is recognized by the industry as an important variable in attracting cinema patrons—if you like the film you are likely to want to talk about it to your friends and recommend they see it—but an answer "yes" to the above question does not necessarily identify nor confirm the likelihood of such an effect taking place. It may only indicate an option the respondent had not considered but, if pressed, might agree to, implying "yes, I'll mention it to friends if the subject crops up, but I won't go out of my way to talk about it." On the other hand an answer "no" does not distinguish between a respondent who means "no, because I don't talk about films I see," from "no, because in spite of the fact that I usually talk to my friends about the films I see I don't make recommendations," nor from what the researcher intends by the

[3] See Austin's criticisms of three of his own studies in 6.

question "no, I will not recommend the film because I didn't like it." Very important differences in meaning lie behind the answers to preformulated questions and make generalizations about psychological processes operating in film contexts (as elsewhere) hazardous. While much of the potential ambiguity of such questions is absent from everyday dialogue where potential misunderstandings of statements uttered in conversation can be quickly cleared up, questionnaires and rating scales generally proscribe such communication which limits understanding of both question and answer (30).

Austin suggests that motivational research to specific films is an important area of concern which will explain why people go to see film A as opposed to film B. Work along these lines (e.g., 3) typically utilizes questionnaires involving supplied statements with which subjects have to indicate their degree of congruence using a graduated scale. The results of these scores are then usually subjected to a multiple correlational analysis, and factor analyzed. The purpose of this procedure is to obtain some underlying anchor points—factors which account for the largest portions of variance amongst the data sets—which are thought to represent fundamental postulates of cognition. Differences between different groups of subjects divided by age, gender, frequency of attendance, etc., can then be estimated by making simple statistical comparisons. Differences emerging are group differences based upon initial categorizations, such as, "high" vs. "low" motivation between "frequent" and "infrequent attenders." This is a well-trodden methodological path in social science research and while it enables the development of some underlying theoretical postulates, the gap between cognition and film viewing as a *specific* cognitive activity has yet to be bridged. Also, there are assumptions about the use of supplied statements which possibly conflict with at least one psychological principle of individual perception (dealt with later) which apply to other methodological approaches discussed below.

Some studies have attempted to measure attitudes to film. Taken together they show a declining attitude to film which parallels a decline in cinema attendance. Even if one accepts these findings at face value, one cannot assume a causal relation between them since the reasons for falling cinema attendances, like any other social behavior, are determined by many factors. Like similar studies of preference and decision making (see below), attitude measurement research relies on the application of an attitude "scale." Such instruments traditionally develop from Likert scales and start with the collection of a large number of *prima facie* statements which are administered to a large group of subjects who are asked to indicate their agreement or disagreement with each. Item analysis or factor analysis is then used to remove from the initial collection those statements that do not show sufficiently high correlations with either the initial total score or other items. This ensures that the scale has a high internal consistency and reliability. More recent "stimulus-" and "response-centered" approaches make use of respondents' answers on rating scales and compute a score based on the median scale values for those statements with which a respondent agrees, as in the former case, or a score based upon general respondent patterns, as in the latter (20).

Thurstone was probably the first to develop a movie attitude scale in 1930 as part of the Payne Studies (33). In a replication study, Austin (7) has shown that Thurstone's scale taps some dimensions of attitude—"educational value," "potential for social injury," "content," and "value in leisure time pursuits"—but omits others. Austin's findings were arrived at using a factor analysis of responses to a modification of the 40 Thurstone statements rated on a 7-point scale. However, neither study circumvents the problem that questions or answers on a rating scale to specific statements do not exhaust all possible construals of an event. What attitude research in film has yet to show is how those who comprise the subject pool of such research construe attitude statements prior to rating them, and how enduring are their attitudes to particular films or to film in general.

Regression Analyses

Paradoxically some studies by Litman (22, 23) and Simonet (31) have attempted to assess audience response by removing the audience from the research altogether, yet strongly implying it. Litman performed a regression analysis of a number of independent variables (type of story, MPAA ratings, cast, production costs, "major" vs. independent distributor, season of release, winning of or nominations for an academy award, and critics' reviews) on a sample of 125 films released in the U.S. between 1972 and 1978. The variables were fitted to an equation in which the dependent variable was film revenues (taken from listings in *Variety*). Regression analysis yields coefficients for each independent explanatory variable in its equations. These coefficients represented the change in revenues resulting from a unit of change in the corresponding independent variable, all other variables being held constant. The higher the statistical fit (R^2), the more the variation in the dependent variable (revenues) is explained, and the greater is the accuracy of the estimating equation. Litman's results showed that many of the variables thought by the industry to be significant in the promotion of attendance, clearly were not. MPAA ratings were not significant, a finding also supported by three studies of the effects of ratings upon movie audiences by Austin (6). Two of these used self-report measures of preferences for film and the third, an "unobtrusive" measure. In Litman's study the type of story and presence of stars were also nonsignificant; critics' ratings, production budget, Christmas release, and presence of awards were the significant variables.

Simonet's study employed a similar regression analysis of revenues with a number of production variables in the equation. Using *Variety* as his source, he sampled 73 of the "all time" top grossing films released between 1936 and 1972. His results indicated that the past box office record of the director and producer of the film were the two significant factors which positively predicted the financial success of a film.

Litman's and Simonet's studies are clearly innovative in their approach to the problem of audience measurement, revealing many of the variables which play a part in a film's ultimate commercial success. But "audience" is understood in these studies as no more than a numerical return at the box office, and in the case of Litman's study some of these returns are unavailable and the weighting for these in his equations is only an estimate. As with some of the assumptions pertaining to market research, an audience is conceived of as a passive holistic "mass" formed at the moment of the right set of pre-projection variables, some of which have been elucidated, as in the studies mentioned above, while others presumably have yet to be determined. No consideration has been given as to how these variables interact in the heads of potential moviegoers, nor to their relative effects. Answers to such questions are unlikely to come from regression analyses of marketing variables alone.

Preference Studies

Film preferences are at the heart of another of Austin's concerns. He reports on a number of studies which have drawn upon such "preferences" but dismisses them as being "unreliable" and their coding categories as being "non-comparable" (5, p. xxx). While members of the public have no difficulty identifying their favorite "type" of film, the difficulty for the researcher is in fathoming what patrons mean by certain labels and understanding the discriminations people are able to make between them.This is an important criticism returning us to the general question of the meaning of an audience's response(s). Clearly we are in need of a tool which will enable members of a film audience, when called upon, to explicate their individual personal (as opposed to collective) responses since film viewing is an individual private experience, even if the context of that experience, in the darkness of a theatre auditorium, is shared with anonymous others. Assessing reactions should ideally be carried out as close to the actual circumstance of the film as possible to avoid contamination from subsequent events which might hinder recall. Every opportunity should be available for each individual to express himself or herself on their own terms, and in this respect the experimenter should also be sensitive to the idiosyncratic meanings with which individuals construe events.

Questionnaires are fundamentally inadequate for this purpose since they invariably frame questions cast in the theoretical perspective of the experimenter. Even "open-ended" questions, which are an advance upon the standard questionnaire in that they allow for some free expression on the part of the respondent, will not enable an assessment of the way individuals impute highly personal shades of meaning into the words they choose to use.

Austin perceives that: "content analysis, coupled with such tools as the semantic differential and multidimensional scaling, suggest a method which could be used to clarify how the audience conceptualizes film types" (5, p. xxx). Austin and Gordon (8) have used precisely these methods to assess subjects' perceptions of film genres. Here 20 genre labels were rated on a set of supplied "attributes" taken from the Gough Adjective Check List, Osgood's Semantic Differential, and Mehrebian's emotional response items. Ratings of attributes on all genres were carried out by a sample of university students and were analyzed by means of multidimensional scaling to assess perceptual relationships among the genres. The results indicated similarities in the way pairs of genres were perceived (notably "war" with "western," "action" with "adventure," "drama" with "comedy") The authors took the findings of this analysis as a validation of their conceptual model of genres which linked all genre subtypes to drama and comedy; unfortunately no attempt was made to identify the perceptual dimensions along which the genre groupings emerged. Likewise no attempt was made to assess individual familiarity with either the meanings of the attributes—a common problem of semantic differential and check-list methods—or the genre classification.

Experimental Studies

While the studies mentioned above deal with questions of audience in different ways they have in common the fact that they are all at one hand removed from the viewing experience. None of the methods so far discussed really enable an examination of the viewer *in vivo*. Studies of the viewer undertaken at the time that he or she is watching a film are usually carried out within a psychophysiological or experimental psychological framework and are intent upon seeking a reductionist level of explanation of viewing experience. In general what these studies aim at doing is to capture some element of an individual viewer's response to usually a small segment or sequence of a film so that fairly precise quantitative relationships between the two can be established.

This approach achieved some popularity in France in the late 1940s and early 1950s where the studies were incorporated under the rubric of "filmology"—the science of film. The subject during this period became the province of a number of different specialities, each of which brought something of its own subject to bear upon film. As Lowry points out however "it was this divergence of interests, and the increasing specialization required in pursuing them separately which marked the definitive end of the eclectic formative period of filmology" (24, p. 141).

The specific criticisms of each filmological study need not be detailed here. Suffice to say that while some physiological responses to films or film segments have been demonstrated, it remains to be seen what these effects actually mean since to date there has been no demonstration of a consistently reliable one-to-one correspondence between psychological and psychophysiological phenomena. For example, studies which have shown correlations between some psychophysiological index, such as GSR or EEG and, say, erotic or pornographic films, fail to establish (i) whether such effects are transient or permanent, (ii) what exactly in the material viewed elicits a response in the viewer, that is, what the precise nature of the stimulus is, (iii) what the stimulus means to the subject, and (iv) how the meaning of the material viewed "translates" into a physiological context.

Also the approach invariably fails to take account of individual differences. Indeed many psychophysiological studies, notably those within filmology, are predicated on the assumption that audiences/viewers/subjects are homogenous—being more or less equally prone to the "effects" of a stimulating environment. In order to demonstrate correlations between events and responses, the viewing context is often (though not always) greatly simplified so that some quantitative measure of filmed events can take place.[4] Where studies have gone beyond the purely physiological level to consider film events cognitively, the response measure has invariably been some form of questionnaire which makes such studies subject to the criticism previously expressed about the ambiguity of meaning of the items and the limitations to the elicitation of personal meaning in respondents' interpretations.

However, there are some interesting exceptions worthy of note which take relatively simple filmed patterns, but derive or infer fairly sophisticated audience response measures. A study by Penn (28) used 450 respondents to evaluate a film sequence in which either vehicles, persons, or rectangles appeared, producing "concepts" of each single object, pair of objects, or "scene as a whole." Each concept was rated on three scales of a semantic differential for each "major dimension of cognitive meaning" (i.e., evaluation, activity, potency) producing nine scales in all. A further variable in this design was the type of editing (cutting) used in the sequence. Cutting was either constant, accelerating, or decelerating. Each subject saw one sequence and was placed in a group of five to 10 subjects who viewed sequences in which type of cutting was the variable. Results indicated a positive relationship of cutting rate with the potency dimension, and fast but constant rates of cutting evoked perception of greater activity than did accelerated cutting for similar subject matter which, taken together, suggest that "meaning" in some aspects is affected by editing. However it is obviously difficult to generalize from the results using the simplified content of these films. Also the dimensions of judgment, as is typical of a semantic differential, were supplied and the precise meanings evoked for different subjects by various styles of editing was obscured in this design.

Based upon information theory concepts, Lynch (25) used a version of the standard verbal cloze procedure of Taylor (32) and Darnell (14) for estimating language proficiency. In this test subjects had to fill in blank words in a verbal passage. Their answers were judged not only according to whether the supplied answer matched that of the tester but also in terms of the relative probability of use in the context dependent upon group norms for language use. Lynch's modification of this technique (called clozentropy) substitutes *shots* for blank words, taking out a shot in a film sequence and asking subjects what would most likely occur next. This was done for different kinds of films with a sample of 93 undergraduates. Ability to predict correctly varied significantly with the sophis-

---

[4] Some of the pertinent criticisms of this reductionistic approach, which was at the height of its popularity in the mid-1950s, are discussed in Edward Lowry's excellent book (24) in the chapter "The Legacies of Filmology."

tication of the audience, the complexity of the film and the level of the analysis. This study was primarily a validational procedure of the instrument in the context of film audience research and showed much promise (as yet unrealized).

The studies of Penn and Lynch map fairly precise relationships of filmic elements to aspects of viewers' responses and hint at possible psychological mechanisms at work in the viewing situation expressed within the informational processing language of cognitive psychology. Yet sophisticated and careful as these studies are, they do not begin to tap the depth of perception of the individual viewer that makes up his or her experience in viewing an entire film. Indeed is it possible to study viewing experience phenomenally?

In one obvious sense the answer is yes, since each viewer is generally able to give some public account of his or her experience of the film and also, upon reflection, privately to him or herself. But if we are to study this experience and try and understand it we will need to have a research tool which will enable us to (i) allow each subject to provide an account of his or her experience on his or her own terms, (ii) discern what those terms mean, such as, how, within the framework of the written or spoken account, meaning is embedded in the particular use of language, and (iii) examine the precise relationship of this account to specific elements of the film relevant to our research interests.

Lynch's clozentropy study appears promising. Individual expectations are assessed throughout the film by periodically stopping it and asking subjects what they think will occur next. In this way perception in terms of expectation can be examined. However the paradigm would appear to be unhelpful in assessing the variety of other perceptual categories in which answers can be structured, and it offers no clues as to how it would deal with individual differences in language use and establish the personal meaning of the terms used by each subject.

Penn's study mentioned earlier makes use of Osgood's semantic differential as a way of assessing the affective meanings different individuals impute to different forms of film editing.[5] This is an instrument which uses seven-point bipolar rating scales, which are based upon an extensive series of factor analytic studies. Comparisons of the meanings of two different words understood by one subject or of the meanings of the same word by different subjects can occur by scoring the rating in terms of three supposedly universal dimensions (evaluation, potency, activity). However while the scales are bipolar, the concepts implied in the adjectives (e.g., beautiful-ugly, cruel-kind, slow-fast) are not. People usually erect their own modes of discrimination when evaluating concepts. But factor analytic procedures are examples of what Bannister and Mair (10) call psychologists looking for hierarchical constructs under which to subsume the constructs of

[5] A similar study using semantic differential to study the effects of editing upon an audience of a TV image, in this case the substitution of a single shot, was carried out by John Baggaley and Steve Duck (9). Other studies of television have made use of the semantic differential, most notably one by George Gerbner (16); however little of this work has been directed specifically at cinema audiences.

their subjects. This presents a problem for there is nothing in the procedures which allows for the possibility that subjects may employ their own hierarchical system of concepts. As they say, "the subject tested by the Semantic Differential cannot reveal hierarchical structure, try as (s)he might; the test permits no ready examination of the way the subject links and organizes concept and concept, scale and scale or concept and scale" (p. 126). Constraints are placed not only upon the type of answer subjects can give by forcing them to use a limited and supplied vocabulary, but upon the type of explanation arrived at, reducing all manner of individual perception to three preformulated categories. This might be statistically convenient and give to those who adopt this method some confidence in their attempts to compare the accounts of different groups of subjects, but it essentially trivializes the idea of comparative perception that it supposedly seeks to uncover.

ALTERNATIVE CURRENTS

At the present time the only available research tool which will meet the stringent demands implied by my criticisms of previous methods is the repertory grid derived from George Kelly's Personal Construct Psychology (21). The repertory grid is an instrument designed to display the person in his or her own terms. It is a record of a set of personal judgments (constructs) amongst a sample of a set of elements. These elements constitute a context and constructs are the basis upon which elements are understood. A construct is a category of thought by which an individual construes or interprets his or her world of personal experience. It represents a consistent way for the person to make sense of some aspects of reality. Once constructs are elicited they can be used to rate a set of elements and the resulting data subjected to a principal components analysis, multidimensional scaling, or cluster analysis (see for example, 15, 29) which identifies components or groups of similarly used constructs central to each subject's construing system.

The value of the rep grid over other methods routinely used in social psychology lies in the fact that it makes no a priori assumptions about what is significant for individuals, nor does it seek to elicit a particular response from subjects regardless of its pertinence, as more traditional methods have done. It also situates the subject at the center of a construing system and enables group patterns of responding to be discerned from individual patterns.

Surprisingly very little film audience research using grids has been carried out. An early unpublished study by Carver (13) compared critics' with laymen's evaluations of films as a way of addressing the questions of whether they construed films in a similar manner. However no attempt in this study was made to ensure that subjects saw the same films, nor viewed them under similar conditions; and constructs were supplied rather than elicited and may have reflected more of the construct system of the experimenter than of his subjects.

Two of my own studies in this area have used elicited rather than supplied constructs. In one of these subjects were drawn from two different cultures as a way of addressing some theoretical assumptions about the range of availability of response to coded elements of a narrative film (11). The other used a small clinical population of agoraphobics and a control group to test a hypothesis about separation anxiety (a feature of the film that both groups watched), namely, that panic disordered subjects would be more affected than controls by viewing the film and consequently would elicit more constructs of anxiety (12). In each of these exploratory studies an attempt was made to link some elements of the film, whether of plot or of formal structure, to the phenomenal experience of the perceiving subject.

At this stage the field is wide open for much more work using this technique. It may well transpire that the best strategy, as has been suggested by others, is some combination of methods and approaches. Certainly I can see links between the ideas proposed by Lynch using his cloze procedure on film and those I have been advocating using a rep grid, as a means of analyzing what subjects experience at different moments in the life of the film. In the area of culture particularly this might prove to be a useful beginning to getting to grips with what is that people from different backgrounds experience when perceiving film.

It might also put to rest the view commonly held in some sectors of the film industry (and of academia) that members of a film audience, like a group of subjects for a psychological study, share the same view as that of the filmmaker or researcher, or for that matter, each other.

REFERENCES

1. Anderson, J. and Anderson, B. "Motion Perception in Motion Pictures." In T. de Lauretis and S. Heath (Eds.), *The Cinematic Apparatus*. London: Macmillan, 1980.
2. Arnheim, R. "The Gestalt Theory of Expression." *Psychological Review* 56, 1949, pp. 156–171.
3. Austin, B. A. "Motivations for Movie Attendance." *Communication Quarterly* 34, 1986, pp. 115–126.
4. Austin, B. A. "1982–85 Update on Film Audience Research." *Journal of Popular Film and Television*, Summer 1986, pp. 33–39.
5. Austin, B. A. *The Film Audience: An International Bibliography of Research*. Metuchen, NJ: Scarecrow Press, 1983.
6. Austin, B.A. "G-PG-R-X: The Purpose, Promise and Performance of the Movie Rating System." *Journal of Arts Management and Law* 12, Summer 1982, pp. 51–74.
7. Austin, B. A. "Factor Analytic Study of Attitudes Towards Motion Pictures." *Journal of Social Psychology* 11, 1982, pp. 211–217.
8. Austin, B. A. and Gordon, T. F. "Movie Genres: Towards a Conceptualised Model and Standardized Definitions." In B. A. Austin (Ed.), *Current Research in Film: Audiences, Economics, and Law* (Vol. 3), Norwood, NJ: Ablex, 1987, pp. 12–33.
9. Baggaley J. and Duck, S. *The Dynamics of Television*. Hants, England: Saxon House, 1976.
10. Bannister, D. and Mair, J. M. M. *The Evaluation of Personal Constructs*. London: Academic Press, 1968.
11. Blowers, G. H. and McCoy, M. M. "Perceiving Cinematic Episodes: A Cross-cultural

Repertory Grid Study of a Narrative Film Segment.'' *International Journal of Psychology* 21, 1986, pp. 317–332.

12. Blowers, G. H., McClenahan, K. and Roth, W. T. ''Panic-Disordered Subjects' Perceptions of Film: A Repertory Grid Study.'' *Perceptual and Motor Skills* 63, 1986, pp. 1119–1128.
13. Carver, M. V. ''The Critical Evaluation of Films by Repertory Grid.'' Unpublished PhD thesis. University of London, 1967.
14. Darnell, D. K. ''Clozentropy: A Procedure for Testing English-Language Proficiency in Foreign Students.'' *Speech Monographs* 37, 1970, pp. 36–46.
15. Fransella F. and Bannister, D. B. *A Manual of Repertory Grid Technique*. London: Wiley, 1977.
16. Gerbner, G. ''Cultural Indicators: The Case of Violence in Television Drama.'' *Annals of the American Academy of Political and Social Science* 338, 1970, pp. 69–81.
17. Hochberg, J. and Brooks, V. ''Perception of Motion Pictures.'' In E. C. Carterette and H. P. Friedman (Eds.), *Handbook of Perception* (Vol. X). London: Academic, 1978, pp. 259–304.
18. Hochberg, J. and Brooks, V. ''Film Cutting and Visual Momentum.'' In R. A. Monty and J. W. Senders (Eds.), *Eye Movements and Psychological Processes*. Hillsdale, NJ: Erlbaum, 1976, pp. 293–313.
19. Hochberg, J. and Brooks, V. ''The Integration of Successive Cinematic Views of Simple Scenes.'' *Bulletin of the Psychonomic Society* 4, 1974, p. 263.
20. Jaspars, J. ''The Nature and Measurement of Attitudes: Determinants of Attitudes and Attitude Change.'' In H. Tajfel and C. Fraser (Eds.), *Introducing Social Psychology*. Harmondsworth: Penguin, 1978.
21. Kelly, G. A. *The Psychology of Personal Constructs*. New York: Norton, 1955.
22. Litman, B. R. ''Predicting Success of Theatrical Movies: An Empirical Study.'' *Journal of Popular Culture* 16, 1983, pp. 159–175.
23. Litman, B. R. ''Decision-making in the Film Industry: The Influence of the TV Market.'' *Journal of Communication* 32, 1982, pp. 33–52.
24. Lowry, E. *the Filmology Movement and Film Study in France*. Ann Arbor, MI: UMI Research Press, 1985.
25. Lynch, F. D. *Clozentropy: A Technique for Studying Audience Responses to Films*. New York: Arno, 1978.
26. Marchetti, G. ''Subcultural Studies and the Film Audience: Rethinking the Film Viewing Context.'' In B. A. Austin (Ed.), *Current Research in Film: Audiences, Economics and Law* (Vol. 2). Norwood, NJ: Ablex, 1986, pp. 62–79.
27. Nichols, B. and Lederman, S. J. ''Flicker and Motion in Film.'' In T. de Lauretis and S. Heath (Eds.), *The Cinematic Apparatus*. London: Macmillan, 1980.
28. Penn, R. ''Effects of Motion and Cutting Rate in Motion Pictures''. *Audio-Visual Communication Review* 19, 1971, pp. 29–50.
29. Rathod, P. ''Methods for the Analysis of Rep Grid Data.'' In H. Bonarius, R. Holland, and S. Rosenberg (Eds.), *Personal Construct Psychology: recent advances in theory and practice*. Chichester: Wiley, 1981.
30. Shotter, J. D. ''Empirical methods in social enquiry.'' In R. Harre and R. Lamb (Eds.), *The Dictionary of Personality and Social Psychology*. Oxford: Basil Blackwell, 1986.
31. Simonet, T. S. ''Regression Analysis of Prior Experiences of Key Production Personnel as Predictors of High Grossing Motion Pictures in American Release.'' *Dissertation Abstracts* 1977/78 38, 3A.
32. Taylor, W. L. '''Cloze' Readability Scores as Indices on Individual Differences in Comprehension and Attitude.'' *Journal of Psychology* 41, 1957, pp. 19–26.
33. Thurstone, L. L. ''A Scale for Measuring Attitude Towards Movies.'' *Journal of Educational Research* 22, 1930, pp. 89–94.

5

Hollywood Genres and the Production of Culture Perspective*

Robert E. Kapsis

Film genres can be defined as broad forms of popular expression, such as Westerns, gangster films, musicals, horror films, romantic comedies, science fiction films, and psychological suspense thrillers that contain predictable combinations of features (cf. 25, 38, 39).[1] The dominant theoretical orientation of most sociological and historical studies of film genres and cycles is that they in some way reflect some aspect of society. According to this viewpoint (henceforth referred to as "the reflection of society perspective"), shifts in film content reflect changes in audience taste preferences which are, in turn, linked to major shifts in the structure of society. The underlying assumption of many studies in this tradition is that popular films are a more or less accurate mirror of social structure, because by choosing the films it attends, the audience reveals its preferences to film studios and distributors which, in turn, passively produce and finance films reflecting audience desires. Siegfried Kracauer's *From Caligari to Hitler* (30) was a pioneering effort in viewing film content as a reflection of the psychological tendencies of a nation as a collectivity.

The reflection approach has also been applied to American cinema. Three important studies are *The Six-Gun Mystique* by John Cawelti (14), *Sixguns and*

* The research reported here was supported by a fellowship from the National Endowment for the Humanities and grant # 665370 from the PSC-CUNY Research Award Program.

[1] Genre films depict familiar, basically one-dimensional characters enacting a predictable story line within a familiar social setting. By contrast, non-genre films generally involve central characters who we relate to more as unique individuals than in terms of previous film experiences and these unique individuals progress through nonconventionalized conflicts toward a not easily predictable resolution (cf. 39).

Society by Will Wright (47), and *Hollywood Genres* by Thomas Schatz (39). All three studies are preoccupied with the mythical qualities of Hollywood genres.[2] In addition, each book treats genre films primarily as symbolic reflections of the society and historical period in which they are created. Wright, for example, describes changes in the content of popular Hollywood westerns between 1930 and 1970, from a concern for solitary heroes fighting it out with villains for the sake of the weak but growing community (which Wright calls the ''Classical Plot'' western) to a preoccupation with elite bands of heroes, who fight not for the community which they have rejected but to affirm themselves as professionals (which Wright calls the ''Professional Plot'' western). According to Wright, this structural progression in the western is the result of a profound change in American economic institutions occurring at roughly the same time, from a free market (the gunfighter as *homo economicus*) to a corporate economy (the gunfighter as technocrat).

Theoretically more ambitious than Wright or Cawelti, Schatz's approach to genre promises to deliver more—to show how genre development reflects not only changes in the wider society but also the way the film industry routinely conducts business. Unfortunately, in the individual chapters devoted to specific genres, such as the Western, screwball comedy, and musicals, Schatz falls back to a societal reflection orientation or simply to describing individual films in relation to the generic form, largely ignoring the role of the Hollywood studio system. What is needed is a study which examines how the industrial process, independent of changes in audience taste preferences, influences both the short- and long-term development of Hollywood genres.

In contrast to the reflection viewpoint, there is what has been termed the production of culture perspective. Developed by sociologists, this orientation is less polemical than either the more general critique of the mass media developed by the Frankfurt School (see, e.g., 22, 32) or recent neo-Marxist criticisms of classical Hollywood films (e.g., *Cahiers du cinéma's* collective text on John Ford's *Young Mr. Lincoln* [11]; but see Buscombe's [10] critique of Marxist attempts to relate the products of Hollywood to the industry which produced them). The production of culture viewpoint begins with the observation that the nature and content of all cultural products (including film) are influenced by or embedded in the immediate organizational, legal, and economic environments in

---

[2] Consider the following passage from Schatz which is typical of this approach:

> Throughout this study we have discussed Hollywood film genres as formal strategies for renegotiating and reinforcing American ideology. Thus genre can be seen as a form of social ritual. Implicit in this viewpoint is the notion that these ritual forms contribute to what might be called a contemporary American mythology. In a genuine ''national cinema'' like that developed in Hollywood, with its mass appeal and distribution, with its efforts to project an idealized cultural self-image, and with its reworking of popular stories, it seems not only reasonable but necessary that we seriously consider the status of commercial filmmaking as a form of contemporary mythmaking. (39, p. 261)

which they are produced (13, 36, 42). The various milieux of symbolic production examined from this perspective have included book publishing, television, popular music, painting, and more recently film (see 7, 35, 42 for good overviews of this work).[3]

A sizable body of literature in this tradition has concentrated on mass media organizations, showing how the complex interorganizational network of production companies, distributors, mass media gatekeepers, and retailers influence the production and dissemination of a wide range of cultural commodities (see, for example, 17, 20, 21). A recurring theme in the literature on television and the movies is that because of uncertainty over the future tastes of the audience, the production process characteristically involves interpersonal conflict between producers, directors, script writers, and distribution executives over what the audience will like or accept (12, 16, 17, 26, 27).

In addition to interorganizational relationships, there are also a number of other extra-artistic factors—the market, pressure groups and censorship, statute law and government regulations, and new technologies which have influenced the production of popular culture independent of actual shifts in audience taste preferences (see 36). Consider, for example, markets. Changes in the types of theatrical films made may result from shrinking or expanding markets having little to do with actual changes in audience desires. One of the most conspicuous developments in Hollywood since the late 1960s has been the production of movies primarily for teenagers and young adults, that is, a shift away from making films for a truly mass audience. That American film studios have become less willing to back films dealing with serious social themes reflects what is now a deeply entrenched belief among film packagers, namely, that Hollywood's core market—young people—are simply not interested in such films.

In this chapter, I will apply a production of culture perspective to Hollywood genre film production. There are two major reasons why I believe this approach is an essential tool for examining Hollywood film genres. First, the very existence of genre films and cycles is a product of the film industry's attempt to overcome the problem of uncertainty, that is, of not knowing the future tastes of the mass audience. To reduce this uncertainty, the movie studios, like other mass entertainment industries, fall back on notions about "live or dead genres, doomed formats, cycles that come and go" (17, p. 23).

A second reason for applying this perspective to Hollywood filmmaking relates to the existence of a complex network of interorganizational relationships which mediates between the movie production company and the consumer. Which genres finally get made depends on how organizational gatekeepers at

[3] In the past decade, film scholars have become increasingly interested in exploring the relationship between the industrial structure of Hollywood and the content of Hollywood feature films (see 1, 2, 3, 9, 15, 23, 24, 29, 33, 40). Still, the bulk of recent industrial, legal, and commercial histories of the American film industry fail to systematically examine how business and economic interests influence the production and aesthetic practices of the films themselves (e.g., 5, 6, 18).

various stages of the film production process assess the product in relation to their perception of the audience's future tastes. For example, film production companies often make films from which marketing executives then determine which generic label is most appropriate for promotion the film. While the audience and, by extension, society have some indirect influence on film content via ticket sales, that influence is filtered through the in-house conflicts and interorganizational decisions that shape what films are made and get released.

In this chapter I will examine the boom and bust cycle that movie genres periodically go through. My objectives are three-fold: (1) to show that genre film production is vastly different during the boom phase of a cycle than when a genre is in decline; (2) to determine the extent to which cyclical change is independent of changes in audience taste preferences; and (3) to explore the relative impact of three factors—markets, pressure groups, and media gatekeepers on the emergence, persistence, and decline of film cycles.

During the boom phase of a film cycle, dozens of films of a particular genre are released or re-released each year while dozens more are either in pre-production, production, or post-production. One factor that might affect the duration of a film cycle is the perception of how markets (audiences) might respond to the genre. According to many movie industry observers, for a genre boom period to emerge and persist, there must be strong indications that the genre will thrive in at least two of the three major theatrical markets—domestic, foreign, and ancillary (such as sales to network and cable television and videotape playback). A second condition to be examined is the impact of pressure groups organized against the genre. A number of historical studies have documented how pressure groups have caused popular genres to either disappear or change their basic formulas (see 8, 34).[4] The third condition to be explored here is the role of media gatekeepers.[5] I hypothesize that in order for a film cycle to persist, media gatekeepers must regularly provide stories about the genre, and feature interviews with persons connected with film projects that are examples of

[4] Since the inception of motion pictures at the turn of the century, groups of concerned citizens have attacked the popular medium, perceiving it as a potential threat to the established order. Fearing government censorship, the film industry imposed its own controls on film content. The National Review Board, the Hays Office, the Production Code Administration, and the Classification and Rating Administration were all manifestations of the film industry's attempt, during different historical periods, to regulate film content on its own without government interference. Pressure from the Catholic Legion of Decency, for example, triggered the strict enforcement of the production code during the mid-1930s, resulting in the sudden disappearance of the then popular gangster genre.

[5] As Hirsch (20) points out, the role of mass media gatekeepers is especially important in cultural industries, such as the movie business, where both demand uncertainty is high and formal vertical integration has been made formally illegal. "Cultural products provide 'copy' and 'programming' for newspapers, magazines, radio stations, and television programs; in exchange, they receive 'free' publicity. The presence or absence of coverage, rather than its favorable or unfavorable interpretation is the important variable here" (20, p. 647).

the form. When a genre is no longer perceived as "newsworthy" by the media, it may lose its appeal to audiences as well.

To explore the cyclical nature of genre film production, I will examine post-1978 developments in the horror genre. In late 1978, a new horror cycle emerged which would last until around 1983.

RESEARCH PROCEDURES

Between February 1981 and January 1986, I interviewed marketing, production, and acquisition executives, senior story editors, and readers at Universal, Twentieth Century-Fox, Paramount, MGM, Columbia, Embassy, and Shapiro Entertainment, and asked them about their views on audiences, genre pictures, and film cycles. During the exploratory phase of the research, personal contacts largely determined which film organizations were selected. When my focus shifted to horror films, the organizations I selected (e.g., Universal, Paramount, Embassy, and Shapiro Entertainment) were those which at that time figured prominently in the production and/or distribution of such films. During the project's first year, I gathered detailed information on the pre-production, filming, post-production, and marketing of several low-budget horror films. For one of the films examined, *Halloween II*, two members of my West Coast research staff were on the set every day during the film's six week shooting schedule and gathered detailed field notes on the shooting of the film. During post-production, we interviewed members of the cast and crew (including the online producer, director, and cinematographer) in order to gain an understanding of the routine factors which influence the content of genre films (e.g., changes in the way the potential audience is perceived). Executives from Universal Studios involved in the marketing and advertising of the film were also interviewed. Subsequently, I interviewed artistic and financial decision makers involved in other recent horror films. Additional valuable information about the horror cycle of the early 1980s was drawn from the newspaper and magazine clipping services at the Margaret Herrick Library of the Academy of Motion Picture Arts and Sciences in Beverly Hills and from the major trade papers of the film industry, especially *Variety* and *The Hollywood Reporter*.

1979–80: HORROR BOOM PERIOD

Horror[6] has been one of the most enduring of Hollywood film genres. The decade of the 1970s was no exception. Three top grossing films, *The Exorcist* (1973), *Jaws* (1975), and *Halloween* (1978), probably did more than anything else to

[6] The basic formula of the horror film is that normality is threatened by the Monster. This formula encompasses the entire range of horror films "being applicable whether the Monster is a vampire, a giant gorilla, an extra terrestrial invader, an amorphous gooey mass, . . . a child possessed by the Devil" (46) or a human psychotic or schizophrenic.

assure that the horror film genre during the 1970s and early 1980s would enjoy the kind of long-term popularity it had experienced throughout the 1930s. The enormous success of *The Exorcist*, for example, resulted in each major studio reaching out to make another film about demonic possession. But by fall 1978, the popularity of such films had already peaked. Horror films were leaving studios in the red, and it would have come as no surprise had Hollywood temporarily stopped making them altogether. The meteoric arrival of the low-budget horror film *Halloween* in October 1978 after the genre had supposedly peaked, assured that movie studio executives would continue to back horror film projects. *Halloween* earned over $50 million in box office receipts after costing under $400,000 to produce. And it performed well in both domestic and foreign markets.

Film companies—first the minors and then the majors—were quick to cash in on *Halloween*'s success. Film executives extracted from *Halloween* the elements or formula believed to have been responsible for its success: (1) the male psychopathic killer terrorizing teenage girls in their social milieu (the world of babysitters, prom queens, and camp counselors), and (2) the graphic depiction of blood and violence (indeed, more explicit than permitted at that time on prime-time television). Over the next two years film companies produced a large number of films so similar to *Halloween* in style and content that a new subgenre of horror emerged, what has been termed "knife-kill," "splatter," or "slasher" movies. From *Prom Night* and *Friday the 13th* to *Terror Train* and *Friday the 13th Part II*, each film contained successively more graphic depictions of violence, blood, and gore. The "slice and dice" horror film had been born.

Other types of horror films also went into production during this period (e.g., ghost stories, werewolf stories, etc.), reflecting the film industry's view that more traditional forms could be revived and rejuvenated by beefing up the violence and through startling special effects. In addition, recent horror film "cult" classics were reissued, such as *Night of the Living Dead*, *The Texas Chain-Saw Massacre*, and *The Last House on the Left*.[7] Indeed, by late 1979, a horror genre boom period had emerged which would last roughly until early 1981.

Between 1979 and 1981, horror films performed strongly in both domestic and foreign markets. In 1978 only nine horror films earned at least one million dollars in domestic rentals. That rate doubled and tripled over the next two years.

---

[7] Another indication of an environment conducive to horror film production is that many young filmmakers who were looking for an opportunity to direct their first feature film were handed horror projects, while veteran filmmakers who were still recovering from a string of commercial failures (e.g., John Frankenheimer, Paul Schrader, and Sidney Furie) found work in horror. Directors Wes Craven and Tobe Hooper, who had offended the Hollywood establishment a decade go with *The Last House on the Left* and *The Texas Chain Saw Massacre*, respectively, suddenly found themselves employable again.

Seventeen horror films in 1979 and 26 in 1980 topped the million dollar mark.[8] Over the same period foreign production of horror films dramatically increased—from only 23 new films starting production in 1978 to 33 in 1979 and 55 in 1980. Another indication that a bullish market for horror had arrived is that roughly one-fourth of all movies screened and pitched at the international sales events at Cannes, Milan, and Los Angeles were horror films (43, 45; see Tables 1 and 2).

During this period, horror projects received considerable coverage from the mass media. Executives at Pickwick/Maslansky/Koenigsberg (PMK)—a public relations firm whose horror film clients during the horror boom included directors Brian De Palma, George Romero, and John Carpenter, producer Debra Hill, and actress Jamie Lee Curtis—reported that at the height of the horror craze, media gatekeepers "were all jumping on our horror films," that is, were willing to plug them in various ways. Said account executive Katie Sweet, "We really got involved with the whole business of horror after *Halloween* . . . We started handling John Carpenter and for whatever reason we became the office for handling alot of this genre of film" (personal interview, fall 1981). According to Sweet, at the height of the horror boom period, PMK could bring together many of its clients working in horror and have them talk to the media about their work. For example, one night on NBC's now defunct Tomorrow Show, Rona Barrett moderated an entire segment which brought together horror directors John Carpenter and George Romero to discuss their work. "In those days," recalled

Table 1. Horror Film Performance*

Year	Film Rentals
1970	$ 6,500,000
1971	19,000,000
1972	31,500,000
1973	6,500,000
1974	80,000,000
1975	166,500,000
1976	73,000,000
1977	118,000,000
1978	109,000,000
1979	204,000,000
1980	168,000,000
1981	133,000,000
1982	227,000,000
1983	107,000,000

*Source: Adapted from *Variety*, January 25, 1984, p. 36.

[8] The rate of change in the profitability of horror is only slightly reduced after controlling for ticket price inflation.

Table 2. Horror Film Production*

Year	U.S.	Foreign	Total
1970	22	71	93
1971	57	88	145
1972	83	106	189
1973	39	76	115
1974	21	50	71
1975	22	36	58
1976	43	37	80
1977	28	33	61
1978	35	23	58
1979	38	33	71
1980	66	55	121
1981	70	45	115
1982	34	35	69
1983 (est.)	35	25	60

*Pictures are dated by the year filming commences, not year of eventual release. The 1970–80 data have been updated from *Variety's* November 19, 1980 chart to include recently discovered films and backdate releases to their earlier production date. Comedy horror spoofs and other borderline fantasies are omitted from the yearly totals. Source: *Variety*, January 25, 1984, p. 36.

Sweet, "there was ease in getting the media to cover horror; it was just not that difficult."

Another characteristic of this horror boom period was that there were no organized crusades against horror films. In fact, for a short time, it became chic to like horror—a trend traceable to the rise of auteur theory in the late 1960s as well as to the attempts of high-culture critics in the 1970s to apply self-sufficient and self-referential aesthetic criteria (derived from high-culture criticism) to popular genres. One outcome of this shift in critical standards was that by the late 1960s a number of the films of popular genre filmmakers, such as Alfred Hitchcock and Howard Hawks, were considered works of art (see 28). This tendency was broadened during the 1970s to include other popular genre filmmakers as well. Indeed, at the start of the horror boom period of the late 1970s, critics who ordinarily regarded horror with disdain were arguing that with the right director (e.g., Hitchcock in *Psycho*), a work of considerable artistry could be achieved within that genre. *Newsweek's* critic David Ansen praised John Carpenter's *Halloween* as "a superb exercise in the art of suspense . . . From the movie's dazzling prologue in 1963 to its chilling conclusion in 1978, we are being pummeled by a master manipulator" (4, p. 116). Apparently, the prestigious literary magazine, the *New Yorker*, agreed with this assessment because in the winter of 1980 it featured a lengthy profile of Carpenter (41).

Fear No Evil is a horror film that was conceived in 1979, shot in 1980, and released in early 1981. The circumstances surrounding the evolution of this film illustrate how the favorable climate for horror between 1979 and 1981 affected filmmaking at that time.

In the Fall of 1978, Frank La Loggia, the director of *Fear No Evil*, started work on a love story but ended up with a horror movie. At that time, according to La Loggia, "Horror films were doing very well and we were looking for a first project that our money people could get behind, and so we developed an idea for a horror fantasy, approached them with that, and were able to raise about a half million dollars" (personal interview, fall 1981).

With that money the director was able to complete principal photography for the film but still needed about $250,000 to add the visual and sound effects.So he took the picture in rough cut form to Avco Embassy—a major distributor of horror films at that time—which agreed to supply the money to complete the film. Recalled the executive who subsequently advised the director on the project, "The sales department thought they could take it to Cannes and get $1 million right off the top in foreign rentals" (31, p. 4). Convinced that it was a safe investment, Avco agreed to cover post-production costs, but with certain strings attached.

Avco Embassy executives wanted more shots of high school kids at school because they believed they could sell the film from the exploitative angle of kids in danger. Yet the film's story line had really little to do with kids in jeopardy. The film centers on three arch angels—Michael, Gabriel, and Raphael—who periodically return to earth in the guise of humans to do battle with the latest incarnation of Lucifer, the fallen angel. The premise of *Fear No Evil* is that Lucifer comes to earth in the form of a high school student who is then pursued by the arch angels. According to La Loggia, in the film's original form, the high school environment was not central to the story. "We included that environment because the horror films that were making it theatrically seemed to revolve around high school kids. When we brought the film to Avco the first time, they found the high school setting the most appealing aspect of the picture." Therefore, Avco insisted that the high school element be more dominant and that more blood and guts be added whenever possible. The director had shot several scenes involving high school kids that were absent from the rough cut form that Avco saw. Recalled La Loggia, "I'd shot the material primarily as a safeguard and sure enough when they began to ask for it, it was a good thing we had it around, because not having the footage might have jeopardized the deal. That's just the way they were thinking at the time." More relevant than how audiences were thinking at the time of the horror boom period was how studio executives were thinking about that audience.

By early fall 1980, it appeared to some well-placed industry observers that the domestic market was once again saturated with horror and that the low-budget horror film was on a downslide (19). Accordingly, worried marketing executives concentrated on positioning the horror films that were already finished, releasing them when national or regional markets were not already glutted with horror.

1981–82: BOOM OR BUST? THE BACKLASH AGAINST HORROR[9]

In January of 1981, the next wave of horror started with Avco Embassy's *Fear No Evil* and *Scanners*. *Fear No Evil* opened in Florida and Texas on January 16 and, according to its director, did "fantastic business." The film's good showing in the South did not escape the notice of the other studios. In a matter of weeks, many of the other horror films that had been sitting on the shelves were released. "We took the first step in the water," said La Loggia. "The water was fine and everybody else came in." By the time *Fear No Evil* opened in New York in February, for example, *Scanners* and *Maniac* had already opened, and *My Bloody Valentine* was to premier the next week. Soon to follow were *Blood Beach*, *The Boogey Man*, and re-release of *The Texas Chain Saw Massacre*.

The 1981 mini-boom in horror provoked a media backlash. Leading the assault of the critics were Chicago reviewers Gene Siskel and Roger Ebert, who devoted an entire "Sneak Previews" television show to denouncing knife-kill movies, while (paradoxically) defending Carpenter's handling of similar material in *Halloween*. The Siskel-Ebert complaints focused on both the explicit and exploitative violence of these films as well as on their rampant misogyny (the victims often were independent young women who, the films implied, were asking for it). Other critics and journalists quickly followed suit (newspaper clipping file, Academy of Motion Picture Arts and Sciences, Beverly Hills). Indeed, by later 1982, many newspapers and national magazines had stopped reviewing low-budget horror films altogether.[10]

The critical attack on low-budget horror movies extended to big-budget productions which are more dependent on the good will of critics and other journalists as they seek a broader appeal. Most of the big-budget horror films released in 1981 and 1982 (e.g., *Ghost Story*, *Cat People*, and *The Thing*) received terrible reviews. They also performed poorly at the box office. Failing to attract a broader audience, these films received most of their business from fans of low-budget horror (newspaper clipping file, Academy of Motion Picture Arts and Sciences, Beverly Hills).

It also became more difficult for horror films to get free media coverage, reflecting not merely the backlash or crusade against horror but that "horror" was no longer perceived as "newsworthy." One might expect free publicity for any type of genre film to be easier to obtain earlier in a cycle than later. According to public relations executive Neil Koenigsberg who I interviewed in 1981, "You can no longer go in and say, 'Oh we have this horror picture.' " He then cited as a hypothetical case the prospects of getting *Life* magazine to do a

---

[9] An earlier version of this section appeared in Kapsis (26).

[10] According to *Variety*, "With the glut of product on the market, and the reluctance of both indies and major distribs to hold press screenings for violent (and gory) films, most national and New York publications have stopped reviewing low-budget horror pictures" (44, p. 7).

story on John Carpenter's *The Thing*—a horror film that was scheduled for release the summer of 1982. Because it's perceived as a horror film, a production story wouldn't get published. What might work, Koenigsberg said, is a story about "this incredible career of a young person named John Carpenter. Look at the career and look at what makes him tick, because that means eventually getting into *The Thing*."

An additional assault against horror films came from the Classification and Rating Administration (CARA) of the Motion Picture Association of America which assigns the ratings to theatrical films. Richard D. Heffner, the chairman of CARA, admitted to me in 1981 that since the arrival of the slasher films in 1978, his office had gotten tougher on violence. Some movies, said Heffner, that received an R rating three years ago would get an X rating today. One movie that received the dreaded X on its first screening for CARA was the sequel to *Halloween*. Heffner admitted that the version of the film CARA first saw was not as violent as some of the earlier films in the "slasher" series that had received an R. But, he stressed, this had nothing to do with punishing the sequel because the original had spawned the slasher cycle, as the film's producers had alleged, but because CARA's standards had stiffened over the last few years. CARA's harder line, Heffner was quick to point out, reflects what the board perceives as changing parental attitudes toward violence. CARA is not a moral agent imposing its position on the film industry, he said, but a "barometer" of the country's changing moral climate.

Despite the chill, horror films continued to be made. The difference was that now skittish directors and producers started to put some distance between themselves and the genre. An early indication came in late October 1981 when critic Stephen Farber hosted a weekend "Harvest of Horror" course at UCLA. At the opening session, Farber apologized to his students for the failure of a number of invited guests to show up and discuss their work. "We had invited Christopher Lee," said Farber at the time, but "he decided he no longer wanted to be associated with horror films. He felt that he had transcended the genre."

Farber went on to cite similar reactions from other people in the industry he had contacted. Filmmaker Paul Schrader, who was completing his remake of *The Cat People*, told Farber that his film wasn't horror but "a phantasy in the tradition of Cocteau." Many producers insisted their movies were "suspense thrillers," "supernatural tales," "intense psychological dramas"—anything but horror films (field notes, October 30, 1981).

Producer Edward Feldman is typical of those who worked on horror projects during the 1981–82 down-turn period who called horror by any other name. "Horror to me always connotes a low-budget maneuvering of the audience," he said. "It is graphically violent. It appeals to a much lower educational level" (personal interview, Fall 1981). According to David Madden, who was feature story editor at Twentieth Century-Fox when we interviewed him in fall 1981, Feldman's film, *The Sender*, was Fox's only horror project then in development. Not surprisingly, Feldman disagreed with Madden's characterization of his film—insisting that his unfinished picture was more suspenseful than graphically violent:

> There is much more intellectual violence. It's more in your mind and in your emotional state. You don't see people chopping people up. You walk a fine line in these kinds of movies. If you don't intellectualize a little and make them more a dramatic vehicle, as *The Exorcist* or *The Shining*, you've got what is known as a "quick-in and quick-out movie," which opens in a thousand theaters and you pray for one or two good weekends. We're trying to make a movie that has some substance.

In the spring of 1980 when plans to make a sequel to *Halloween* got underway, the boom in low-budget horror films was in full swing. However, by the fall of 1981, when *Halloween II* was about to be released, industry uncertainty about the marketability of horror had become widespread and the media backlash against horror films had reached its zenith. The making of this film illustrates that audience uncertainty among filmmakers and studio marketing people intensifies as it becomes less and less clear whether the genre cycle in question will continue to boom or suddenly bust.[11]

According to its producers, the challenge of *Halloween II* was to make a film that would end the slasher cycle but would not be as bloody as recent films in the genre. The game plan was to create a thriller or suspense film rather than simply a horror film. The director, Rick Rosenthal, said he was hired for *Halloween II* because of his work on a short which "was not a horror film but a psychological thriller." Co-producer Debra Hill concurred that the premise of the sequel as with the original was to build fear and suspense—Hitchcockian virtues—rather than repulse the audience with graphic displays of blood and guts. At the same time, the filmmakers recognized that because of recent developments in the horror genre, the sequel would have to be more graphic and violent than the original. Indeed, the original script was most compatible with this strategy, calling for no less than a dozen grisly killings.

After shooting the film, the director was given about five weeks to prepare his cut or version of the film. Once his rough cut (minus a sound track) was completed, the producers, still unsure about what audiences hoped to find in their film, proceeded to show the unfinished film to high school students, soliciting their opinions. And, according to one of the producers, the students wanted more blood and guts. As the director described it, the producers became scared that there wasn't enough blood and gore in their film, so they went out and shot a few new scenes that were extremely violent. Although the rough-cut version of the film did include a dozen or so brutal killings, none of the victims was a teenage girl. Killing off at least one teenage girl had become a staple of the genre. So a new scene was shot and inserted early in the picture depicting the fatal slashing

[11] For a detailed account of the making of *Halloween II* see Kapsis (27).

of a high school girl. Also, the producers drastically shortened several scenes where there were no immediate payoffs, that is, where no gory killings occurred.

Late in the film, one of the female characters is trying to escape from the killer. She gets in a car, tries to start it, can't start it, and gets out. In the director's original cut, the scene lasts several minutes and functions to build suspense in the audience. "It goes on and on and on when I cut it," the director told us (personal interview, Fall 1981). "The viewer is supposed to think, 'Oh shit, the car doesn't start' and then you say 'Wait a minute. This isn't a scene bout a car not starting. He's in the back seat. Get out! Get out of the car!' And just when you are saying, 'Oh, no! He's coming out of the back seat,' she gets out of the car." According to the director, because there was no payoff in the scene, that is, the girl was not brutally murdered, the producers shortened it. In the final version, she gets in and out of the car in a matter of seconds—not long enough for the audience to say, "Look Out!"

Halloween II was a big success at the box office but nearly all reviews of it were strongly negative. In fact, the vast majority of horror films released in 1981 and 1982 were panned, including several that many of today's critics admire (e.g., *Deadly Blessing*, 1981; *The Thing*, 1982; and *The Entity*, 1982; see newspaper clipping file, Academy of Motion Picture Arts and Sciences, Beverly Hills). One of John Carpenter's best films, *The Thing*, was "reviled by critics as loathsome, disgusting and horrible" (37). Despite the backlash, horror remained a potentially big winner at the box office. While film rentals for horror were somewhat down in 1981, they climbed to an all-time high in 1982.

1983: BUST

Horror films performed badly at the box office in 1983, a trend which has continued right up to the present. Domestic film rentals declined by over 50 percent from 1982 levels. "In absolute dollar terms, not correcting for inflation," reported *Variety* (45), "this represented the worst performance for shock pictures since 1976" (see Table 1). In addition, none of the horror films released by independent producers earned over five million dollars, while virtually all the big-budget horror films flopped. In fact, the only commercially successful films were the moderately budgeted and well-publicized projects from the major distributers (*Jaws 3D*, *Psycho II*, *Cujo*, *The Dead Zone*, and *Christine*). And even these films enjoyed only a modest success at the box office. What happened?

Contrary to the reflection thesis, the sudden collapse of a genre may result from shrinking or expanding markets having little to do with actual shifts in audience taste preferences. As mentioned earlier, current studio practices dictate that in order for most film deals to be consummated, there must be some degree of certainty that the movie will perform well in at least two of the three major markets—domestic, foreign, and ancillary. That the domestic market for a particular genre may be good is no guarantee that film studios will back future projects in that genre. Thus, if a type of genre film remains popular with American audiences but fails overseas, Hollywood will schedule fewer such films for production in the future, especially if the ancillary market for such films is limited.

The sudden bust of horror films in 1983 is largely explained by the perceived failure of the genre overseas two years earlier and Hollywood's subsequent decision to start pulling out of horror. This decision is reflected in the relatively few number of American-made horror films that went into production in 1982—less than half the figure for 1981 (see Table 2). Also note in Table 2 that the decline in the production of foreign-made horror films started in 1981—one year before the decline of American-made horror films. Indeed, the 1981 decline of horror in foreign territories was interpreted by a number of industry observers as a signal to pull out of horror. "It was the overseas market that sent the signal," explained Leonard Shapiro, President of Shapiro Entertainment, who during the early 1980s was vice-president of film acquisitions and marketing services at Avco Embassy. "That market dried up six months before the U.S. market did. So the writing was definitely on the wall that the making of horror film deals was in for a slow-down period" (personal interviews, fall 1981 and winter 1986).

Yet horror remained popular with American audiences in 1982. As we recall, horror film rentals were higher that year than for any other year (see Table 1). A record 31 horror films earned at least one million dollars in domestic rentals in 1982 compared to 22 in 1981 and 26 in 1980 at the height of the horror craze. But because of Hollywood's decision before 1982 to start cutting back drastically in the production of horror, 1983 found relatively few new horror films available to American audiences. Indeed, *Variety* (45, p. 3) reported that of the 51 new horror films released during 1983, "over half (some 27 titles) were shelved pictures actually filmed in 1981 or earlier and dumped on the market at this time." One might speculate that if audiences in 1983 had been offered a fresher product, the horror genre would have survived longer than it did. Moreover, the dismal performance of horror in 1983 suggests that genre films need to be produced in sufficient numbers in order to create a sense that they are the hallmark of a group (generational or subcultural) consciousness.

The media backlash against horror may also have influenced Hollywood's decision to cut back on horror. However, its influence was probably small compared to the market constraints described above. Filmmakers working in horror are willing to risk a hostile press. "I make films for audiences, not critics," said Debra Hill, line producer of the *Halloween* series (personal interview, Fall 1981). "It is a business. I'm not dumb." And for distributors of horror, media ads or spots are more important than reviews as a means of selling their films. Thus, the reluctance of certain newspapers and magazines during the height of the backlash to publish movie ads depicting explicit violence may have discouraged some film companies from competing in the horror sweepstakes (see 26).

IMPLICATIONS AND FINAL REMARKS

The research reported in this chapter has implications for the scholarly debate about the role of the audience in popular culture production (see 13, pp. 97–115). Are audiences active or passive? This debate is important because of its concern about who is responsible for the content and quality of a society's popular entertainment. According to the reflection of society perspective, Hollywood's audience is sovereign because by choosing the films it attends, the audience reveals its preferences to the Hollywood studios which, in turn, passively produce films reflecting audience desires.[12] By contrast, the research on Hollywood genre filmmaking reported here supports the production of culture perspective by suggesting that the audience's influence is more passive since it is filtered through conflicting perceptions of the audience's future tastes, other in-house conflicts, and interorganizational decisions regarding expanding and contracting markets. For example, early in the genre boom period we found that the secondary audience was a more important force in influencing a director's or producer's decision regarding content than their image of the primary audience. That is, more relevant than how audiences were thinking at the time of the genre boom period was how studio executives were thinking about that audience. During the making of *Fear No Evil*, studio executives acted as if they knew what the audience wanted. Later in the cycle, uncertainty intensified as it became problematic whether the genre craze would continue or suddenly bust. Under these conditions, as exemplified in the discussion of *Halloween II*, conflicting images of audience expectations emerged which affected the overall coherence of the emerging film.

This chapter assessed the role of markets, media hype, and pressure groups as constraints on genre film production. Two other constraints that have been important in the development of movie genres should be briefly noted here.

Innovations in film technologies have influenced the artistic conditions within which films have evolved. Hollywood's conversion to sound movies in the late 1920s, for example, proved to be a catalyst in the evolution of certain movie genres such as the musical and the gangster film. As Schatz (39) points out, "synchronous sound affected both the visual and editing strategies of gangster movies. The new audio effects (gunshots, screams, screeching tires, etc.) encouraged filmmakers to focus upon action and urban violence, and also to develop a fast-paced narrative and editing style" (39, p. 85). Technological innovations have also affected the horror film. Recent advances in special makeup effects partially explain why the depiction of explicit violence and gore became the vehicle for innovation within the horror cycle described in this

---

[12] A key flaw in this argument is that the audience presumably "votes" by paying at the box office. Yet paying does not tap the reasons for attendance nor, importantly, subsequent levels of enjoyment.

chapter. Of course, this argument presupposes that behind the technological advances was the search for heightening the means of sensationalism.

Another important constraint, especially on long-term genre development, which has received surprisingly little scholarly attention, is the competition between Hollywood and other sources of entertainment, such as television, Broadway, and the recording industry. As mentioned earlier, Wright attributed the post-1950 decline of the "classic plot" western and the rise of the "professional plot" formula during the same period to a shift in popular ideology brought about by the transformation in American society from a free market to a planned economy. If Wright's reflection interpretation is sound, then, the TV western should have undergone a parallel development during the same period. It did not. The classical plot western remained the dominant TV western format throughout the 1960s. In an effort to differentiate its product from the TV western, Hollywood experimented with several different western formats, culminating in the eventual commercial success of the professional plot western and other types of theatrical westerns that displayed more graphic depictions of violence than was then permitted on network television. Examining recent developments in other genres from this perspective might also prove especially fruitful. Consider, for example, the Hollywood musical. Many of the classical movie musicals of the early 1950s (e.g., *Singin' in the Rain* and *Bandwagon*) glorified Hollywood as the great inheritor of the spirit of musical entertainment while criticizing other sources of musical entertainment, such as Broadway and television. By contrast, post-1975 Hollywood musicals (e.g., *Footloose* and *Purple Rain*) tend to be less critical of alternative sources of popular entertainment. I suspect that this development is in someway related to the fact that movie production since the early 1970s has become more firmly entrenched in the economic and industrial complex that produces other forms of mass culture. Showing how changes in the nature of competition between Hollywood and other entertainment centers involved in producing similar generic forms have dramatically affected both the long-term and short-term development of movie genres and cycles could open up a whole new area for future research in the popular arts.

REFERENCES

1. Allen, J. "The Film Viewer as Consumer." *Quarterly Review of Film Studies* 5, Fall 1980, pp. 481–499.
2. Allen, R. C. and Gomery, D. *Film History Theory and Practice*. New York: Alfred A. Knopf, 1985.
3. Altman, R. "A Semantic Syntactic Approach to Film Genre." *Cinema Journal* 23, 1984, pp. 6–18.
4. Ansen, D. "Trick or Treat." *Newsweek*, December 4, 1978, pp. 116, 120.
5. Balio, T. (Ed.). *The American Film Industry*. Revised Edition. Madison: University of Wisconsin Press, 1985.
6. Balio, T. *United Artists: The Company Built by the Stars*. Madison: University of Wisconsin Press, 1976.

7. Becker, H. S. *Art Worlds*. Berkeley: University of California Press, 1982.
8. Bergman, A. *We're in the Money*. New York: New York University Press, 1971.
9. Bordwell, D., Staiger, J. and Thompson, K. *The Classical Hollywood Cinema: Film Style & Mode of Production to 1960*. New York: Columbia University Press, 1985.
10. Buscombe, E. "The Idea of Genre in the American Cinema." *Screen* 11, 1970, pp. 33–45.
11. "Young Mr. Lincoln de John Ford." *Cahiers du Cinéma* August 1970, pp. 29–47.
12. Cantor, M. G. *The Hollywood TV Producer: His Work and His Audience*. New York: Basic Books, 1971.
13. Cantor, M. G. *Prime-Time Television: Content and Control*. Beverly Hills: Sage, 1980.
14. Cawelti, J. G. *The Six-Gun Mystique*. Bowling Green, Ohio: Bowling Green Popular Press, 1971.
15. Davies, P. and Neve, B. (Eds.). *Cinema, Politics and Society in America*. Manchester, England: Manchester University Press, 1981.
16. Gans, H. J. "The Creator Audience Relationship in the Mass Media: An Analysis of Movie Making." In B. Rosenberg and D. White (Eds.), *Mass Culture: The Popular Arts in America*. New York: Free Press, 1957, pp. 315–324.
17. Gitlin, T. *Inside Prime Time*. New York: Pantheon, 1983.
18. Gomery, D. "The American Film Industry of the 1970s: Stasis in the New Hollywood." *Wide Angle* 5, 1983, pp. 52–59.
19. Harmetz. A. "Quick End of Low-Budget Horror Film." *New York Times*, October 2, 1980, section 6, p. 15.
20. Hirsch, P. M. "Processing Fads and Fashions: An Organization-set Analysis of Cultural Industry Systems." *American Journal of Sociology* 77, 1972, pp. 639–659.
21. Hirsch, P. M. "Occupational, Organizational and Institutional Models in Mass Media Research." In P. Hirsch, P. Miller, and F. G. Kline (Eds.), *Strategies for Mass Communication Research*. Beverly Hills: Sage. 1978, pp. 13–42.
22. Horkheimer, M. and Adorno, T. W. *Dialectic of Enlightment*. New York: Herder and Herder, 1972.
23. Jowett, G. *Film: The Democratic Art*. Boston: Little, Brown, 1976.
24. Jowett, G. and Linton, J. M. *Movies as Mass Communication*. Beverly Hills: Sage, 1980.
25. Kaminsky, S. M. *American Film Genres*. New York: Dell, 1974.
26. Kapsis, R. E. "Dressed to Kill." *American Film*, March 1982, pp. 52–56.
27. Kapsis, R. E. "Hollywood Filmmaking and Audience Image." In S. Ball-Rokeach and M. Cantor (Eds.), *Media, Audience, and Social Structure*. Beverly Hills: Sage, 1986, pp. 161–173.
28. Kapsis, R. E. "Hitchcock: Auteur or Hack—How the Filmmaker Reshaped His Reputation Among the Critics." *Cineaste* 14, 1986, pp. 30–35.
29. Kerr, P. "Out of What Past? Notes on the B Film Noir." *Screen Education*, 1979/80, pp. 45–65.
30. Kracauer, S. *From Caligari to Hitler: A Psychological History of the German Film*. Princeton: Princeton University Press, 1947.
31. "Devil and Mr. LaLoggia." *Los Angeles Times*, Calendar Section, November 9, 1980, p. 4.
32. Marcuse, H. *One-Dimensional Man: Studies in the Ideology of Advanced Industrial Society*. Boston: Beacon, 1964.
33. May, L. *Screening Out the Past*. New York: Oxford University Press, 1980.
34. Parker, J. J. "Organizational Environment of the Motion Picture Sector." In S. Ball-Rokeach and M. Cantor (Eds.), *Media, Audience, and Social Structure*. Beverly Hills: Sage, 1986, pp. 143–160.
35. Peterson, R. A. "Revitalizing the Culture Concept." *Annual Review of Sociology* 5, 1979, pp. 137–166.
36. Peterson, R. A. "Five Constraints on the Production of Culture: Law, Technology, Market,

Organizational Structure and Occupational Careers." *Journal of Popular Culture* 16, 1982, pp. 143–153.

37. Pollock, D. "Carpenter: Doing His 'Thing' Despite Critics." *Los Angeles Times*, Calendar Section, July 9, 1982, pp. 1, 8.
38. Rosenblum, B. "Style as Social Process." *American Sociological Review* 43, 1978, pp. 422–438.
39. Schatz. T. *Hollywood Genres, Formulas, Filmmaking, and the Studio System*. Philadelphia: Temple University Press, 1981.
40. Sklar, R. *Movie-Made America*. New York: Random House, 1975.
41. Stevenson, J. "Profiles" (John Carpenter). *New Yorker*, January 28, 1980, pp. 41–42.
42. Tuchman, G. "Consciousness Industries and the Production of Culture." *Journal of Communication* 33, 1983, pp. 330–341.
43. "Fear 'Stalk & Slash' Horror." *Variety*, May 26, 1982, pp. 7, 36.
44. "Incredible Shrinking Horror Market." *Variety*, February 16, 1983, pp. 7, 24.
45. "Horrid Year for Horror." *Variety*, January 25, 1984, pp. 3, 36.
46. Wood, R. "Return of the Repressed." *Film Comment* July, 1978, pp. 25–32.
47. Wright, W. *Sixguns and Society: A Structural Study of the Western*. Berkeley: University of California Press, 1975.

6

High Concept, Product Differentiation, and the Contemporary U.S. Film Industry

Justin Wyatt

In describing the past two decades of American film, many historians and critics have labeled these films as homogeneous—lacking in diversity and ingenuity. While this tag has been widely accepted, homogeneity inadequately describes recent film for several reasons. In this chapter, I explore the theoretical and applied uses of product differentiation for film in the current industry—how studios differentiate their product to garner larger market shares, and the methods through which the product of film is differentiated. One primary method of differentiation is the high-concept picture: a film which relies heavily upon a surface stylishness and extensive marketing. These films are significant as a differentiated product since they are clearly marked as distinct from other films through their design and packaging. Therefore my exploration of product differentiation charts the development of high concept, an increasingly important economic factor within the recent industry. Additionally, an empirical model accounting for the difference of the high-concept films will be developed.

THE THEORY OF PRODUCT DIFFERENTIATION

To examine the methods through which the marketplace for film has been shaped by product differentiation, I will discuss the theoretical framework behind the economic concepts of product differentiation and market segmentation. Considering film as a good/service, we could state that the demand for a particular film depends upon price of admission and a large number of product characteristics. The nature of the functional relationship (between the demand for film and the various characteristics of the product) depends upon the individual consumer's tastes, competitive entertainment offerings (such as television, cable, theater), the level of disposable income, and many other factors. The importance of consumer taste introduces a very important facet of the marketplace for film—market segmentation. Most films are targeted at a certain well-defined audience demographic, for example, a film such as Paramount's *Flashdance* obviously targets a young, female audience. The story, the concept, the development, and the marketing of the film initially were designed to appeal to this audience (5). As a contrast, Paramount's *A New Life* (an Alan Alda film dealing with post-marital problems) was designed to target an older, predominately female audience (12). How much overlap would there really be between the two audiences? The heterogeneity in the demand functions for the different groups allows for the entire market of filmgoers to be disaggregated into segments with distinct demand functions (8). In this way, market segmentation appears to be a useful method to discuss the film audience.

The problem with discussing market segmentation alone is that it interacts with product differentiation as a marketplace condition. A market may be segmented according to specific demand functions for a homogeneous product, but, within the single product of "film," films are also clearly different from each other. Unlike the function played by a laundry detergent, different films serve different purposes for each person. For example, within a young female audience, the function fulfilled by *Flashdance* would be much different than the needs fulfilled by *Terms of Endearment*. The product (film) is perceived to be different from other products based on perceived product characteristics. Therefore, the market is split by (a) the different demand functions of consumers, and (b) by the differences within the competing products. Product differentiation can be seen as a complement or means of implementing market segmentation (8, p. 1).

Product differentiation can be implemented through two different routes. Hirshleifer makes the distinction in terms of *variety* and *quality* (15, p. 385). Differentiation over product variety relates to the characteristics of a commodity: consumer preferences are distributed over a range of some characteristic of the product. These product characteristics may be either objective or subjective (on the part of the consumer). As the number of differentiated versions of the product increase, so does the consumer satisfaction. In this manner, firms are able to ascertain certain segments of the market through their slightly differentiated products. Variations in product quality assume that consumers value some underlying attribute contained within the product (31). The greater the amount of the attribute contained within the product, the greater the satisfaction of the consumer.

The description of product differentiation may be explained with the example of film. The variations in product quality are fairly self-evident: the evaluation of the film by the consumer as "good" or "worth seeing," relate to the ex-post perceived quality of the film. Of course, variations in the product quality are also established *before* the viewer purchases a ticket since reviews, publicity, and word of mouth all create an expectation of a certain level of quality. Films which are perceived as being of a higher quality ("better entertainment value") will garner a larger market share, other things equal. Since each viewer has a different demand and utility function, the evaluation of quality will differ from consumer to consumer; otherwise, in the extreme case, one film would corner the entire audience of filmgoers. Variations in product variety are more difficult to ascertain. The attributes of film from which the viewer derives utility might include such factors as plotline, stars, production value, genre, social relevance, and difference/similarity to other films (originality). Additionally, in the more global choice of film attendance versus other entertainment products, factors related to the exhibition of the film clearly are also attributes to the viewer: geographic location, convenience, theater maintenance, staff courtesy and service, and projection/sound quality. If consumers are perceived as valuing each of these attributes approximately equally, then the model of product differentiation collapses into variations of product quality. Otherwise, differentiation depends upon the varied attributes inherent in the moviegoing experience (7).

With the addition of the concept of product differentiation, the traditional accounts of the marketplace for film become increasingly inadequate. The marketplace can be conceived as split into many different smaller markets, each catering to specific audience segments with distinct demand functions. The marketplace is split as is the "good" of film itself: Film can be conceptualized more fruitfully as a product with a large number of attributes which can be varied to meet the needs of specific audiences. This atomized model of the film marketplace obviously has some problems in practice (i.e., "cross-over" films would complicate the model considerably), yet it also offers some specific routes to explain the status of the 1980s film industry. Perhaps the model of market segmentation and product differentiation could be utilized in an examination of specific studio product and strategies in the marketplace. High concept might be conceptualized as a specific form of differentiated product which has the potential for crossing into more than one audience segment.

HIGH CONCEPT AS PRODUCT DIFFERENTIATION

In his analysis of the relationship between film content and economic determinants, Dominick comments that "the tighter the oligopoly and the risk, the more similar will be the 'look' of films produced by each studio" (9, p. 138). Dominick argues that the new technologies have not increased the variety of films produced: Hollywood is only producing more of the same. While the kinds or genres of film may be the same, I disagree with Dominick's contention regarding the aesthetics of these films. The most successful studios are those which can identify and exploit a particular market segment in their films. In particular, Paramount realizes this strategy through a significant percentage of their release schedule. While Paramount is most clearly aligned with the high concept film, other studies (such as Touchstone/Disney) also have a distinctive look or type of project. Accordingly in the past several years, studio films *have* become differentiated through their look and style; for example, one can talk about the "personality" of a Paramount film just as authors have discussed the classic MGM or Warners films of fifty years ago. While I would not want to claim that a studio's production schedule is not diversified, there does appear to be continuity between some elements of certain studios' output.

The continuity suggests that a form of product differentiation is being undertaken by the majors. The advantages to this strategy are many, as Chamberlain summarizes, "Where the possibility of differentiation exists, sales depend on the skill with which the good is distinguished from others and made to appeal to a specific groups of buyers" (6, p. 283). Studio manipulation of product characteristics intersects with the category of high concept: the most financially successful studio of the past decade has been the studio most associated with the term high concept. High concept seems to be a more exact category of differentiation because, in several respects, there are decisive breaks from the usual narrational and compositional structure of the Hollywood film. I will highlight the breaks which offer a differentiated product.

As a form of product differentiation, high concept operates through two channels: through an emphasis on screen style, and through integration with marketing and merchandising. Miller and LeRoy discuss style changes as a type of product differentiation unrelated to quality or durability (7, p. 326). Innovations in style result in the obsolescence of the already existing products: the most dramatic results occur in the auto and fashion industries. This strategy thereby aids elimination of competing products. Style in the high concept films embodies many facets: style in the production, narrative, and use of genre. The most obvious of these traits is the high-tech style of the production. Working from a tradition which architectural historian Reyner Banham referred to as "the Second Industrial Revolution" for its emphasis upon electronic devices and controlled environments, these films offer a distinctive look.[1] Peter McAlevey refers to the style as a "high-tech gloss;" this explanation seems useful as it refers to the superficial rendering of high technology which controls the films (2, p. 86). The look of the films includes a minimal (often almost black and white) color scheme, a predominance of reflected images, use of extreme backlighting, and a tendency towards settings of an industrial nature (without industry as an ostensible narrative point) (41). Additionally style or stylishness often centers the narrative. Plots are built around events which concern style as an issue of performance; for example, consider the importance of style in aviation (*Top Gun*), dance (*Flashdance*, *Footloose*), or demeanor (*American Gigolo*, *9½ Weeks*) to the functioning of the various films. The style of these films represents one configuration of attributes (production, narrative, design) which serves to effectively differentiate the high-concept films. The other major differentiating factor involves packaging, rather than product design.

---

[1] For a brief explanation of "the high tech style" in design, see Alan Johnson's entry in *What's What in the 1980s* (29, pp. 150–151).

High-concept films have a greater focus upon their marketing and merchandising. They are designed to be marketed and merchandised to a particular audience. The majority of the films are targeted to a certain audience in conception thereby making their media campaigns much more specific and directed. In general the film skew to a younger group, although the large-scale high-concept hits do cross-over into other audience segments during their run.[2] The difference between the promotion of the high-concept films seems to be a reliance upon the image and the replication of this image through different media. By image, I am referring to both the figures from the print campaign ads and to the "persona" of the entire film (i.e., the connotations which the entire campaign, including publicity and promotion, create for the film). The viewer's impression of the film is strengthened by the repetition of the image from the ad campaign, media buys, and, most importantly, the licensing of the film through different products. While all films are supported by ad campaigns, only a minority are based on a concept which lends itself to this cross-fertilization of promotion; for example, *Top Gun's* concept depends upon strong visuals and a generically based story which lead easily to the film's presentation in the media. Other Paramount films (perhaps *Heartburn* or *Children of a Lesser God*) contain concepts which cannot be contained succinctly through promotion, and which therefore do not operate via the same form of product differentiation. The image-based media campaigns represent segment-based product differentiation: through the advertising, the company is able to appeal to particular market segments thereby differentiating its product from the rest. Frequently this form augments the differentiation in terms of style which also marks the high-concept film.

THE MAJORS, HIGH CONCEPT, AND PRODUCT DIFFERENTIATION

Of the majors, Paramount and Disney have been most successful in practicing these forms of product differentiation. Between both companies, there are important connections which explain their successful manipulation of the market and high concept. Paramount's position within the contemporary industry grew under the supervision of Gulf and Western's Charles Bludhorn, who appointed Barry Diller as the chairman of Paramount in 1974. Diller, whose background was in television, re-organized the studio, and made a relentless effort to focus upon the story in his films.[3] Along with Michael Eisner, Diller was responsible for a remarkable number of hit films, including *Raiders of the Lost Ark*, *Ordinary People*, and *Flashdance* (11, p. 107). Paramount's salient trait might

[2] Although demographics on this cross-over trend are not available, films such as *Top Gun* and *Rambo* are frequently discussed as opening to a fairly specific audience and broadening out later.

[3] Tony Schwartz's article (33) offers some very interesting anecdotes about the Diller regime at Paramount, including some interviews with the notoriously low-key Paramount executives.

well be their need to maintain close control and attention to every project. The desire to treat each project on an individual basis, rather than as merely part of a large release schedule, separates Paramount from other studios. Tony Schwartz' investigation of the Diller regime at Paramount includes a quote from an independent (anonymous) producer: "Are they smarter than the executives at other studios? The answer is yes. Are the movies better for their input? Probably. But who wants to work all the time in a bunker atmosphere, under the constant threat of the guillotine?" (33, p. 27). Interviews with many of the key marketing and distribution executives produce the other side of the coin however: Paramount's involvement is meant to foster and expand the work of the individual filmmaker (12, 26, 39).

Diller left Paramount in 1984 after disagreements with Martin S. Davis, the new chairman of Gulf and Western (14). Almost simultaneously, Eisner left for Walt Disney Productions, as did many of the key production executives (10, p. 83). Nevertheless, 24-year Paramount veteran Frank Mancuso became the new Paramount chairman, and, after an initially rough start, continued Paramount's winning streak.[4] Paramount has also benefited from the cross-fertilization made possible from its television and movie divisions: Successful television series have been recently developed from the *Star Trek* and *Friday the Thirteenth* series, and lucrative licensing campaigns have also been developed from these "tele" -films.[5] Regarding the managerial style at Paramount and the reasons for their tremendous success, several upper-level executives expressed the opinion that the movement of information between the different departments makes Paramount unique; for example, Diana Widom, senior vice-president of publicity, in a telephone interview, commented, "There is a tremendous interaction between the marketing department, production and distribution. All these key departments are working together. There's a flow of information, of ideas, and exchange of ideas—that's what makes Paramount unique. There's a friendship and a respect between the key members of all these departments" (39). Perhaps this openness is one component of Paramount's creative and professional success story in the past two decades.

Many of Paramount's films play into utopian fantasies; as Tony Schwartz suggests, "a remarkable number of Paramount's movies mine the mainstream fantasy of struggling against odds to realize a dream" (33, p. 27). Just as important is Paramount's adherence to established genre patterns. While other studios offer films which defy genre description, Paramount works within genre: from the musical (*Footloose*, *Staying Alive*, *Flashdance*), the adventure/action

---

[4] Martin S. Davis blames Paramount's poor 1985 showing upon a list of pictures (i.e., *The River Rat*, *Joy of Sex*, *Top Secret!*) instituted by Diller, not Mancuso. For more information on the transition from Diller to Mancuso, see Farley's (10) and Trachtenberg's (36) articles.

[5] Of course, the *Star Trek* films were based on the Paramount television series from the 1960s. In 1986, the company developed *Star Trek: The Next Generation* as a series for first-run syndication.

film (*Raiders, 48 Hrs, Indiana Jones, The Untouchables*), and the "fish out of water" comedy (*Beverly Hills Cop, Crocodile Dundee, The Golden Child, Trading Places, Planes, Trains, and Automobiles*), to the teenage comedy (*Pretty in Pink, Some Kind of Wonderful*). While Paramount does undertake cross-generic products (i.e., the film noir comedy *The Blue Iguana*, the comedy-romance-thriller *Atlantic City*), typically these films are not integral to the company's release schedule.[6] Nevertheless, Paramount's genre films are certainly not classical genre examples either. More than other studios, Paramount utilizes the viewer's knowledge and understanding of mass/popular culture. The audience's recognition of, for example, musical conventions (in the case of *Staying Alive* or *Flashdance*), action/adventure serials (*Indiana Jones*), television series (*Star Trek, Untouchables*), and even board games (*Clue*), gives the studio license to "update" the films through the look of the films. The studio's style has been described as "urban, hip, gutsy," and this evaluation certainly grows from the surface appearance of the Paramount films (19, p. 63). This look is most closely aligned with the high-concept style discussed above. The fusion of this stylishness with the saturated genre narratives offers the method that Paramount has utilized to differentiate its product. Producer Don Simpson's assessment of *Flashdance*'s success could well describe Paramount's modus operandi: "I though there was a chance for popular art, not high art, in the concept. *Flashdance* had a quality known as top spin, in which the casting, the concept and the look and sound of the movie all come together" (30, p. 84).

Although one could not tell from the market share charts, another company has been making great strides in the past three years—Walt Disney Productions. Growing from a dismal three percent of the market at the beginning of the decade, Disney has risen to 14 percent in 1987, placing it second only to Paramount.[7] Disney's success seems due to three principle components: the formation of Touchstone Pictures in 1984, the exodus of the Paramount team Eisner-Jeffrey Katzenberg in the same year, and the entry of Disney into other entertainment ventures (21, p. 68). Touchstone was formed primarily to supply more adult-oriented films without losing the family stamp of the Disney name (38). In its first year, Touchstone produced *Splash* (revenues $62.1 million) and the less successful *Country* ($8.3 million). The new team's influence was not felt until two years later with *Down and Out in Beverly Hills, Ruthless People, The Color of Money*, and *Tough Guys*.

By the time Disney had begun to make a real dent into the marketplace, several traits became clear within the films and, indeed, within the operation of Disney. One cannot underestimate the importance of Eisner and Katzenberg to

---

[6] Some obvious exceptions would include the films *Ragtime, Reds*, and *Heartburn*—all of which deviated from traditional genre definitions and also were positioned as key products for the company.

[7] During January 1988, Paramount actually lost its lead to Disney due to the phenomenally successful *Three Men and a Baby* and *Good Morning Vietnam*.

the development: especially important is their emphasis upon story, causation, medium-budget projects, and the desire for close control and interaction with the filmmakers. While these traits have become internalized within Paramount, the orchestraters (Diller, Eisner, and Katzenberg) have spread their philosophy to other companies; since Disney is not beset by the grave structural problems of Fox, the company has been able to adapt its strategies to the configuration of the new company. While Disney has been most successful with up-scale comedies, their production schedule has become more varied, with forays into action adventure (*Shoot to Kill*) and domestic drama (*The Good Mother*). Whether Disney will be able to compete on a long-term basis with majors such as Paramount is open to debate, although the substantial assets of The Disney Channel, Disney Home Video, and especially the theme parks, offer a large cushion for experimentation (17).[8]

The product from Disney follows some of the same guidelines as the Paramount films. The connection is not coincidental. The connection between the two studios begins with the close control which both have over the projects and, in particular, over the films' budgets (1, p. 63). With the formation of Touchstone in 1984, Disney solved their own diversification problem by creating an adult-oriented film arm. Significantly, Disney did not dilute the tradition of the Disney name and its connection with family entertainment. In a statement which indicates the importance of product differentiation for the company, Richard Berger, president of Disney Pictures, states the reason for the two divisions: "People don't know who [studio] made *Star Wars* or *Raiders*, but they can tell you who made *Tron*" (23, p. 1). While maintaining the Disney product, the company also produced a consistent Touchstone product. With *Down and Out in Beverly Hills* in 1986, Touchstone began to produce films which contained many similarities to each other, while remaining individual projects. The company has profited from a series of comedies featuring established actors, directors, and tight comic timing. The comedies have mainly been light-hearted social commentaries containing larger-than-life personalities, such as Bette Midler or Robin Williams. The difference between these stars' other films and their Disney films underlines Disney's method: the films are able to contain the stars' persona, rather than being overwhelmed. The comedies (such as *Ruthless People, Outrageous Fortune, Three Men and a Baby, Hello Again,* and *Good Morning Vietnam*) have also been balanced by more personal projects, such as Martin Scorsese's *The Color of Money* and Barry Levinson's *Tin Men*. In this way, Disney has been able to develop continuing working relationships with more famous, "auteur" directors, while still having the financial security of their

[8] Disney's venture into pay cable and other media has proven their expertise beyond the theatrical window. Both the Disney Channel and Disney Home Video have been extremely successful. Under the supervision of Jim Jimmiro, Disney Home Video have parlayed their film library into an extremely lucrative enterprise (DHV's *Lady and the Tramp* is the bestselling video of all time).

comedies. Among the other majors, one cannot discern distinctive studio styles—at this time, only Paramount and Disney have successfully practiced product differentiation (via their high-concept projects) on a continual basis.

High-concept films represent perhaps the most blatant form of differentiation. Nevertheless these films illuminate many of the problems with traditional definitions of the marketplace. A description of the industry as mature oligopoly must be thrown into question due to several reasons. Principal among these is the heterogeneity of the product "film" and the market segmentation which certainly is important to the film marketplace. While attention has been paid to the various new technologies and their impact upon the theatrical film industry, some of the basic assumptions of the economic nature of film need to be re-examined. High concept—the most "commercial" and market-driven of all films—indicates the direction that a critical examination of the industry might take.

Since the model of high concept suggests that, in some ways, these films are "more commercial" than the rest of the mainstream product, I have sought to pursue this issue through the development of an empirical model explaining box office revenue. In effect, the model tests the difference of high concept, and the assumption of formulism which is often associated with high concept. The model presented below illustrates some of the more basic findings of my empirical investigation.

A MODEL FOR THE DETERMINATION OF BOX OFFICE REVENUE

While the narrative, cinematic, and economic parameters of high concept explain the operation of the films, these arguments omit the key component of commerciality which seems to underlie many of the industry and trade definitions of high concept. Schickel summarizes this tendency, "What the phrase really means is that the concept is so low it can be summarized and sold on the basis of one simple sentence" (32, p. 86). The sales possibility of high concept is reiterated by Hoberman, who stresses the connection between presold qualities, marketing, and high concept: "*Jaws* was something else: its presold property and media-blitz saturation release pattern heralded the rise of marketing men and 'high concept' " (16, p. 36). In some sense, therefore, high concept is often utilized to describe projects which are immediately (and obviously) commercial.

Underlying the connection between the commercial and high concept is the premise that film can somehow be reduced to a formula. Certainly the industry usage suggests that the high-concept film "ensures" financial success due to the configuration of several elements, including storyline, genre, stars, and bankable directors. One method to investigate this connection is offered through regression and correlational analysis—methods popular within several disciplines, especially the social sciences. This type of analysis is based upon formulating a model and positing a relationship between a dependent variable and one or more explanatory variables.[9] Given the connection between high concept and the commercial, the type of model which seems most appropriate would be a consumer demand model with box office revenue as the dependent variable.

The problem might be approached in two stages: Firstly, through the specification of a model with box office revenue as the dependent variable, several quantifiable explanatory variables, and a sample of all films released from a number of consecutive years. The regression equation yields a model of the relative causal effect of the explanatory variables upon box office gross—this model will be accountable for all films in general. Secondly, a subset of high-concept films can be identified and contained within the larger set. These high-concept films can be evaluated in comparison with the larger model. This evaluation might take several forms: an analysis of the difference between values of explanatory variables in the high-concept films versus the rest of the large sample; a comparison of the predicted gross for the high-concept films to the other films within the larger model; and a separate regression model utilizing only the high-concept films as the sample.

DERIVATION AND SPECIFICATION OF THE MODEL

The dependent variable in the model is theatrical rentals accruing to the distributor per film. A. D. Murphy's *Boxoffice Register* offers both weekly and cumulative yearly figures for box office gross (28). All those films between 1983 and 1986 which grossed more than one million dollars at the box office are in the sample. The vast majority of releases are included within this group since, if a film is given a wide release, a total revenue of at least one million dollars is extremely probable. The sample considers 512 films in total. Since the sample covers four consecutive years, the price of admission during this period does not remain constant. The yearly *International Motion Picture Almanac* offers figures on admission prices, and indeed the price did gradually increase: 1983—$3.15; 1984—$3.34; 1985—$3.51; 1986—$3.67 (18). To adjust the revenue for this increase in admission price, an index for admission was created with 1983 as the base year (1984—1.06; 1985—1.11; 1986—1.17). The rentals are then deflated by this index. The observations themselves skew positively as a result of the extraordinary grosses of several films; for example, *Return of the Jedi* ($252.3 million), *Ghostbusters* ($208.3 million adjusted), and *Beverly Hills Cop* ($216.8 million adjusted).

The first set of independent variables involves the distributor for each film. A binary variable is set to one if the film is distributed by a major (or mini-major), and zero if distributed by an independent. The six major distributors are Para-

[9] Given the values on the dependent and independent variables, the task of regression analysis is to fit an $(n\text{-}1)$ dimensional "line" in n-dimensional space to approximate the values of the dependent variable. The relationship is therefore causal: the equation specifies that the dependent variable is explained by the set of explanatory variables.

mount, Twentieth-Century Fox, Universal, Columbia, Warner Brothers, and MGM/UA. During the period of the sample, MGM/UA was split into two individual companies (MGM and UA), which in conjunction utilized the same distribution functions. For this analysis, I am considering the output of both companies as part of only MGM/UA. The mini-majors are Orion, Tri-Star, and Disney/Touchstone. These companies typically do not have as large a release slate as the majors, and they lack the advantages of economies of scale offered through large-scale production and integration of the different windows of release. Companies such as DEG, Cannon, New World, New Line, and Embassay are considered as independents. In the model, I have also attached a binary variable for each major and mini-major (nine categories and one additional for the independents). The expectation is that the coefficients on the majors will be substantially larger and positive compared to the coefficient on the independents.

The second independent variable comes from the MPAA rating system: a series of binary variables accounts for the categories G-PG-PG13-R. The X rating was excluded since no films in the sample had been assigned this rating. In addition, the categories G and PG were pooled together to form the "base/control category" as this group was the most frequent rating applied by the board. For the regression analysis, the base category was omitted from the specification of the model since all the other ratings are compared to the base category. Data for the MPAA ratings is from *Boxoffice* and the annual index of *Variety* reviews. Since Austin (3) concluded from his model that there was no significant different between grosses on PG- and R-rated films, the MPAA variables were not expected to have any particular sign or coefficient size. (3).

The third independent variable concerns release date. Since the phenomenally successful release of *Jaws* in 1975, summer has been seen increasingly as the most favorable period for release. This pattern has developed in conjunction with the targeting of a youth audience for pictures. Alternately, the Christmas vacation period has remained very important as a release season. To discover if these periods do in fact have a positive effect on box office revenue, I introduced two binary variables for the two periods. It is expected that both variables would have positive coefficients signifying that a Christmas or summer release adds to the revenue of a film all other variables held constant. Release dates are from the first wide-release week for the film listed in Murphy's *Boxoffice Register*.

The presence of bankable stars in a film constitutes the fourth independent variable (27, 34, 35). Utilizing a method for Litman's study, I consider the top ten box office stars from the Quigley Publications' "Annual Poll of Circuit and Independent Exhibitors in the United States" (22). For the current year, a film has a bankable star (a binary variable, 1 = film with star, 0 = no star) if it features any actor or actress from the three previous top ten lists. Therefore a film released in 1986 contains a bankable star if it contains any person from the top ten for 1983–1985. A few minor problems arise from this procedure through. For example, some stars may not make a film for several years and have dropped off the Quigley lists, yet they are still considered potent box office stars to the extent that projects are designed around them—Jane Fonda, Robert Redford, and Warren Beatty all fit this category. In certain cases, therefore, the value 1 is assigned to a film whose star would seem to be bankable despite exclusion form the Quigley lists.[10] The other problem centers around Kindem's argument: the Quigley poll ignores stars from other media who are bankable in their first performance (20, p. 92). Nevertheless, the inconsistency of this phenomenon made the addition of these stars seem too arbitrary: Major media stars, such as Michael J. Fox, Prince, and Dolly Parton, all seem very bankable in their first films, whereas other stars like Tom Selleck, Paul McCartney, and Howie Mandel create little interest in theatrical motion pictures.

Similarly the variable account for the bankable directors is also constructed based upon track record. The directors behind the top twenty films in each of the past three years are utilized—if any of these directors made a film in the current year, the binary variable "marketable director" is set to one. Since a director may have helmed more than one top film in the past three years, the list of marketable directors for each year is less than sixty. The data for the top twenty films is derived from the *Boxoffice Register* and *Variety's* chart of "The Big Rental Films" for each year. The expected coefficient on this variable would be positive since a director with a previous top twenty film would be expected to produce another bankable film. Again the problem would seem to be accounting for the "occasional" director—for example, Stanley Kubrick's *The Shining* was a box office hit in 1980, therefore placing him on the marketable directors lists for 1981–83, yet his next film (*Full Metal Jacket*) was not released until 1987.

The next independent variable is an index of critical reception (4). *Boxoffice* magazine—an industry trade paper targeted primarily for exhibitors—publishes their "Review Digest." Each film in the digest is assigned a rating form one (very poor) to five (excellent). This cumulative rating is based upon an average of the individual ratings from *Boxoffice, Variety, The Los Angeles Times, The New York Times,* and *USA Today*. The sample of films is remarkably comprehensive—the Digest only omitted 54 (out of 512) films from my larger sample of all releases. For the missing critical ratings, I utilized a conversion of Leonard Maltin's ratings (25). Maltin's *TV Movies and Video Guide* offers a 4-point scale, therefore a conversion of these numbers to the 5-point scale was necessary for consistency.[11] One would expect that the coefficient on the rating variable would be small and positive—if a film has a low rating, the effect will be insubstantial; if a film has a very positive rating, the effect will be more pronounced.

A series of seven binary variables accounts for the genre of each film. The

---

[10] The exceptions include Arnold Schwarznegger in *Commando* and Jane Fonda in *Agnes of God*.

[11] Conversion of Maltin ratings followed this method: M(Maltin) 4—C(Converted) 5.0; M3.5—C4.5; M3.0—C4.0; M2.5—C3.5; M2.0—C3.0; M1.5—C2.5; M1.0—C2.0; M Bomb—C1.0.

possible genres are drama, comedy, action/adventure, horror/mystery/suspense, family, musical, and science fiction. Since all films are placed within a single genre, one genre (drama) is omitted for the specification of the regression model. The size of the coefficients on each genre variable are not expected to be any particular sign or size—although the recent trend towards horror and science fiction films would seem to indicate that these variables might have a positive sign in relation to the base (drama) category. Cost figures are also utilized as explanatory variables. While Litman constrained his study to include only films on which he could find cost data, I propose to instead specify a binary variable for high-cost films: set to one if a film has a negative cost of over $15 million, zero otherwise. Data on these high-cost films are available in *Variety's* annual "Big Buck Scorecard" (22). For those high-cost films, another variable lists the actual cost (as a number over $15 million). A priori we would expect that somehow the extra production quality in the high-cost films should correlate with larger box office grosses.

To be more precise about the quantification of high concept, three separate facets of high concept are isolated: the style of the films, the links to merchandising and licensing, and the "repetition" through either remakes, sequels, or series. The high-concept style might be the most amorphous—as I defined previously, these films rely upon the distinctive hard-edged, high-tech style in their production. This style works in conjunction with marketing and merchandising to form the high-concept picture. A binary variable accounting for the high-concept style of the films is therefore specified. Certainly a variable could be defined which would analyze the merchandising aspect; for example, a binary variable equalling one if the film is merchandised through, for instance, soundtracks, book tie-ins, posters, toys, zero otherwise. A more exact model could be determined if more data was available on the types and revenues from merchandising. Finally, high concept can be seen as a type of "economy" on the part of producers—the repetition of bankable material to guarantee audience interest. One of the most obvious forms of this repetition are remakes, sequels, or series films. All of these groups represent one formula for commercial success. With high concept as constituted through some combination of these three factors, the model can be completed. A binary variable is set to one if the film is a remake, sequel, or part of a series; zero otherwise. The high-concept variables will be used to isolate a subset of films which can be considered "high concept." These films will then be compared with the larger set of films, and the differences between the sets will be analyzed.

The final explanatory variables involve the Academy Awards. Two numerical variables list the number of nominations for a film and the actual number of awards won. Therefore the full regression model is composed of the following relationship: box office revenue (dependent variable) is posited to be explained by distribution company, MPAA rating, release pattern, bankable stars, bankable director, critical reception, genre, cost, awards, and the series of high-concept variables. Multiple regression analysis estimates an equation which fits the exact relationship between the dependent and independent variables. Tests of significance and correlation are also run to locate those variables which have a greater effect on revenue (24, 37).

REGRESSION RESULTS

The computer program "SHAZAM" was utilized for the regression and correlation estimates (37). After assessment of the regression results the following variables were found to be consistently insignificant in the model: the MPAA ratings variables (thus confirming the conclusions from earlier studies), the Christmas release season, the academy awards, the mini-majors and independents, the musical genre, and the family genre. The method utilized to derive the best linear model is commonly refered to as "stepwise backward regression." This technique involves specifying a model with all the possible explanatory variables, and then rejecting the explanatory variables one at a time based upon their significance (13, p. 191). The statistical significance of a variable relates to the variables' contribution to the overall explanatory power of the model.[12] The best linear regression model can be found in Table 1. The model considers *only* those variables which proved to be significant in the initial regressions, and shows that 42 percent of the variance in box office revenue was explained by the independent variables specified in the model. Although the results agree basically with the larger model, some individual coefficients warrant mention. The large negative coefficient on the high-cost variable is especially interesting—indicating that a high-cost film will lower the overall box office revenue of a film by $18.6 million! This surprising statistic indicates that high budget films actually lower the prospects for revenue. Films in the sample, such as *Something Wicked This Way Comes, The King of Comedy, Cotton Club, The Bounty, Once Upon a Time in America, King David*, and *Enemy Mine*, all cost more than $20 million each; each grossed substantially less than 50 percent of their budget! These big budget disasters greatly outweigh high-budget hits, such as *Return of the Jedi, Rambo*, and *A View to a Kill*. Although not all the studio variables are significant, all the majors (except Universal) have positive signs. The interpretation of the sign on Universal would indicate that Universal actually has a negative effect on box office revenue. This result has several possible explanations, which might relate to Universal's choice of projects, marketing, and distribution schemes. As expected, both Paramount and Warner Brothers carry the largest positive signs, thereby attesting to their superior distribution and marketing practices. Both the comedy and action genres are significant and carry large positive signs. The bankable director variable is insignificant at the 5%

[12] For a discussion of this relationship, see Gujarati's analysis of the incremental contribution of an explanatory variable (13, pp. 132–135).

Table 1. Regression on Box Office Revenue for Theatrical Movies, 1983–1986

Independent Variables	Estimated Coefficient	Standard Error	*T*-Ratio
Summer release	8.885*	2.117	4.196
Critical rating	4.821*	1.156	4.168
Cost	−18.668*	7.054	−2.646
Value of Cost	−0.912*	0.296	3.081
Academy nominations	4.985*	0.655	7.610
Box office stars	13.864*	3.320	4.175
Bankable director	3.718	2.798	1.328
Merchandising	6.028*	2.154	2.798
High concept style	19.364*	2.833	6.833
Tie-ins	7.726*	2.694	2.868
Paramount	13.624*	3.607	3.776
20th Century-Fox	4.540	3.395	1.337
Universal	−1.298	3.330	−0.389
MGM/UA	0.433	3.453	0.125
Columbia	3.068	3.496	0.877
Warners	5.412**	3.236	1.672
Comedy	11.704*	2.489	4.701
Action	15.119*	2.776	5.446
Horror	8.276*	3.711	2.229
Science-Fiction	8.187**	4.454	1.838
Constant	−22.485*	4.311	−5.214

R-squared: 0.446; R-squared adjusted: 0.423; sample size: 512
*significant at 5% level
**significant at 10% level

level, yet significant at the 20% level (*t*-ratio of 1.328, critical *t* value of 1.282). Especially since the box office star variable is retained in the model, I sought to also include the bankable director variable as a complement.

An analysis of the plotted "observed" versus "predicted" (from the regression equation) grosses uncovers some trends among the types of films which may be projected with the most accuracy. The largest errors occur among the outliers—those films which have phenomenally large grosses.[13] For example, *Back to the Future* grossed $188.77 million in adjusted 1983 dollars; the regression specified a figure of $63.01 million, which is amongst the largest figures predicted in the model, yet obviously quite far away from the actual gross. *Top Gun* is another outlier problem: an actual gross of $154.59 million, with a predicted gross of $87.84 million—again a very high figure for the model, but not very close to the actual gross.

[13] Restricted models were run to limit the number of these outliers. One model considered films with an adjusted gross between $10 million and $60 million (214 observations); another model considered films with an adjusted gross between $5 million and $65 million (334 observations). The former model had few significant variables and a low explained sum of squares; the latter model replicated the results from the larger sample, with a smaller *r* squared value.

Other large errors seem associated with large budget "surprises"—films which had been highly touted, yet failed to live up to their expectations. *The Right Stuff*, *Brainstorm*, and *Brazil* fit into this category. In many ways, these films were expected to perform much stronger and their eventual failure remains a mystery. Perhaps their failure could be explained in terms of high concept: the lack of a clear, marketable concept partially caused the films' failure. The most striking case would be *The Right Stuff*: a film which was well-received by the critics, garnered many Academy award nominations, and considered a fascinating and very American subject. The film grossed only $21.5 million—well below the expected revenues, and far below the predicted value of $78.28 million. This failure seems extremely difficult to account for: all indications before and during release would seem to dictate a much higher gross.

Given the emphasis of the high-concept projects upon simple and definable storylines, interestingly the model's large errors also occur with films which have been widely criticized for their confusing narratives. For example, consider the narratives of *The Hunger*, *The Keep*, *Against All Odds*, *The Cotton Club*, and *Swing Shift*.[14] All of these films are torn in several different directions, confounding the viewer's expectations and the limitations of their genres. These films cannot be conceptually reduced in the same manner as *Flashdance* or *Top Gun*. What is the concept behind, for example, Francis Coppola's sprawling gangster-musical *The Cotton Club*? In the regression model, these "complicated" narratives all performed below their predicted values. In part an argument could be made for their failure in terms of high concept: the lack of a clear concept behind these films hampered their performance at the box office.

The best linear model does possess some undesirable statistical qualities for the estimation of gross. Most importantly the model allows for negative predictive grosses. Since the model is linear in the variables and parameters, the predicted values range from largely negative to largely positive. Obviously in my study, a negative box office revenue is nonsensical. While in my model, there are only a few negative predicted values, the problem can be solved by specifying an alternative functional form for the relationship between box office revenue and the explanatory variables. One such form is the semilog model in which the dependent variable is logged, while the independent variables remain in an unlogged form. In the simple regression case this relationship therefore becomes:

$$\ln y_i = \propto_o + x_I x_I + e$$

This specification constrains the predicted values for gross to be positive. The results of the semilog regression are contained in Table 2. The coefficients on the explanatory variables agree with the findings in the linear model, with the exception of the cost variable which is now insignificant at the five percent level.

---

[14] Other films with unclear concepts fitting this pattern in the model include *Videodrome*, *Prizzi's Honor*, *Heartburn*, *Out of Bounds*, and *Buckaroo Banzai*.

The adjusted R squared (converted for comparison) for the log model shows a slightly better "fit" than for the linear model: 0.436 for the semilog model, 0.423 for the linear model. The size of this difference is not statistically significant. Transforming the predicted values for the semilog model into an unlogged form, we find that generally the semilog model is able to predict the large grossing outliers more accurately. The model has greater problems though with predictions at the lower end of the spectrum for gross. Especially within the one to three million dollars range, the semilog model yields consistently negative errors. The predicted values do not trend downwards as with the linear model, consequently the gain in prediction for the large grossing films is more than outweighed by the loss in accuracy for the smaller films.

To identify the difference of the high-concept films, I isolated a subset consisting of only high-concept films. For this model, a film was considered as high concept if it was both merchandised and possessed the high-concept style. Based upon these criteria, a subset of 67 films (from 512) were classified as high concept. The composition of the sample was derived and appears in Table 3. The most striking comparison between the high-concept sample and the larger sample is the mean for box office revenue: $47.86 million for the high concept films, $18.86 million for the large sample. The increased revenue is also matched by a greater percentage of high-cost films (37.3 percent vs. 21.2 percent) and distri-

Table 2. Regression on Log of Box Office Revenue for Theatrical Movies, 1983–1986

Independent Variables	Estimated Coefficient	Standard Error	*T*-Ratio
Summer release	0.320*	0.086	3.720
Critical rating	0.260*	0.047	5.531
Cost	−0.145	0.287	−0.505
Value of Cost	0.015	0.012	1.296
Academy nominations	0.173*	0.026	6.527
Box office stars	0.598*	0.135	4.431
Bankable director	0.085	0.113	0.752
Merchandising	0.475*	0.087	5.426
High-concept style	0.484*	0.115	4.202
Tie-ins	0.425*	0.109	3.880
Paramount	0.418*	0.146	2.853
20th Century-Fox	0.159	0.138	1.154
Universal	0.015	0.135	0.118
MGM/UA	0.001	0.140	0.008
Columbia	0.293*	0.142	2.065
Warners	0.360*	0.131	2.735
Comedy	0.585*	0.101	5.782
Action	0.545*	0.112	4.826
Horror	0.520*	0.151	3.445
Science-Fiction	0.261	0.181	1.444
Constant	0.234	0.175	1.337

R-squared: 0.458; R-squared adjusted: 0.436; sample size: 512
*significant at 5% level

bution by majors (97.0 percent vs. 81.1 percent). High-concept films also tended to include more action and musical films, and were twice as likely to feature a box office star. As expected, Paramount's share of the high-concept films (16.4 percent) is greater than any other studios, and the independent distributors' share of the high-concept films is substantially smaller than their share of all films.

A regression on box office revenue was constructed utilizing the explanatory variables from the best linear model (Table 3). The model has an adjusted *r* squared of 51 percent, an improvement over the linear model for the large

Table 3. Distribution of the High-Concept Sample and the Entire Sample

	High Concept	Entire Set
sample size:	67	512
Box Office revenue—mean	$47.86 m	($18.86m)
standard deviation	$56.12 m	($28.19m)
films released by majors:	97%	(80.6%)
films released by independents:	3%	(19.4%)
films released during Christmas season:	14.9%	(10.9%)
films released during the Summer season:	43.2%	(33.0%)
films released apart from Christmas or summer:	41.9%	(56.1%)
films containing a box office star:	23.3%	(10.7%)
films containing a bankable director:	23.8%	(16.4%)
high-cost films:	37.3%	(21.2%)
films with G or PG rating:	34.4%	(37.4%)
films with PG13 rating:	17.9%	(14.6%)
films with R rating:	47.7%	(48.0%)
genre breakdown:		
comedy:	22.4%	(30.2%)
drama:	20.9%	(23.0%)
action:	26.8%	(21.1%)
horror:	4.5%	(9.4%)
science fiction:	12.0%	(5.8%)
family:	0%	(5.1%)
musical:	13.4%	(5.1%)
studio breakdown:		
Warners:	13.4%	(12.7%)
Universal:	15.0%	(11.3%)
20th C-F:	12.0%	(10.7%)
Columbia:	13.4%	(9.8%)
MGM/UA:	10.4%	(9.8%)
Paramount:	16.4%	(9.2%)
Orion:	5.9%	(7.4%)
Tri-Star:	5.9%	(6.4%)
Disney:	4.4%	(3.5%)
Independent:	3.0%	(18.9%)

sample. The coefficients on the variables correlate with the previous findings with two exceptions: firstly, the Christmas season variable is significant and positive in the high-concept model; secondly, the horror genre variable carries a negative sign here, indicating that horror scenarios and high concept do not produce positive results at the box office.

From this regression, one can conclude that the specified explanatory variables do not seem to predict high-concept films significantly better than other films in the sample. Despite the high-concept films' large statistical differences from the means of the larger sample, the high-concept films do not appear to be inherently much more explainable. Perhaps the most illuminating facets of the study are the results which demonstrate the overall trends in the "successful" prediction: the poor prediction of big budget/highly touted and elaborate films seems to indicate that "low concept" movies are more difficult to predict in terms of box office revenue. Inclusion of more nuanced marketing and production data might strengthen this finding. Still regression analysis offers one method through which to quantify and investigate the difference of these films—a technique which complements the economic and industrial issues explaining the differentiated product of high-concept films. The importance of these films to the current industry has been established through their financial success. Just as significant though, high concept is crucial to our theoretical understanding of the entire film marketplace and the methods through which contemporary Hollywood is able to economically and aesthetically differentiate its product.

REFERENCES

1. Ansen, D. and McAlevey, P. "The Mouse That Roared." *Newsweek*, March 3, 1986, pp. 62–65.
2. Ansen, D. and McAlevey, P. "The Producer is King Again." *Newsweek*, May 20, 1985, pp. 84–89.
3. Austin, B. A. "Do Movie Ratings Affect a Film's Performance At the Ticket Window?" *Boxoffice*, pp. 40+.
4. Austin, B. A. "Critics' and Consumers' Evaluations of Motion Pictures: A Longitudinal Test of the Taste Culture and Elitist Hypotheses." *Journal of Popular Film and Television*, no. 4, 1983, pp. 156–165.
5. Bruckheimer, J. Telephone interview, October 26, 1987.
6. Chamberlain, E. *The Theory of Monopolistic Competition*. Cambridge, MA: Harvard University Press, 1965.
7. Clarkson, K. and Miller, R. L. *Industrial Organization: Theory, Evidence and Public Policy*. New York, NY: McGraw-Hill, 1982.
8. Dickson, P. R. and Ginter, J. L. "Market Segmentation, Product Differentiation, and Marketing Strategy." *Journal of Marketing*, April 1987, pp. 1–10.
9. Dominick, J. R. "Film Economics and Film Content: 1964–1983." In B. A. Austin (Ed.), *Current Research in Film: Audiences, Economics and Law* (Volume 3). Norwood, NJ: Ablex Publishing Corporation, 1987, pp. 136–153.
10. Farley, E. "Paramount Pictures, The Turnaround: A Frank Mancuso Production." *Business Week*. March 24, 1986, p. 83.
11. Frons, M. and Green, C. "Barry Diller: The Man Who Has to Make It All Happen." *Business Week*. May 20, 1985, p. 107.

12. Goliger, N. Paramount Marketing/Production Vice-President. Interview, March 19, 1988.
13. Gujarati, D. *Basic Econometrics*. New York: McGraw-Hill, 1978.
14. "Gulf & Western: From Grab Bag to Lean, Mean, Marketing Machine." *Business Week*, September 14, 1987, p. 152.
15. Hirshleifer, J. *Price Theory and Applications*. Englewood Cliffs, NJ: Prentice-Hall, 1980.
16. Hoberman, J. "1975–1985: Ten Years That Shook the World." *American Film*, June 1985, pp. 34–60.
17. Horowitz, J. "Touchstone's Magic Touch." *Premiere*, October 1987, pp. 32–38.
18. *International Motion Picture Almanac*. New York: Quigley Publishing Company, 1982–1986.
19. Kilday, G. "Ninth Annual Grosses Gloss." *Film Comment*, March/April 1984, pp. 62–66.
20. Kindem, G. "Hollywood's Movie Star System: A Historical Overview." In G. Kindem (Ed.), *The American Movie Industry: The Business of Motion Pictures*. Carbondale: Southern Illinois University Press, 1982.
21. Koepp, S. "Do You Believe in Magic?" *Time*, April 25, 1988, pp. 66–73.
22. Litman, B. R. "Predicting Success of Theatrical Movies: New Empirical Evidence." Paper presented at the National Convention of the Association for Education in Journalism, Boston, August 1980.
23. Loynd, R. "Disney Unfurls a New Banner: Touchstone Films to Handle Non-Traditional Product." *Daily Variety*, February 16, 1984, p. 1.
24. Maddala, G. S. *Econometrics*. New York, NY: McGraw-Hill Inc., 1977.
25. Maltin, L. *Tv Movies and Video Guide: 1988 Edition*. New York, NY: New American Library, 1987.
26. Marans, M. Paramount Marketing Vice-President. Interview, April 15, 1988.
27. McLeod, D. K. "Bankability Reconsidered." *Movieline*, September 25, 1987, pp. 22–23.
28. Murphy, A. *Boxoffice Register*. Published independently.
29. Pick, C. (Ed.). *What's What in the 1980s*. Detroit: The Gale Research Company, 1982.
30. Pollock, D. "Flashfight." *The Los Angeles Times*, Calendar Section, July 10, 1983, p. 1+.
31. Saving, T. R. "Market Organization and Product Quality." *Southern Economic Journal*, April 1982, pp. 855–867.
32. Schickel, R. "Review of "Irreconcilable Differences." *Time*, October 8, 1984, p. 86.
33. Schwartz, T. "Hollywood's Hottest Stars." *New York*, July 30, 1984, pp. 25–33.
34. Simonet, T. "Performers' Marquee Values in Relation to Top-Grossing Films." Paper presented at the Society for Cinema Studies Conference, Temple University, March 1978.
35. Simonet, T. and Harwood, K. "Popular Favorites and Critics' Darlings Among Film Directors in American Release, 1930–1971." Paper presented at the Society for Cinema Studies Conference, Northwestern University, March 1977.
36. Trachtenburg, J. "G&W After Bludhorn." *Forbes*, December 3, 1984, pp. 39–40.
37. White, K. J. "A General Computer Program for Econometric Methods—SHAZAM." *Econometrica*, January 1978, pp. 239–240.
38. "Who Makes the Movies: A Hollywood Guide." *The New York Times*, January 10, 1988, p. H–26.
39. Widom, D. Paramount Promotion and Publicity Senior Vice-President. Telephone interview, February 21, 1988.
40. Wyatt, J. "High Concept and Classical Hollywood Cinema: Modes of Narration and Style." Paper presented at the University Film and Video Association Conference, Loyola Marymount University, Los Angeles, August 1987.

7

"Understand Thoroughly What You Are Selling": U.S. Film Exhibition Practices in World War I

Leslie Midkiff DeBauche

On December 27, 1917, the Rivoli opened at Broadway and 49th, New York City. Described by a writer for *Moving Picture World* as "The Last Word in Picture Palaces," Roxy Rothapfel's newest theater included an illumination system capable of flooding the auditorium with colored lights, a scent dispersal system capable of filling the auditorium with "suggestive" aromas, and a stage setting entitled "The Conservatory of Jewels," promising ". . . to make even blase Broadway open its eyes" (29, p. 55). The film chosen to inaugurate the Rivoli was a Paramount-Artcraft release, *The Modern Musketeer*, starring Douglas Fairbanks, but this feature film made up only the second half of the program.

> For the opening week the introductory number will be a modified pageant which has been styled 'The Victory for Democracy' . . . it traces the progress of democracy in this country from the time the Pilgrim Fathers landed until the United States entered the present war to make the world safe for the principles on which the nation was founded.
>
> The remainder of the program will be set up of selected soloists, film novelties of every sort, orchestral numbers and a miniature ballet each presented in a manner quite different from anything which has been attempted heretofore. (29, p. 55)

The United States had been fighting World War I for eight months at the time the Rivoli opened. The events of the war filled the newspapers, the Treasury Department had conducted two Liberty Bond Drives, and the United States Food Administration had enrolled 10.5 million people in its Food Conservation Campaign. Representatives of all branches of the motion picture industry had met with representatives from a broad spectrum of governmental agencies to plan how its members could best aid the war effort. It is an understatement to say that the war—its homefront preparations and its battlefront news—preoccupied the government, the American people, and the U.S. film industry. In opening his 2,500 seat theater, Roxy Rothapfel bowed to the important topicality of the war, but not, as might be expected, through his choice of a feature film. (*The Modern Musketeer* contains references to the war appropriate to a narrative set in a contemporary time period, but the war itself does not constitute the narrative.) Instead, the war entered the Rivoli through the "Victory for Democracy" pageant and, no doubt through some of the other live acts, newsreels, and film novelties with which he introduced that film.

The films of World War I were a varied lot: comedy and drama, feature length and short, fiction and nonfiction, some with war-related content, most with no narrative or documentary relation to the war. However, to base interpretation of the films produced during this period strictly on numerical data would be misleading. The most prestigious films, exemplified by D. W. Griffith's *Hearts of the World*, were war-related. Likewise, to base historical interpretation of the role played by the film industry in the war on the homefront strictly on the feature films which it produced, distributed, and exhibited would also be misleading as much, in addition to the feature film, was being exhibited at movie theaters. Almost redundantly the report on the Rivoli's opening concluded:

> The entertainment he [Rothapfel] will provide will be entirely institutional in any event, and it will be a case of going to the Rivoli to see a show, not going to see a certain picture at the Rivoli. (29, p. 55)

While the Rivoli, larger and grander than most theaters in the United States, may have been exceptional in the scale of the programming with which it surrounded its feature film, it was not exceptional in the variety and character of that programming.

The basic premise of this article is that any accurate understanding or fair evaluation of the role played by the film industry in the social, political, or cultural life of the U.S. must rest on an analysis of all the functions of the industry—production, distribution, and exhibition. Further, it is important to realize that films were just one of the products which the industry sought to sell. To assess the role played by the United States film industry during World War I, it is important to describe the films which it produced, but it is equally important to describe the manner in which those films were exhibited. I will survey the ways in which film exhibitors responded to the situation created by the entrance of the United States into the war, particularly the ways exhibitors incorporated the realities and demands of the war into the programming and merchandising of their theaters. I will argue first, that it was through the filmic and nonfilmic programming with which they surrounded the feature film, and through the advertising and promotion with which they merchandised their theaters, that film exhibitors most often invoked the war. Second, I will argue that the film industry, in this case film exhibition, did not change its methods of operation so much as it adapted them. Feature films had been components of total entertainment packages long before April of 1917, and as early as 1915, Epes Winthrop Sargent, author of *Picture Theater Advertising*, had urged managers to promote their theaters as vigorously as they promoted their entertainment programs.

> Your house is a permanent feature. Films are transient. Take some of your advertising space to tell about your house . . . Films are but a part of what you have to sell. Advertise all your features. (35, p. 27)

In film programming and exploitation, the tactics of film exhibitors reflected the impact and influence of the war, however the long-term strategies already enunciated by exhibitors remained constant.

Third, I will argue that the sort of war-related activities in which film exhibitors participated aided them in their ultimate goal of making their theater an integral part of their community, thus ensuring the success of their business enterprise. In other words, film exhibitors were operating well within the boundries set by the principles of "practical patriotism."

"A LITTLE SOMETHING OF SPECIAL EFFECTIVENESS": THEATER PROGRAMMING AND THEATER MERCHANDISING

Harold Edel, manager of one of New York City's biggest picture palaces, The Strand, addressed the issue of theater programming in the first installment of his column, "How It Is Done at the Strand," which appeared in the exhibitor's trade paper, *Moving Picture World* December 22, 1917. Offering his expertise to other exhibitors, he wrote:

> It is up to every exhibitor in the country to bend every effort toward doing his 'bit' whenever and wherever possible. The exhibitor is a potent factor affecting that all important thing, public opinion. I do not mean by this that he should clutter his program with war films and news pictures of soldiers . . . Each week I endeavor to present a little something of special effectiveness in addition to my regular films, bearing on the war. (12, p. 1767)

What were these patriotic features? We can start our tour at the theater's box office, move through its lobby, enter its auditorium, and finally focus on its screen. Although the examples I cite are localized and very specific, they are representative of the range of activity engaged in by the film exhibitor. It is also significant that many of these examples are culled from the pages of exhibitor trade papers, particularly *Moving Picture World* and *Motion Picture News*. Film exhibitors sent items in to such columns as "Advertising for Exhibitors," and "Live Wire Exhibitors," sharing tactics which had worked and asking for feedback from their colleagues. Thus specific examples may have sparked imitation, and as well as being descriptions of what exhibitors were actually doing, these examples are also indicative of what exhibitors thought to be appropriate and found to be effective when promoting their theaters.

In my selection of examples, I have attempted to cover the various geographical areas of the United States and to span the nineteen months of United States involvement in World War I. It is important to note that while this catalog of exhibition practices is illustrative of theater managers' responses to a specific situation, the war, it is also illustrative of a general set of promotional strategies already practiced by exhibitors and already espoused by the trade press. In *Picture Theater Advertising* Sargent had pointed out:

> advertising as it is generally understood, is the art of selling by means of publicity, but advertising is not merely a matter of printing from types, of posting lithographs, of sending out a sandwich man. The real advertising is everything that may attract the trade. (35, p. v)

The following examples of exhibition practices must be considered in this light, as forms of advertising designed to attract trade. While these examples of war-related activities do call attention to certain aspects and needs of the war on the homefront, they simultaneously call attention to the movie theater sponsoring them. It is also important to note that these war-related exhibition practices were not necessarily part of a coordinated promotional campaign for a certain film with war-related content. Instead, they more often occupied an autonomous status vis á vis the film program. Thus, their advertising value lay in attracting trade first to a specific theater, and secondly, to the feature film being shown.

In programming and promoting their theaters during the period of the United States involvement in World War I, theater managers had many options.

Decoration could be used outside the movie theater which served both to locate it prominently on the block and to manifest a patriotic attitude. In Boston, the front of the Globe theater was decked with flags and bunting which would remain, said manager Frank Meagher, until "something more definite breaks regarding the war" (14, p. 2823). Not to be outdone, the manager of the Modern Theater, also in Boston, "arranged for the unfurling of the second largest flag in the city. Manager Pinanski has arranged with the R. H. White Company across the street to fly this mammoth flag on a steel cable between the two buildings over Washington Street" (14, p. 2823).

Theater managers could invoke the war by the very act of selling tickets. In May of 1917, the Stanley Theater in Philadelphia sold its tickets to customers on provision that they agree to respect the flag (38, p. 789). When Catherine Russell Bleeker took over management duties at the Broadway Theater in New York City, she announced that soldiers and sailors would be admitted free, "all days except Sat. and Sun. and holidays" (24, x, p. 5). In July, 1918, *Variety* reported that "A Milwaukee theater is admitting free any patron who presents a letter from a soldier who is overseas" (41, p. 38). Free admission was not the only way an exhibitor could demonstrate his civic-mindedness at the door. He could, and often did, donate a portion of the ticket receipts to various war fund drives. In Seattle, in the summer of 1917, the manager of the Clemmer Theater announced that the "entire receipts on June 25 as well as the salaries of theater employees for that day would be donated to the Red Cross'' (37, p. 273). The Clemmer further drew attention to itself by hiring small boys to walk around town customed as huge red crosses. C. W. Martin of the Temple Theater in McCook, Nebraska donated his proceeds for a week to the first Liberty Bond Drive (30, p. 789). While this strategy of donating to the Red Cross or the Liberty Bond drives was a tactical response to the war, the strategy of donating to worthy causes was already a part of the theater manager's promotional repertoire. *Picture Theater Advertising*, 1915, advised:

> If there is a movement to collect a fund, let him [the manager] not only be a contributor to the fund. He should aid to influence others. He should let his house be designated as a depository. He should give a benefit matinee. He should make his theater a rallying point. (35, p. 4)

Sargent went on to point out the benefits to the manager of such activity.

> This not alone brings prominence to the house, but a leader in the movement, he comes into contact with the newspapers, and the chairman of a fund, is to the editor, a person of greater importance than the man who runs the picture show. (35, p. 4)

The theater's lobby offered the exhibitor further opportunities to do ''a little something of special effectiveness'' (12, p. 1767) whether he was showing Mary Pickford in *Johanna Enlists* or Mary Pickford in *Rebecca of Sunnybrook Farm*. *Moving Picture World* apprised its exhibitor subscribers of the availability of a ''Beautiful FacSimile Painting'' with dimensions of thirty inches by forty inches, presented in a three-inch gold frame and selling for ten dollars.

> The President's face is done in water color and oils, and the American Flag is worked up beautifully in artistic reproduction of the proper shade of red and blue, giving in all a permanent display for the lobby. (20, p. 630)

The United States Food Administration offered a free, six-color poster which they urged exhibitors to have ''framed and kept permanently on exhibition in the theaters'' (40). Douglas Fairbanks linked promotion of a western, *Wild and Wooly*, in which he starred, with a campaign to raise money for the Red Cross. Exhibitors were encouraged to

> present an attractive lobby display with placards urging patrons of the theater to contribute to the Red Cross Fund. A coin box will be placed in the lobby of the theater so that patrons may donate their 'bit' on passing in and out of the theater. (13, p. 64)

Harold Edel was still concerned with nonfilmic gestures in support of the war effort a year after his initial column appeared in *Moving Picture World*. On February 18, 1918, in the lobby of the Strand, he unveiled a bronze tablet bearing the names of all the Strand employees in the Service (21, p. 1350). As the advertising value of donating money to civic projects was recognized and advocated as good theater management, so the use of the lobby to attract trade had likewise been recognized. *Picture Theater Advertising* devoted a chapter to "The Lobby as Advertisement," and a 1927 handbook on theater management by Sargent and John Barry more clearly specified the role played by decoration in the lobby. "The theater lobby, like any other show window, sells the institution (36, p. 183). During World War I, the theater manager often chose to fill his show window with war-related decoration.

By the time the patron had bought or been given his ticket and had passed through the theater lobby to his seat in the auditorium, the theater manager, or "live wire exhibitor," as *Motion Picture News* called its most innovative constituents, had had ample opportunity to call attention to his patriotism and to his theater financially as well as decoratively. Once inside the auditorium another set of strategies was available to him. *Motion Picture News* suggested to its subscribers that they contact their local recruiting officer and offer him access to their theaters, both for actual recruitment and for less direct recruitment through posters. *Motion Picture News* suggested, "It is good policy to do this. Your patrons will know you are doing it for the common good, and it will help the standing of any theater to be always first in such thoughtfulness" (18, p. 2327).

Music was another medium available to the theater manager for reminding patrons of his and their patriotic feelings and duties, and it was another example of adapting existing exhibition strategy to a specific exhibition situation. *Picture Theater Advertising* also noted that music could serve as an advertisement for the theater. In January 1918, *Moving Picture World* reported that Baltimore had made the playing of the National Anthem obligatory at every "public function, concert or entertainment" (6, p. 272). *The New York Times* reported that the Rialto Theater had received so many requests for patriotic music that they had hired two additional trumpeters (45, x, p. 10). In Milwaukee and Chicago, theaters instituted the practice of community singing of patriotic songs as well as other contemporary songs before the feature film was shown. An advertisement for Milwaukee's Alhambra Theater read, "We started Community Singing as an experiment. Now it's an assured success. We yield to the public demand and will continue it one more week with Frederick Carberry directing" (1, II, p. 10).

The stages of the theaters were available for war-related purposes. In Buffalo, New York, the managers of the Star and Teck Theaters placed large signs on their stages asking, "Have you bought a second Liberty Bond?" (9, p. 897). The government's propaganda bureau, the Committee for Public Information, sponsored the Four Minute Men, a corps of 35,000 men and women available to make talks of four minutes duration during the reel changes at motion picture theaters. It is worthwhile to make a side trip in this tour through the movie theater to discuss the conception and functioning of the Four Minute Men. Close study of this organization yields information about the contemporary assessment of the audience for movies, a topic important to an understanding of the impact of the film industry during wartime. It also shows how the film exhibitor was able to incorporate leading citizens of his community into his programing, thus aiding his strategy of integrating his theater into its local setting. And finally, it demonstrates the reciprocity of practical patriotism. Both the government and the film exhibitor gained from their cooperation.

On March 31, 1917, Donald M. Ryerson made a speech, most likely on the importance of military preparedness, during intermission at the Strand Theater in Chicago (11, p. 18). Ryerson with Medill McCormick was a founder of a group calling itself the Four Minute Men, a title alluding to the Minute Men of the Revolutionary War and referring directly to the amount of time it took to make reel changes in the movie theater. The function of the Four Minute Men, as conceived by Ryerson and McCormick was to provide an organization of public speakers, who, using movie theaters as their forum, would inform the attending public of the need for military preparedness.

Under the auspices of George Creel's Committee on Public Information, the structure of the Four Minute Men was a military one. A national director in Washington, D.C. supervised associate directors who were assigned various sections of the country. Under these associate directors were state chairmen supervising local chairmen and finally the Four Minute Men themselves. The director in Washington assigned speaking topics. With the assignment of each topic came a "Bulletin of Instructions" for preparing the speech and a "Budget of Material" containing facts deemed necessary to that preparation. Sample outlines of major points to be stressed and sample speeches were also provided. An array of topics was covered in the various speaking campaigns of the Four Minute Men. For instance, from the beginning of the war until January 1918, movie audiences across the country could have heard speeches on:

The Liberty Loan, May 23–June 15
The Red Cross Hundred Million Dollar Campaign, June 18–June 25
Food Conservation, July 1–July 14
Why We Are Fighting, July 23–Aug. 5
A Nation in Arms, Aug. 6–Aug. 26
What Our Enemy Really Is, Aug. 26–Sept. 23
Onward to Victory, Sept. 24–Oct. 7
The Second Liberty Loan, Oct. 8–Oct. 28
The Food Pledge Campaign, Oct. 29–Nov. 4
Maintaining Morals and Morale, Nov. 12–Nov. 25
Carrying the Message, Nov. 27–Dec. 23 (23, p. 255)

The goal of the Four Minute Men was to provide the government with a network of speakers carrying essentially the same message, at the same time to people throughout the country. This goal was literally realized on July 4, 1918 when 35,000 Four Minute Men joined President Wilson in, simultaneously, delivering his Fourth of July speech (42, p. 368). Speakers were encouraged to tailor the material they were provided to suit their individual personalities, but they were not to veer from the assigned topic and they were not to exclude any of the main points. Mock and Larson, historians of the Committee for Public Information, describe the Four Minute Men and their function.

> America's nation-wide hook-up . . . Instead of the voice of a single speaker carried through the ether to distant points there was a mighty chorus . . . united under CPI leadership for coordinated and synchronized expression of Wilsonian doctrine. (16, p. 113)

Who was this "mighty chorus" addressing? Fred A. Wirth, the state winner in Illinois for his composition on "The Part of the Four Minute Men in the War," identified them and himself with some passion, writing, "I am a stoker for the Great Melting Pot. In four minutes I breathe the flame of true American patriotism to people of all kinds and creeds (11, pp. 93-94). Bertram Nelson further characterized the movie audience.

> There are a surprisingly large number of people in every community who do not read; there are others who read no English; and a still larger number who read nothing but headlines . . . How can we reach them? Not through the press, for they do not read; not through patriotic rallies, for they do not come. Every night eight to ten million people of all classes, all degrees of intelligence, black and white, young and old, rich and poor, meet in the moving picture houses of this country, and among them are many of these silent ones who do not read or attend meetings, but who must be reached. (23, p. 252)

The assumption was that at the movies a speaker had access to the broad spectrum of the American public. The estimate of eight to ten million in daily attendance is echoed, more loudly by other contemporary sources such as *Exhibitors Trade Review* and the *New York Times* (43, p. 552, x, p. 6). The perception by those in a position to judge was that through movie theaters one speaker could be assured a large, representative audience for his message of food conservation, his pitch for war bonds, or his information on the reason for U.S. entry into the war. In a speech addressed to the "15,000 Four Minute Men of the United States" President Wilson acknowledged the "hearty cooperation of the managers of moving picture theaters" and he repeated the contemporary assessment of their attitude to the addition of Four Minute Men to their programs (23, p. 253). Curry, writing his history of the Four Minute Men in Illinois, notes

> The movement never could have been a success without the spontaneous cordial cooperation of the big figures of the motion picture industry. Messers Brady and Zukor in New York, and Messers Ascher and Schaefer in Chicago were quick to see the great patriotic service they might do the nation by giving the movement their personal support. (11, p. 90)

Curry also reports that the actual arrangements between the Four Minute Men and the theater managers in Illinois were worked out between representatives of the Four Minute Men and Joseph Hopp, chairman of the Executive Committee of the Motion Picture Exhibitors League of America. At a national level, the Four Minute Men obtained the sanction of the National Association of the Motion

Picture Industry (NAMPI), which named that speaking group alone the official representative of the government in the movie theaters of the United States. Curry points out that this guarantee of exclusive access may also have been in the film exhibitors' best interest as it insulated him from "scores of unreasonable demands which might be made upon them from a multiplicity of so-called 'patriotic' organizations or individuals of good, bad and indifferent character" (11, p. 90). The government officially recognized the contribution of theater owners and managers in the fall of 1918, by issuing a certificate, "in recognition of the patriotic service of granting to the Four Minute Men the exclusive privilege of speaking to the audience" (10, p. 27).

There was an appreciation on the part of the government that care must be taken not to take advantage of the good will of its theatrical host. Reminders occurred with some consistency even as late as December 24, 1918 that Four Minute Men must not speak longer than four minutes (26, p. 633). The final bulletin stated, "Let us not yield to the sentiment that this is our last appearance . . . and permit ourselves to exceed our distinguishing time limit" (26, p. 633). There is also some evidence that care was taken in the selection, assignment and training of speakers. For instance, in Cincinnati, a board composed of a teacher of speech, a movie theater manager and a Four Minute Man screened all aspiring Four Minute Men to "see that they are up to a minimum standard of effectiveness, classifying them according to their relative abilities so that the very best men may be sent to the more important theaters" (42, p. 396). Chicago had a school for Four Minute Men established by Bertram Nelson of the University of Chicago. Four Minute Men were not the only people allowed to address the more or less captive movie audience. An advertisement in the July 21, 1918 issue of the *Milwaukee Journal* advised readers that they could come to the Alhambra Theater to see William S. Hart as "Shark Monroe, the savage master of a sealing schooner . . . and also hear Lieut. John Hewitt who had just spent thirty-one months at the Front" (2, II, p. 6). Four Minute Men and other speakers on war-related topics became components of and not intrusions into the exhibitor's program. The theater manager benefited from the ready-made and representative audience.

Once the houselights dimmed and the moviegoers' attention was directed to the screen, the theater manager had a final opportunity to promote his theater by striking the patriotic chord. An advertisement in *Motion Picture News* for the American Bioscope Company read, "Attention Patriots Do Your Bit. Open or close every show with the Stars and Stripes. 60 feet or longer at only 10 cents a foot" (3, II, p. 8). Slides were another option. The Excelsior Illustrating Company of New York offered, "A few of the other beautifully handcolored patriotic slides, 25 cents" (4, p. 269). Or exhibitors could make their own slides, "Joseph Yeager, who had just added a third theater to his string in Raton, New Mexico is using slides of local boys who have enlisted. They are making a hit now and he has a full set for later use should they be killed or perform some unusual service" (34, p. 1235). Exhibitors also made use of newsreels showing hometown boys at bootcamp. On October 28, 1917, the Butterfly Theater in Milwaukee offered "Local Boys at Camp McArthur" programmed with *The Pricemark* (5, p. 2876). Later in the war "smiles" films provided another way for exhibitors to connect their theaters both to the community and to the war in Europe. People were invited to be photographed and the resulting film was to be sent to Europe and shown to the soldiers. These films were first screened in the local movie house, however, providing the exhibitor another time-honored way to attract the trade.

Finally, in addition to these gimmicks, the exhibitor also had access to a variety of newsreels, cartoons, and short documentaries picturing the war and war-related activities with which he could surround his feature film.

Clearly, it was difficult for the theater goer in Seattle, Washington, or McCook, Nebraska to escape the war by going to the movies. Even if the featured film starred Fatty Arbuckle as *The Bellboy* or Theda Bara as *Cleopatra*, chances were that the screening would begin with a rendition of the "Star Spangled Banner," that slides would be shown advising patrons to substitute corn for wheat and fish for meat. Even cartoons like "O U U-Boat" would serve to remind those in attendance of the world outside the theater.

In so programming his entertainment and promoting his theater, the film exhibitor was not acting alone, nor was patriotism his sole impetus. In adapting his business practices to the exigencies of the times, the exhibitor was behaving like the businesses which surrounded his theater. During the World War I period, advertising urged consumers to not only buy house dresses and pots and pans, but it also urged consumers to buy War Savings Stamps. Gimbels in Milwaukee hosted a Liberty Bond rally which was addressed by Douglas Fairbanks. The Feagins Company in Los Angeles decorated its front window with models of missiles in a patriotic display, and the ranks of the Four Minute Men were filled with doctors, lawyers, and community businessmen. The film exhibitor was proving himself a fit member of any chamber of commerce; nor was the exhibitor conducting his business in a totally new way on account of the war. The specific exhibition practices he employed—collecting money for war drives, programing patriotic music, decorating his theater with flags—all fall within the scope of accepted principles for successful theater management, and as I will now suggest, these tactics were also in keeping with the film exhibitor's long-range business strategy, to make his theater a permanent and influential institution within his community.

"UNDERSTAND THOROUGHLY WHAT YOU ARE SELLING": THEATER MANAGEMENT

In his 1915 handbook for film exhibitors, *Picture Theater Advertising*, Epes Winthrop Sargent stressed the importance of advertising, and he characterized the advertising problem faced by the theater manager.

> To gain a regular sales the article must be good. The motion picture theater is no different in this respect from a patent breakfast food or a folding bed, the article must sustain that advertising or the advertising will have been done in vain.
>
> In the case of the motion picture theater the advertising implies a contract not only to show certain specified subjects, but to show these to the best possible advantage. There is an understood promise that the pictures shall be seen under the most advantegous conditions of comfort, cleanliness and service. (35, p. 2)

Theater managers were selling two ''articles'' simultaneously—feature film programs and the amenities of their theaters. In 1927 Sargent collaborated with John F. Barry, director of the Publix Theater Managers Training School, in writing the more comprehensive *Building Theater Patronage: Management and Merchandising*. This handbook included the topics, such as ''The Lobby as Advertisement,'' ''Music as an Advertisement,'' ''Doing Presswork,'' ''Copy,'' ''Form Letters,'' covered in the preceding book, and it reasserted the dual nature of the product theater managers had to sell. In the chapter on selecting advertising copy, Barry and Sargent stressed, ''Understand thoroughly what you are selling—your theater and the program'' (36, p. 292).

Although these handbooks are separated by twelve years, and although the place of exhibition within the structure of the film industry was changing during that span from independent or horizontally integrated, local theater chains to chains of theaters vertically integrated with film production, the advice being offered to the theater manager and the assumptions being made about the nature of his enterprise are remarkably consistent. In 1915 Sargent baptized the film exhibitor as a businessman.

> Throughout the book 'Exhibitor' is used in preference to 'manager' because Exhibitor has come to mean one who exhibits or presents motion picture programs. In the early days of the 'Biograph Theater,' it was a term of reproach, for then the exhibitor was any sort of itinerant showman presenting in a tent or vacant store some attraction to catch the nickels and dimes of the unwary . . . Today the term remains, but through the efforts of real businessmen, the reproach has been removed and it has come to have a definite meaning as applying to this one particular form of amusement enterprise . . . It is distinctive and exact and in no way a thing to be ashamed of. (36, p. vi)

By 1927 Barry and Sargent, who in the interim had continued to edit the ''Advertising for Exhibitors'' column for *Moving Picture World*, confirmed the exhibitor as businessman.

> There was a time when they spoke of it as the motion picture *game*! The word implied the elements of luck, chance, gamble, haphazard, hit or miss operation. Today theater operation is not a game, but a business that is coolly [sic] and calculatingly well planned . . . The manager is a businessman with both eyes on profits. (36, p. 40)

It is necessary to understand how the exhibitor defined his business and what the exhibitor perceived to be his long-range business goals in order to accurately rationalize and contextualize the various methods of theater promotion and programming discussed earlier in this chapter. These questions can best be answered by information gathered from Sargent and Barry, as well as from exhibitor trade papers. As primary documents, these handbooks and trade papers are important in two ways. First, they do record specific exhibition practices and points of view and so serve the researcher as a compilation of the social, political, and film industrial events of concern to film exhibitors. Second, the livelihood of these authors and publications depended on the longevity of the film industry and particularly on the success of the film exhibition. Thus at the same time as they offered advertising strategies, management tips and in the case of trade journals, news items, film reviews and advertisements for upcoming releases, they were also in business to inculcate a sense of professionalism and pride in the trade, encouraging the long-term goal of industry stability.

My reliance upon the ideas and strategies in Barry and Sargent's text is also an implicit argument for understanding film exhibition in 1917–1918 to be a mature business enterprise. In other words, I assume that the business practices and goals espoused by Barry and Sargent in 1927 hold true for exhibitors ten years earlier. This historiographical decision is based on several historical factors. First, by 1917 film exhibition was already a business augmented by trade journals as well as local and national trade associations. Second, there is a thematic and topical consistency from the 1915 text by Sargent, through the intervening columns of *Moving Picture World* to *Building Theater Patronage*. From *Picture Theater Advertising* to *Building Theater Patronage*, ideas are not changed, they are refined. Notions implicit in Sargent's earlier book are made explicit in the 1927 joint venture. *Picture Theater Advertising* delivers specific promotional strategies; *Building Theater Patronage* resubmits those strategies as functions of a method for successful theater management.

What kind of business was the film exhibitor in? Barry and Sargent offer a brief history which summarizes the work of the exhibitor.

> At a time when the motion picture theater was a seemingly temporary enterprise, when equipment, service, lighting and other details were not worthy of consideration or return, it was natural that the program alone was relied on for patronage. Even today when the program is exceptional, the program primarily will be responsible for business. But exceptional programs are relatively rare. Regular attendance must be built with other things which go to make a theater an institution. They include every detail of operation—admission price, location, accessibility, seating comforts, projection, music, personnel, ventilation, patron conveniences, starting hours program management no matter what the program is, distinctive novelties of every kind. The theater as an institution is the prominent factor that makes regular patrons. (36, p. 24)

In other words, the feature film becomes, except in the case of the rare exceptional program, the equal to location, ventilation, and music as a selling point to lure the consumer into the theater.

The notion that it is important to establish the theater as an institution within the community pervades the trade press writing of 1917–1918, as well as providing the major themes of both *Picture Theater Advertising* and *Building Theater Patronage*. Specifically, as Barry and Sargent point out, institutionality is a function of every detail of theater operation. Generally, the concept of the theater as an institution results from an implicit distinction between the theater as a business enterprise and its nominal product, the feature film. This is a distinction which rests on an opposition between the relative permanence of the theater building and the transience of the film product which plays a two- or three-day run and then is gone. As a business person, the theater manager's concern was for the economic health of his theater. Popular films helped to insure that health, but only just helped.

At another level such a distinction between the theater and the film may also manifest a structural tension within the film industry between production and exhibition. Sargent sets the stakes of this competition in a December 29, 1917 column in *Moving Picture World*. The prize is the loyalty of the moviegoer.

> Make people come to the theater because your house is the trademark of good shows. Don't ride on the popularity of a brand. Do just what the brand has done. Take your own personal trademark to the public and drive it home. Get all the benefit you can from the popular trademarks if you use brands, but make it plain that the reason that a show is good is because it is at the Star or the Lyceum . . . Paramount and Goldwyn and others in advertising to the patron seek to create a demand that will necessitate your use of the product. Follow the leader and create in the minds of the local public that your house is as necessary to the enjoyment of the films as are the films themselves. Then make is so. (33, p. 1939)

In other words, the local theater and the nationally distributed, trademark-bearing motion picture producer were both competing for the brand loyalty of the moviegoer. The goal of the theater manager was to build a regular clientele who came to his *theater* regardless of the show. (Recall the review commenting on the institutional nature of the Rivoli's programming.) The goal of the film producer was to build a regular clientele for his particular brand of film, regardless of theater. I characterize this tension as competition rather than conflict between these two arms of the industry because a necessary symbiosis also characterizes their relationship during this time. In 1917–1918 producing studios, such as Paramount, did spend large sums on national advertising campaigns promoting their product; but Paramount also spent much money sending "exploiteres" into the field to work with theater managers in the advertising and promotion of specific films at specific theaters (39, p. 56–57).

Establishing the theater as an institution serving an increasing and regular clientele was a result of more than just proper management. Conventional wisdom within the industry also pointed to the importance of actively integrating the theater and the theater manager into the daily affairs of the local community. In September of 1917, "Advertising for Exhibitors" published an "Exhibitor's Catechism;" this list of questions served as an examination of theater manager's conscience, pointing him to a variety of areas which needed to be considered if he wanted to attain fiscal salvation. Among those questions addressing management issues, such as cleanliness, admission price, and projection, are questions which assume the need for a certain relationship between the theater manager and his community.

> What have I done to make my theater one of the community's social centers?
> Am I a member of the local merchant's organization?
> Have I ever attempted to get local merchants to cooperate with me for mutual benefit? (31, p. 1846)

Implicit in these questions is the belief that the theater should be a civic forum, and that the theater manager should be a leading citizen as well as a showman. The point is made more explicitly in a short cautionary tale published in an April 1917 issue of *Motion Picture News*. Under the title, "Be A Town Figure," the story of an "old timer" and a "bright young fellow" is told.

> The older timer ran a picture show in the "opera house." He charged an unvarying price of admission. His program was liked as he was liked—because both could be depended upon.
> Along came a bright young fellow with new-fangled notions who built himself a dazzling theater, installed sensational pictures and charged ten cents against the old timer's fifteen. (19, p. 2472)

In the face of this business competition, or opposition as it was called, the old timer did not change his business practices and more importantly he did continue to be active in town affairs, unlike the bright young fellow who pinned his success solely to flashy exhibition practice.

> The old timer changed his attitude—not a hair's breath! . . . When Main Street was to be repaved, his voice carried its usual weight. When the question of a new wing for the high school came up, his opinion was taken as seriously as the town banker's. (19, p. 2472)

This fable culminates in a moral lesson for the exhibitor.

> At the end of the third year, the newcomer sprinted out of town on a trail of debts. Is the older timer still doing business? The last we heard of him he had been elected to the town board of trustees. (19, p. 2472)

Cooperation with other businesses and taking part in community activities were ways of building good will for the movie theater. The assumption was that the more good will which accrued to your house, the firmer the foundation on which that institution rested.

Barry and Sargent echo the importance of good will.

> One of the assets of any business institution is good will. Though intangible, it is very real. A habit of coming to a particular institution rather than elsewhere, because of satisfaction with past service or confidence in the product and the values

> offered is good will. But as far as a theater is concerned, good will does not depend upon the merchandise and the prices offered because programs alone are generally looked upon as the theater's product and programs are a changing factor . . . Good will for a theater is determined by every detail of operation . . . It is developed over a period of time . . . It sells tickets when special production and outstanding bargain programs are not offered. Good will is one of the strongest assets of the showman, because public confidence in his statements is necessary if his advertising is to get results. (36, p. 32)

Reviewing the war-related exhibition practices catalogued earlier in this chapter in the light of Barry and Sargent's admonition to "Understand thoroughly what you are selling—your theater and the program" contextualizes those practices in a way which shifts attention from their charming quirkiness to their strategic value. It also helps to temper any reading of them as pure expressions of naive patriotism emanating from the good old days. This is not to say that film exhibitors were not enthusiastic or patriotic. The rhetoric of the trade papers fairly glows red, white, and blue. It is to say that these people were engaged in a business, and while they recognized a national responsibility, they also recognized and exploited a business opportunity. Adolph Zukor was interviewed early in 1918 by *Moving Picture World* for the weekly column, "The Motion Picture and the War." Under the heading, "Importance of the Exhibitor in the Present Crisis," Zukor makes this point.

> A golden opportunity lies before the motion picture theater exhibitor of today, which should be grasped at the psychological time . . . Our everyday life is being filled with little inconveniences due to the enormous help this country is giving the Allies, and the newspapers teem with war news. Now is the time for the exhibitor to make his house the court of happiness and gladness for his locality where patrons will gather to relax the tension of the times, which fact he should bring out in his advertisement in newspapers and in slides.
>
> The year 1918 should be a memorable one in the industry, for it will mark the culmination of important events that had their birth in 1917. Within a few months spring will arrive and with it the great offensives on the battlefronts of Europe. The tension of the war will be at its maximum, and the exhibitor has sufficient time by beginning now, to decide the part his house will play in his locality. And when the war is over and the country again filled with gladness, it will be a difficult matter to wean patrons from the theaters that established a clientele during the dark hour when entertainment was not merely a pleasure but a necessity. (17, p. 678)

So, theater managers allied themselves with the war effort in visible ways designed to attract trade and to build the base of their regular clientele. Flags were displayed, as were photographs of Wilson, exploitation stunts like costuming children as red crosses and sending them into the streets were tried, advertisements in newspapers offered free tickets to soldiers and bona fide families of soldiers. Newsreels of local boys in uniform or of local folk were screened to attract patrons. Advertisements for movies urged consumers to buy Liberty

Bonds and also to come to the theater. Film exhibitors identified themselves with other businessmen in collecting for war funds, promoting recruitment, and providing their theaters to serve as forums for civic events. In the short term these tactics helped the exhibitor to fill the seats in his theater; in the long term the hope was that they would function strategically, and help to institutionalize the theater within the community.

"DO YOUR BIT CHEERFULLY": WARTIME REGULATIONS

At the same time that World War I offered the exhibitor the opportunity to increase his trade and more firmly establish his theater, it also presented him with a specific set of challenges in the form of the war tax, the imposition of ten weeks of Fuelless Tuesdays, and other more localized restrictions on exhibition.

A three-pronged tax was levied on the motion picture industry beginning in October 1917. Both raw film and the positive print were taxed, and beginning November 1, 1917, a 10 percent tax on theater admissions over a nickel was instituted. The film producers, responsible for the tax on film footage, passed their costs on to the exhibitor in the form of a uniform fee of fifteen cents per reel per day. Within the exhibition branch of the industry this move provoked much anger. Film producers argued that all taxes should be paid by the ultimate consumer of their product, the moviegoer, and it was up to the exhibitor to collect those taxes. Film exhibitors argued that the increase in their cost of doing business caused by such a surcharge would drive them out of business. What is important for the argument being made here is that this often vitriolic exchange between producer and exhibitor took place in the trade press and in their business correspondence; it did not attract attention in the popular press. Instead, the public heard about the tax on theater tickets, a tax exhibitors were less loath to pass on to the consumer. Sargent devoted an installment of his column, "Advertising for Exhibitors," to sharing suggestions from exhibitors for advertising this tax and for countering patron displeasure.

> Everyone lately has been wrestling with the new tax on tickets. This tax was so generally commented on in the newspapers that the public was ready for it, but there is a difference between a tax in the newspaper and a tax in the box office. (31, p. 1775)

Sargent relates how exhibitors in Cleveland formed a committee to educate the public about the amount and method of payment for the tax, but of special concern was the need to reassure consumers that, "Uncle Sam gets it—we don't" (32, p. 1775). The manager of the Elmwood Theater in Buffalo, New York sent in a copy of his newspaper advertising which also explained the new tax and urged, "Do your bit cheerfully! Help win the war. The tax on admission to this theater helps to keep the firing line intact" (32, p. 1775). The tax on theater admission gave the exhibitor yet another advertising point. Buying a ticket to a theater, paying the ten percent tax was helping "To swell this great Liberty-for-the-World-Fund" (15, XIII, p. 8).

The film exhibitor was also able to turn the United States Fuel Administration's Monday closing order to his advantage. In January 1918, the Fuel Administration ruled that for the ten Mondays from January 21 through March 25, no fuel could be used to heat such places as theaters, business offices, or stores in territory east of the Mississippi. The film industry acted quickly and in concert. On January 20 the *New York Times* reported that Harry A. Garfield, head of the Fuel Administration, had amended the order.

> Theaters, moving picture houses and other places of amusement where alcoholic drinks are not sold are to be permitted to remain open on the ten Mondays beginning January 21, so that the vast army of workers in the territory east of the Mississippi who must remain idle . . . may have some place to go. The theaters and amusement places, however must remain closed on ten Tuesdays instead. (25, X, p. 4)

The article reported that Garfield reached this decision after being contacted by President Wilson who "expressed sympathy with the plea of the theatrical managers. The President received a delegation of the managers at the White House on Thursday" (25, X, p. 4). On February 8, 1918, *Variety* reported "Picture Business Satisfied with Garfield's Holidays." The article noted that neither producers, distributors, nor exhibitors were adversely affected by the closing order.

> Despite pessimistic predictions, the heatless and workless Mondays have not caused the picture industry any material losses . . . One exchangeman said to a *Variety* representative "I doubt if any manufacturer suffered a material loss under the unusual conditions. Exhibitors themselves have been doing such phenomenal business Mondays that few complaints have come from that quarter. Exhibitors have virtually been having a series of three holidays with Saturday, Sunday and the new Monday holiday bunched. I place my loss at a minimum." (27, p. 46)

Moving Picture World reported "Blue Tuesday Means Good Mondays, Telegrams to Goldwyn Tell of Big Business Sunday, Monday and Wednesday" (22, p. 885). Even the *Chicago Tribune*'s move column, "Right Off the Reel," quoted a local exhibitor.

> When we were told that we had to close on Mondays my heart was like lead. That meant decided loss. But when the order was changed and Tuesday named as closing day, things looked bright . . . Monday being closing day for stores and offices gives us enough business to make up for dark Tuesday. (28, VIII, p. 3)

CONCLUSION

Entrance of the United States into World War I presented the film exhibitor with a set of challenges to his business. I have argued that he attempted to turn those challenges into opportunities. Moviegoers were encouraged, through advertising, to see the theater as a necessary, inexpensive, and entertaining relief from the worries and inconveniences of the war, and conversely they were encouraged to consider attendance at the theater as a way of participating in the war effort by paying their portion of the theater tax or contributing to war funds. Yet another advertising angle was exploited as the exhibitor promoted the educational value of newsreels and other programming for those interested in seeing the preparations for and actions of World War I. In general, film exhibitors were successful. *Moving Picture World* sent reporters to various parts of the United States in January 1918 to report on business conditions. While some exhibitors pointed to the war as a problem, most pointed to non-war-related factors like weather: excessive cold and snow in the middle west, drought in Texas and around San Francisco as the major obstacle to their business (44, pp. 793–798). In July 1918, the time of the annual convention of the motion picture industry, *Exhibitors Trade Review* published a summary of the events of the year. The editors noted:

> The most significant—and the sorriest—feature of the year, however is this: in itself, the motion picture industry is very largely the industry it was a year ago . . .
>
> The industry is the same in 1918 that it was in 1917. It is the world that is different . . .
>
> We are the same today that we were a year ago—as individual human beings, no; as Americans, no; as motion picture business men, unfortunately, yes. (46, p. 539)

Rhetorically graceful, this assessment is not precisely accurate. There were changes taking place in the exhibition branch of the film industry, and not all exhibitors would benefit from those changes.

This chapter has argued specifically for an understanding of film industry behavior during World War I as a manifestation of the principle of "practical patriotism." This term, derived from contemporary trade papers, referred to a blending of nationalistic impulses with business acumen (7, X, p. 10). Producers, distributors, and exhibitors were encouraged to merge their country's needs and wants with their own commercial needs and wants. I have shown how, in this case film exhibitors, were able to incorporate war-related tactics into their own long-term business strategies. Further, I have shown how these war-related activities were adaptations of existing promotion and exploitation procedures.

More generally, I am arguing for a certain approach to the historical study of the U.S. film industry during any time period. Bordwell, Staiger, and Thompson in *The Classical Hollywood Cinema* stress the important application of "adjacent histories"—theater history, economics, business history—to the work of film history (8). I support this broadening of the referential context, but urge first, a more comprehensive view of the film industry itself. This view would take account of the dynamic relationship among all three branches of the industry in any one period and would also take account of the continuity of production, distribution, and exhibition strategies and tactics over time.

The historian works within temporal boundaries. In film history, those boundaries have included the beginnings and endings of decades and the beginnings and endings of significant events, such as a war, a "golden age," a rise and fall. These boundaries serve usefully to limit and may help to focus the historian's task. However, working within such temporal boundaries also poses certain risks. There is a tendency to adopt a view of the industry and its products which is as circumscribed as the time period under study. The dangers are several. First, industry practice is seen in a vacuum, and the tendency is to attribute that practice to the times. In other words, insufficient account is taken of preexisting strategies and tactics, with the result that these are found to be novelties, invention instead of innovation. An inaccurate account of the industry results.

The dangers of inaccuracy which result when temporal boundaries cease to be permeable also exist in studies which look solely at the films produced in any period without accounting for their promotion and exhibition. The majority of films produced during World War I were not war-related, however, that lack of narrative topicality was probably countered by the topicality of the programming which surrounded them. Historians trying to argue for the influence of a film or a group of films in a society need to take a broad view in their analysis and consider advertising and promotion, and they also need to take into account other conditions of exhibition.

REFERENCES

1. Advertisement. *Milwaukee Journal*, July 14, 1918, II, p. 10.
2. Advertisement. *Milwaukee Journal*, July 21, 1918, II, p. 6.
3. Advertisement. *Milwaukee Journal*, October 28, 1917, II, p. 8.
4. Advertisement. *Motion Picture News*, April 28, 1917, p. 2692.
5. Advertisement. *Motion Picture News*, May 5, 1917, p. 2876.
6. "Baltimore Makes Anthem Obligatory." *Moving Picture World*, 12 January 12, 1918, p. 272.
7. "The Bar Sinister." Advertisement. *New York Times* June 3, 1917, X. p. 6.
8. Bordwell, D., Staiger, J. and Thompson, K. *The Classical Hollywood Cinema: Film Style and Mode of Production to 1960*. New York: Columbia University Press, 1985.
9. "Buffalo Exhibitors Praised for Patriotism." *Moving Picture World*, November 10, 1917, p. 897.
10. Creel, G. *Complete Report of the Chairman of the Committee on Public Information, 1917, 1918, 1919*. Washington, DC: Government Printing Office, 1920; New York: DaCapo Press, rpt. 1972.
11. Curry, J. S. *Illinois Activities in the World War*, I. Chicago: Thomas B. Poole Co, 1921.
12. Edel, H. "How It Is Done at the Strand." *Moving Picture World*, December 22, 1917, p. 1767.
13. "Fairbanks Starts Red Cross Fund." *Moving Picture World*, July 7, 1917, p. 64.
14. "Live Wire Exhibitors." *Motion Picture News*, May 5, 1917, p. 2823.
15. *Minneapolis Tribune*, October 28, 1917, XIII, p. 8.
16. Mock, J. R. and Larson, C. *Words That Won the War: The Story of the Committee on Public Information*. Princeton: Princeton University Press, 1939.
17. "The Motion Picture and the War." *Moving Picture World*, February 2, 1918, p. 678.
18. *Motion Picture News*, April 14, 1917, p. 2327.
19. *Motion Picture News*, April 21, 1917, p. 2472.
20. *Moving Picture World*, April 28, 1917, p. 630.

21. *Moving Picture World*, February 9, 1918, p. 1350.
22. *Moving Picture World*, February 9, 1918, p. 885.
23. Flowers, M., ed, *What Every American should know about The War*. New York: George H. Doren Co, 1918.
24. *New York Times*, December 23, 1917, X, p. 5.
25. *New York Times*, January 20, 1918, X, p. 4.
26. Oukrop, C. "The Four Minute Men Became a National Network during World War I." *Journalism Quarterly*, Winter 1975, p. 633.
27. "Picture Business Satisfied with Garfield Holidays." *Variety*, February 8, 1918, p. 46.
28. "Right Off the Reel." *Chicago Tribune*, January 27, 1918, VII, p. 3.
29. "Rivoli Opens to the Public Dec. 27." *Moving Picture World*, January 5, 1918, p. 55.
30. Sargent, E. W. "Advertising for Exhibitors." *Moving Picture World*, August 4, 1917, p. 789.
31. Sargent, E. W. "Advertising for Exhibitors." *Moving Picture World*, September 22, 1917, p. 1846.
32. Sargent, E. W. "Advertising for Exhibitors." *Moving Picture World*, December 22, 1917, p. 1775.
33. Sargent, E. W. "Advertising for Exhibitors." *Moving Picture World*, December 29, 1917, p. 1939.
34. Sargent, E. W. "Advertising for Exhibitors." *Moving Picture World*, March 2, 1918, pp. 1235–1236.
35. Sargent, E. W. *Picture Theater Advertising*. New York: Chalmers Publishing Company, 1915.
36. Sargent, E. W. and Barry, J. F. *Building Theater Patronage: Management and Merchandising*. New York: Chalmers Publishing Company, 1927.
37. "Seattle Film Men Aid Red Cross Drive." *Moving Picture World*, July 14, 1918, p. 273.
38. "Stanley Sells Tickets Subject to Agreement to Respect Flag." *Moving Picture World*, May 5, 1917, p. 789.
39. *The Story of the Famous Players-Lasky Company*. Unpublished document in the Museum of Modern Art Archives 1919.
40. United States Food Administration, Letter, October 2, 1917, National Archives, Record Group 4 (12 Hc-A4, box 505).
41. *Variety*, July 12, 1918, p. 38.
42. Van Wye, B. C. "Speech Training for Patriotic Service." *Quarterly Journal of Speech*, October 4, 1918, p. 368.
43. "War Achievements of the Motion Picture Industry Set Forth in Brief to Federal Officials by National Association." *Exhibitors Trade Review*, July 20, 1918 p. 552; Advertisement. *New York Times*, April 28, 1918, X, p. 6.
44. "World Correspondents Describe Business Conditions." *Moving Picture World*, February 9, 1918, pp. 793–798.
45. "Written on the Screen." *New York Times*, May 6, 1917, X, p. 6.
46. "The Year in Review." *Exhibitors Trade Review*, July 20, 1918, p. 539.

8

Capital, Labor Power, and the Identity of Film*

Thomas Guback

Research and study involving any medium proceed from questions that investigators pose. These questions, in turn, reflect certain assumptions—implicit and often unstated—about the nature of reality and the particular identity of the process, relationship, or object under study. Such questions reveal what an investigator considers to be important and what is worth knowing, but they are shaped to a great extent by the social context in which research takes place. Implicit assumptions frame and structure the subject, and delineate the perspective from which an investigator examines it. Raising these assumptions to the level of consciousness not only permits a careful inspection of them but also clarifies the foundation of research. It provides, as well, an occasion to reflect about how study may be expanded, and what latent possibilities exist for fresh illumination of a field. Such inquiry, particularly as it addresses cinema, offers the luxury of looking at how we look at the field, and situating it in a context that heretofore may not have been explored at length.

Several lines of inquiry have come to dominate cinema studies. We have approached film as statement, through which we can know its maker or makers as individual creators and people of talent. Beyond that, we have confronted film as text, to be read and dissected for its own internal structure and meaning. In addition, we have considered film, at times, to be a form of amusement and diversion, by means of which we can infer something about the audience or the cultural and social atmosphere in which particular films were made. Historical studies in the field not infrequently use one or another of these approaches as the starting place for a chronological ordering of what has been happening.

These perspectives have a common ground: they revolve around the embedded content of film. Content is what the medium is all about, or so it would seem. These perspectives also share another point: Generally, they abstract film from the *institutional* environment surrounding production, marketing, and consumption. In this regard, I mean "production" in the large, systematic sense that applies to film as industrial output, irrespective of any film's personalized maker, rather than in the limited sense of the actual planning and shooting of a *particular* film.

While emphasis on content and content-related matters has illuminated important aspects of the medium, we also need to understand the medium in another frame of reference in order to grasp an entirely different identity. I am suggesting that the nature of film is clarified if we acknowledge the medium within its institutional setting. This shifts the terms of analysis from what we see to the social relations that are implicit in the industry and that govern the terms on which the industry operates. I believe, as well, that these social relations must be open to critique of the broadest kind, rather than being accepted as immutable givens that are subject only to occasional reform for the sake of maximizing profit.

I am proposing, then, to look at a set of relationships between the medium and the capitalist economic system (such as in North America and western Europe) and to examine how film is embedded in it. It should be clear that I am addressing film that has some commercial purpose or value, although I am not limiting the discussion to the typical Hollywood picture. "Commercial" is not meant to distinguish certain films from so-called "art" or "experimental" films, because these too can be made under capitalist conditions of production. This chapter is concerned with these conditions and relations of production, rather than with an arbitrary evaluative label assigned to a picture by a critic or someone engaged in criticism. This in no way denies that individuals' artistic contributions constitute a variable that separates one particular film from another or, alternatively, may lead to groups of particular films with shared elements of content or style. I am suggesting, though, that there is something more fundamental about the medium that shapes its character and that provides the arena in which individual inclinations are allowed to work themselves out.

This set of relationships hardly can be explored in depth in this chapter, but they do need to be identified and put on the agenda of study. The three that I am introducing do not constitute an exhaustive inventory by any means, yet they help to delineate some basic areas. Briefly, these concern:

1. The implicit identity and nature of film in a capitalist economy.
2. The allocation of capital for factors of production, and how this bears on the character of film as a business undertaking.
3. The place of film in an economy increasingly typified by the furnishing of services rather than the manufacturing of goods.

These may be restated in the following way as questions:

1. Within the context of our economic system, what is the objective character of film?

2. Is film production more properly considered a labor-intensive or capital-intensive enterprise?
3. Although film is often considered to be a service industry, does the concept "productive labor" suitably and accurately describe the activity of workers in the industry?

FILM AS COMMODITY

The motion picture industry is an institutionalized form built upon machines and technology. The medium represents the intersection of optics, mechanics, and chemistry, but the functions assigned to the medium and the industrial structure in which the medium has developed, flow from the logic of a particular economic system. It is clear that the medium could not exist apart from the technology. This distinguishes film production from many other kinds of production, such as the making of pottery, clothing, or jewelry, for example. Although hand production in those fields can be supplanted by machinery in order to increase the output of purchased labor power, this does not necessarily create a unique product. On the other hand, film is a qualitatively distinct product and form, but it too has permitted vast increases in productivity, as far as labor power is concerned.

The innovation of motion pictures (as well as recorded music and broadcasting) significantly changed the method of presenting and distributing information, understood in the broadest sense of the term. The cost of providing a given hour of amusement to each member of the audience is extremely modest because of the way the economic system has shaped the terms of production and consumption. To use the example of cinema: with 1,000 prints of a film in circulation, each exhibited three times daily, a given photoplay has 90,000 monthly shows, and all are derived from only a single "performance" recorded on film. This is a tremendous increase in worker productively, compared to live theatre.[1] The economic system, through appropriation and application of machinery and technology, has created conditions in which its workers are able to produce more—but more *what*?

The output of the motion picture industry is not just the motion picture. Its generalized *final* product is the valorization of capital, and in this context, the motion picture is but the *means* used to achieve that goal. Another product can be ideological cultivation, through which the property system and class structure, and their attendant values, are reinforced rather than demystified or critiqued. The ideological function might be relatively automatic, in that it flows from the particular nature of reality that is taken for granted throughout the system and

---

[1] There is an interesting discussion of productivity increases by Peter Bächlin (1, p. 158). He points out that although cinema cannot readily be adapted to the mass production system or to Taylorism, there are other ways in which given labor power can be made to increase output per unit of time. He notes as well that for producers the problem is to find a balance in film between a unique form and a standard form.

never debated. The valorization function, on the other hand, is a consciously identified goal that companies unabashedly strive to achieve.

Because the motion picture is used to valorize capital, the medium can be said to be instrumentalized, and, consequently, skills and artistic talent are channeled for particular purposes. The nature of film production is such that it offers extraordinary possibilities for valorization and accumulation of capital. This is the case not only because the medium's machinery is able to increase labor productivity, but also because employers pay for some labor power only *once*,[2] even though the product of labor power (a film) can continue to generate revenue with each exhibition. Returns, therefore, can be very high relative to investment, while amortization of costs can be quite rapid. From the perspective of the economic system and class that dominate the industry, the ultimate result of production is valorization, and this is achieved through creation of surplus value embodied in the commodity that is produced.

All too often, the product of the film industry in a capitalist economy is considered to be just films, and they are studied as if they were *only* objects of utility. But this removes film from its institutional setting. It also overlooks that, basically, film is a *commodity* with a dual nature. It is not only an object of utility that, through consumption, satisfies some human need. It also is a repository of value, which is materialized through the commercial exchange process. Film, as a commodity, is a good that is produced so it can be introduced into the flow of trade. Films are not made for their own sake, not for the exclusive use of, or direct consumption by, their makers. They are produced to be exchanged in the marketplace against consumers' revenue. Receipts constitute the measure of exchange value, although they do not necessarily measure use value. Indeed, the anticipated exchange value for a given film can determine the amount of capital to be invested and can influence how this capital will be used to purchase factors of production.

Compared to labor power, capital is highly mobile and largely indifferent to the special attributes of any sphere of economic activity (see 3, pp. 1012–1013). It has no particular affinity for, or loyalty to, the film industry, and can be diverted to other uses with comparative freedom. The wave of runaway production in the 1950s and 1960s showed how easily capital could be diverted from the United States to foreign sites of film making. But capital also can leave the film industry altogether, as is evident when production companies shift investment from motion pictures to nonmedia businesses, or exhibition chains move into real estate or soft drink bottling.

---

[2] Flat-rate salary payments are customary in the production side of the business, especially for administrative and technical workers. No matter how much money the film earns that they have worked on their salary level remains unchanged. On the artistic side, employment contracts customarily call for a basic salary plus percentage residual payments derived from the producer's receipts from other media such as pay television, home video, etc. Labor unions representing artistic workers have struggled over the years to have residual payments included in contracts. Compensation for individual major stars sometimes includes a percentage of the producer's receipts from all media.

Where capital is invested is conditioned to a great degree by the general ease or difficulty of realizing the exchange value of the commodity produced. Because wage labor is essential for capital formation, it is important that the individual or collective capitalist be able to supervise and discipline the individual or collective laborer (3, p. 986). This control assures that the produced commodity meets general specifications for use and exchange values—that is, that the commodity measures up to the requirements of capital.[3] In this regard, while it is true in a technical sense that workers use the means of production, it is nonetheless the case that capital uses workers to produce commodities.

As intellectual property, films are rather unique commodities within the generalized capitalist mode of production. In a system characterized by private *property*, it is not surprising to find that films, even when they are considered as artistic statements, have been subsumed by this system and brought within its sway as exclusive property, although not necessarily property of those who create it. These conditions are codified by copyright law that makes each production a legal monopoly whose use is entirely controlled by the copyright owner. Each economic transaction is for the benefit of that owner.[4]

To answer the original question: In a capitalist economy, the objective character of film is its existence as a commodity. That it is made by wage labor, and that its purpose is exchange value, unite it with virtually everything else in capitalism. In a systemic view, then, the primary function of film is valorization of capital. The varieties of content reflect the ways individual repositories of capital set out to attain that goal, and the conditions they impose on the allocation and use of resources. The producer of a film is not, in reality, the person whose name flashes on the screen. That person is the surrogate who carries out the generalized logic of the institutional order in which the film industry exists. The ultimate producer of the commodity is the set of property relations that are specific to a historical epoch.

LABOR-INTENSIVE PRODUCTION

It is common knowledge that production budgets for typical films produced in the United States in the late 1980s are around $20 million, to which must be added marketing and distribution costs. It is a truism that this enterprise requires considerable sums of capital to make a unique product, the demand for which is highly unstable and relatively unpredictable. But does this imply that film production is a capital intensive industry like other kinds of manufacturing?

---

[3] This is evident in conditions imposed by banks on production-distribution companies that borrow finance capital. To protect their loans, banks receive considerable latitude to monitor and change corporate behavior as it affects film making or the borrower's acquisition of independently produced pictures.

[4] The exception to this is the rental of video cassettes. The first sale doctrine in the copyright law prevents owners of films that have been distributed on cassettes from having a legal claim to a share of the revenue received by stores that rent cassettes to the public.

The problem is clarified when two elements are distinguished and separated. On the one hand, as we know, there is the general demand for substantial amounts of money *as capital* used to make a film. On the other, there is the use of this capital to purchase various factors of production, such as equipment, raw materials, and labor power.

Although film making, like many other business activities, can be very expensive, the important point is which factors of production, and in what relative quantities, are acquired with capital. There are variations from one picture to the next, of course, but the bulk of capital is spent typically to purchase direct labor power[5] of various kinds: artistic, technical, skilled, managerial, and administrative. Comparatively smaller amounts cover costs of capital equipment (such as studios) and other nonlabor expenses, among them rights, interest payments, materials, raw stock and processing, insurance, vehicles and transportation, costume rental, and so on.

Although it is frequently claimed that the studio system mass produced certain kinds of films, and that a few companies in the past concentrated mainly on churning out endless variations of a basic type,[6] these analogies with the factory manufacturing system depend on a great deal of poetic license. It is true, of course, that sets and costumes can be reused, and that themes and story lines are subject to frequent repetition. It also is clear that shooting can be organized so that efficient and rational use is made of resources. However, while all these examples can result in greater productivity of labor, they are not synonymous with mass production. Customarily, mass production involves machine-made replicas with interchangeable parts and limited intervention by human operatives during the production process. As well, it frequently requires large investment in equipment.

A capital intensive industry typically relies on much capital equipment, compared to labor power. This is the case for the manufacture of raw stock or the processing and printing of films. Occasionally, one finds that a particular aspect of cinema, such as colored images, slips from one category to the other. Hand coloring of motion picture frames was labor intensive, but it was superceded by color stock that was comparatively capital intensive. In this respect, capital was shifted away from the purchase of labor power, which was engaged to paint frames, to the purchase of an industrially produced substitute that did the work chemically.

---

[5] I am making a distinction between direct and indirect labor power. The former is purchased and applied immediately, as when musicians are engaged to play for the music track of a film, or a film crew shoots background footage on location. Indirect labor power is stored or accumulated for use at a subsequent time, as when a producer buys or rents canned music, stock library footage, costumes, etc. In the first instance, there is a direct purchase of labor power, whereas in the second, there is the purchase of a completed product in which activity has been stored. The labor power accumulated in it was paid for previously by the original employer who hired the workers. It is clear that some production expenditures, such as for the rental of costumes, etc., really are payments for labor power once or twice removed.

[6] Monogram's westerns come to mind immediately.

Film making is not amenable to the same kind of manufacturing techniques that characterize production of, say, toasters or automobiles. (The duplicating of prints and the manufacturing of raw stock, of course, are quite amenable to mass production techniques.) Compared to them, film is almost a handcrafted commodity. As an activity that tends toward being labor intensive, film production involves considerable use of labor power relative to the amount of capital equipment, per unit of output. Underscoring that film production is labor intensive recalls to our attention the crucial role of labor power for creating value, and thus for valorizing capital.

PRODUCTIVITY OF LABOR

Labor intensiveness is a characteristic film production shares with what are called service industries. Particularly during the last half century, the service sector has grown enormously, just as decades earlier, manufacturing overtook agriculture as the primary employer.

Several features distinguish the service sector, which includes transportation, hotels, telecommunications, advertising, data processing and a variety of professional fields such as counseling, law, brokerage, accounting, medicine, and teaching. One distinction is that a tangible good is not necessarily produced or manufactured; consequently, an economic transaction does not need to involve a product physically changing hands. Moreover, there often is a personal relationship between the provider of the service and its purchaser. In many cases, the furnisher of the service cannot readily be replaced by a machine (although technology has become important to many services).

The United States Department of Commerce classifies the motion picture business as a service industry, and every five years its Bureau of the Census releases a special report on film in the *Selected Service Industries* series. It could be argued that the film business deserves to be part of the service sector because the typical transaction in the film business does not involve the sale of a product, least of all to the public. The basis of the industry consists of the sale of rights that allow the purchaser to use the film only under specific conditions, and ordinarily for a given time period. As tangible private property, the film continues to be owned by the seller of those rights, who normally has exclusivity. In the retail end of the industry, the theatre patron's ticket buys the right to view the film, and usually only one time. The purchase of a video recording of the same film gives the buyer ownership of the cassette, not the motion picture or its copyright, and the transaction carries an implicit agreement about how that recording can be used.

Even though rights are at the center of the film business, we must not overlook another aspect. The production side of the industry still is very much a manufacturer. It is clear that labor power, raw materials, and equipment are organized by the capitalist to yield a tangible output, the initial print of which can be duplicated infinitely. Not only can this product be sold outright, it *was* in the early days of the industry. The making of raw stock, equipment, and obviously the film itself, are properly considered manufacturing, so only the other parts of the industry—distribution and exhibition—are in the service sector.

The distinction between the manufacturing and service sectors involves another problem having to do with whether labor is productive or nonproductive. Sometimes it is argued that in the service sector, labor yields no tangible product, and therefore labor is nonproductive, whereas in the manufacturing sector, labor results in a tangible product, and therefore it is productive. Translating that to the entertainment business, the argument would be that the actor on a theatre stage, as well as the play's director and electricians, all are laboring in the service sector since no tangible product is produced—whereas on the film set, these same people participate in the manufacture of a motion picture. On the stage, they are nonproductive, but on the film set, they are productive.

This line of argument obscures the economic context in which paid labor takes place and separates kinds of labor that ultimately have the same function. Given the set of property relations that are the bases for the capitalist economic system, it is more appropriate to define and analyze labor power in relation to that system, rather than in relation to the physical nature of the output. In this way, whether in service or manufacturing, labor needs to be recognized in the role it plays for capital—that is, in its *relationship* to capital. Productive labor is any labor power that is exchanged with capital; it is productive in the sense that it functions to valorize capital (3, pp. 1038–1049). Neither the content of labor nor the physical nature of the output should be decisive. The actor engaged by capital to perform, whether on the stage or on the film set, is still expanding the value of capital through labor power, even though one performance may yield no tangible product while the other does. Similarly, workers in distribution and exhibition are productive laborers in the sense that their activity also contributes, although sometimes indirectly, to valorization of capital.[7] Indeed, workers in these sectors are structurally indispensable to the functioning of the film business.

---

[7] There is considerable debate about workers in the commercial sector (for example, cashiers, salespeople, office clerks, etc.), their relation to merchant and industrial capital, and their roles in the valorization of capital. Because of the highly integrated nature of the economic system, and certainly the film business in it, I prefer to take a broad view that combines many diverse occupations into a collective laborer. While it can be argued that the labor powers of commercial workers do not produce surplus value, in the same sense that it is created by workers hired by industrial capital, it is true nonetheless that all these workers *together* function to increase their employers' capital, be it applied in commerce or manufacturing.

Furthermore, to make distinctions among a variety of tasks carried out by the same worker seems arbitrary, if not irrelevant. Productive labor is performed by an actor or actress on a film set; productive labor also may include making a public appearance for publicity's sake.

The debate about productive labor has been explored by Ian Gough (2) and by Peter Meiksins (4). Each provides abundant footnotes and references to other germane work, including that of Ernest Mandel.

Just as various kinds of occupational specialties in film production are combined to form a collective laborer in that phase, collective laborers exist in each of the other levels of the business, too. Beyond that, workers in all phases of the motion picture industry constitute a more generalized collective laborer.[8] The worker in exhibition, for example, is contributing to valorizing the capital of the exhibitor, as well as that of the film producer.

Ultimately, the distinction between manufacturing and service is quite irrelevant for analytical purposes. It does not recognize the property relationship inherent in the economic system, and thus glosses over the core of capitalism and how capital is multiplied and reproduced. In terms of the film business, labor power should be regarded as productive whenever it is exchanged with capital, regardless of the nature of the product or its degree of usefulness.

CONCLUSION

This chapter is a prospectus for a different approach to the film medium and the film industry, as they exist under capitalism. All too often, it is only film content that is subject to analysis. I have suggested that, given the economic context in which the film industry operates, there is another starting point and another dimension of reality about film that is more fundamental.

The objective character of film is its status as a commodity. In this respect, films, as output of the industry, are means to expand capital, and this derives from their exchange value as commodities. Although to make a given film may require large sums of capital, the production sector is basically labor intensive. We are reminded, perhaps more clearly than in other industrial activities, of the role labor power plays in capital multiplication.

REFERENCES

1. Bächlin, P. *Histoire Economique du Cinéma*. Paris: La Nouvelle Edition, 1947.
2. Gough, I. "Marx's Theory of Productive and Unproductive Labor." *New Left Review* 76, November–December 1972, pp. 47–72.
3. Marx, K. "Results of the Immediate Process of Production." Appendix to *Capital*, volume 1. New York: Vintage Books, 1977.
4. Meiksins, P. "Productive and Unproductive Labor and Marx's Theory of Class." *The Review of Radical Political Economics* 13 (3), Fall 1981, pp. 34–42.

[8] An analogy is the collective capitalist: the modern conglomerate or diversified company doing business not only throughout the nations, but worldwide as well. The major corporations in the film business typically also have interest in other mass media and in sectors far removed from communications. The collective capitalist label also applies to vertically integrated film companies, and especially to those engaged in production, distribution, and exhibition.

9

The Guise of the Propagandist: Governmental Classification of Foreign Political Films

Richard A. Parker

In its role as guardian of the national security, the federal government has assumed a variety of guises. Among the most controversial is the Justice Department's role as classifier of foreign films. Pursuant to the provisions of the Foreign Agents Registration Act (FARA) (12), the Attorney General possesses and exercises the power to categorize films and other materials produced by a foreign government as "political propaganda." In *Block v. Meese* (3), the United States Court of Appeals for the District of Columbia Circuit upheld the constitutionality of this classification scheme, and the Supreme Court declined review. Instead, the nation's highest court overturned the decision of the United States District Court for the Eastern District of California in a companion case, *Meese v. Keene* (20). The Supreme Court ruled that FARA did not abridge the First Amendment right of exhibitors to show films classified as "political propaganda."

The *Block* and *Keene* decisions affect the film industry in a variety of ways. The catalyst is the judicially sanctioned requirement that foreign films perceived as influencing the American political decision-making process be classified as "political propaganda." First, the *Keene* ruling will stifle the sale and distribution of foreign political films to libraries, schools, political organizations, and other potential consumers in this country. This de facto system of censorship stigmatizes award-winning documentaries, financially handicaps foreign film producers, and deprives Americans of the salutary corrective influence of an international perspective on the vital issues of our day. Second, the system encourages other governments to initiate retaliatory measures against American producers of documentaries reflecting on their political problems—a "trade war" is fostered in the film industry. Third, the review program sanctioned in FARA sets a chilling precedent: The federal government has established a right to review and to classify films to attain political objectives. The potential for abuse in times of perceived crisis is frightening to contemplate. In short, these judicial decisions are likely to amplify a hesitance on the part of film producers both at home and abroad to produce documentary films critical of United States government policy and practices.

The fundamental issue of government classification of foreign films as "political propaganda" merits reargument, the Court's denial of certiorari in *Block* notwithstanding. A constitutional challenge to FARA is justifiable because the classification system must satisfy a basic requirement: That government intrusions upon basic rights employ the "least restrictive means" requisite to fulfillment of their purpose. Absent satisfaction of this requirement the FARA classification scheme constitutes abridgment of the right to free expression for producers, distributors, and exhibitors of foreign political films.

Why reargue court decisions? Two reasons come readily to mind. At a pragmatic level it is noteworthy to observe that, of the five Justices comprising the *Keene* majority, one has already resigned from the Court. A reargument here might preface reconsideration of these same issues in the federal appellate courts. The second reason for reargument is more substantial. The *Block* and *Keene* cases challenge the authority of the federal government to classify (and thereby stigmatize) political expression on national-security grounds. The implications of these rulings for the right of free expression are staggering to contemplate. If the government can assert a right to classify foreign films today, what obstacle precludes an impassioned Congress, rife with hysteria, from endowing a federal agent with the authority to similarly classify domestic films during some future "crisis"? If the government can safely classify films, why not radio and television broadcasts, books and speeches? The Supreme Court's decision in *Burstyn v. Wilson* (7, p. 502) that "expression by means of motion pictures is included within the free speech and free press guarantees of the First and Fourteenth Amendments" potentially cuts both ways. We cannot afford to blithely ignore the implications of intrusions upon the right of free expression simply because their evolution appears unlikely. As Justice Holmes intoned, "When a nation is at war many things that might be said in times of peace are such a hindrance to its effort that their utterance will not be endured so long as men fight, and that no court could regard them as protected by any constitutional right" (27, p. 52). Our experience with the "Red Scare" era confirms that a time of war may be more psychological than real and yet constitutes a genuine threat to civil liberties (31).

This chapter finds the judicial assertion of a need to classify foreign films as "political propaganda" unsatisfying. The FARA categorization fails the constitutional requirement that any constraint upon free expression must utilize the least restrictive means requisite in fulfillment of its function. An examination of the probable rationale for upholding the constitutionality of the classification system despite these objections invites the reader into the realm of national security ideology, where rights are trumped for reasons that are questionable at best and sinister at worst.

BACKGROUND

Congress enacted FARA in 1938 to require registration of all persons employed by foreign principals for the purpose of disseminating propaganda in the United States (1, p. 937; 32, p. 591). In 1942 Congress amended the Act in several significant ways. First, the purpose of the Act was specified: "to protect the national defense, internal security, and foreign relations of the United States by requiring public disclosure by persons engaging in propaganda activities . . . so that the Government and the people of the United States may be informed of the identity of such persons and may appraise their statements and actions in the light of their associations and activities." Second, the Act empowered the Attorney General to label foreign communications, including films, as "political propaganda." This term is comprehensively defined in the amended Act and includes all materials that may "influence a recipient . . . with reference to the political or public interests, policies or relations of a government of a foreign country or a foreign political party or with reference to the foreign policies of the United States." It also applies to any communication of foreign origin "which advocates, advises, instigates, or promotes any racial, social, political, or religious disorder, civil riot, or other conflict involving the use of force or violence" in the United States or in any other American republic. Third, the Act requires disseminators of "political propaganda" to label the material as such and to identify both the agent and the agent's principal (i.e., the country of origin) (12, 28). Fourth, the Act requires report of the pattern of dissemination of the materials. For example, with regard to films, a report on the names of exhibitors and the number of exhibitions is required of the agent. Any material produced by or for a foreign government is subject to review and classification under the provisions of the Act.

In 1982 the Department of Justice identified three Canadian films, two concerning acid rain and one examining the effects of nuclear war, as "political propaganda" according to FARA specifications. Two federal lawsuits were filed challenging the constitutionality of the designations. A. Mitchell Block, sole distributor of one of the films, joined with several potential exhibitors claiming both economic injury and abridgment of the First Amendment right to disseminate ideas (4). Barry Keene, a California State Senator and potential exhibitor, contended that the classification compelled him to choose between the risk of damage to his personal, political and professional reputation in the eyes of his constituents for showing films so designated, or denial of his First Amendment right to exhibit the films (16, p. 1120).

These objections were rebuffed in the highest federal appellate courts. This chapter cannot exhaustively review the reasons for decision; it therefore focuses upon a single constitutional ground for protecting films from classification as political propaganda.

THE "LEAST RESTRICTIVE MEANS" TEST

Among the standards for assessing the constitutionality of a statute or governmental regulation is the "least restrictive means" test. This test requires that, when governmental intrusion is otherwise justified, restraints upon freedom of expression "must be as narrowly drawn as possible to effectuate legitimate governmental goals and to minimize the adverse impact on First Amendment rights" (16, p. 1125, citing 9, 11, & 25). It specifies that the goal of a regulation cannot "be pursued by means that broadly stifle personal liberties when the end can be more narrowly achieved" (29, p. 488). The test, while applicable in a variety of situations (8, 21, 22, 23, 26, 27, 30, 35), is particularly appropriate when the regulation advances "a substantial Government interest unrelated to the suppression of free expression" (6, p. 354). Although the test is often used in conjunction with balancing of government interests against free-speech rights (13, p. 195), the conjunction is not a necessary one (35, p. 426, note 20). In fact, the regulation at issue in *Block* and *Keene* is especially amenable to resolution using the "least drastic means" test. In most First Amendment adjudications, judges do not articulate an alternative means because they are reluctant to issue advisory opinions (32, p. 1002; 17, p. 471). In both *Block* and *Keene* an alternative means was not only available to the courts—it was proposed by the Department of Justice, the very agent employing the restriction!

Recall that the offending phrase in both cases was the arguably perjorative label—"political propaganda"—applied to the films in question. Among the documents considered by both courts was a letter from Edward C. Schmults, Deputy Attorney General, to the Hon. Robert W. Kastenmeier, Chairman, Subcommittee on Courts, Civil Liberties, and the Administration of Justice, of the House Committee on the Judiciary. The letter reads in relevant part:

> We believe Congress should . . . consider replacing the broad definition of "political propaganda" . . . with a more concise definition, more narrowly focused on the United States political process. We would also support the use of a more neutral term like political "advocacy" or "information" to designate information that must be labeled. (20, p. 1879 [Blackmun, J., dissenting])

Pursuant to this letter, counsel representing both Block and Keene explicitly argued that an injunction against the use of the term, "political propaganda," would compel legislative reform of the offending regulation. In both cases the majority rebuffed this argument for reasons that merit careful attention. At this point, however, it is important to realize that the courts could have chosen one of two means to achieve the goal of informing the public regarding the origin and nature of the films: (1) they could have sanctified continued use of the term "political propaganda," or (2) they could have invalidated the use of that term on constitutional grounds, compelling legislative resort to an alternative designation, such as "political advocacy."

Application of the "least restrictive means" test suggests two reasons why the latter course of action is superior to the former. Both reasons presume that the language used in classifying the films may deter their use in political argument, an assumption explored below. The first reason for rejecting "political propaganda" in favor of "political advocacy" is that the former language is perjorative while the latter is neutral. The second reason is that the former language misrepresents some information, such as the films in question, whereas the designation, "political advocacy," accurately classifies the information. Both of these reasons were explicitly considered and rejected (wrongly, in the analysis adduced here) by the majority of the judges in the cases reviewed herein. These reasons merit detailed reconsideration.

More Neutral Language is Least Restrictive

It should be noted at the outset that the government has a legitimate interest in informing the public regarding the origin of foreign materials. This interest is considerable regardless of whether or not the government possess a "right" to communicate (37, Part III). The question is not whether the public should be so informed, but how.

It should likewise be recognized that both Block and Keene raise legitimate First Amendment concerns regarding the onerous implications of the appellation, "political propaganda." In *Block* the judges recognized that this categorization had the practical effect of foreclosing sale and distribution of the Oscar award-winning foreign documentary, *If You Love this Planet*, to schools, colleges, and libraries, whose "principal 'problem', obviously, is the political aversion of these public instrumentalities to being identified as distributors of a 'propaganda' film" (3, p. 1308). In *Keene* a majority of the Supreme Court accepted without challenge Keene's assertion that exhibition of the films "while they bore such characterization" would harm his reputation and impair his chances for reelection. Keene offered unchallenged support for his allegation: (1) a Gallup poll indicating that 49.1 percent of the public would be less inclined to vote for a candidate who arranged to exhibit foreign films so classified by the federal government; (2) the opinion of the researcher who designed the survey, who concluded that exhibition of films so designated would seriously impair a candidate's chances for reelection; and (3) the testimony of one of Keene's political advisors, who claimed that opponents would undoubtedly seize the opportunity to portray the Senator as a "disseminator of 'foreign political propaganda' " were he to show the films (20, pp. 1867–1868). Paradoxically, in the face of this uncontested evidence, both courts called the statutory classification "neutral". The *Keene* court went so far as to assert that no evidence suggested that the designation produced "any adverse impact upon the distribution" of the films (20, p. 1873) and that disseminators could remedy the problem simply by adding ''any further information they think germane to the public's viewing of the materials'' (20, p. 1871).

Evidence of inconsistencies such as those identified herein is crucial to comprehension of the real motives of the judges, an issue confronted at the conclusion of this chapter. For now it will suffice to simply recognize the incongruities. First, to claim that language which intimidates purchasers of designated materials and destroys the careers of exhibitors is ''neutral'' defies both logic and common sense. To accept an artificial distinction between ''statutorily neutral'' and ''pragmatically neutral'' language, as the courts would have us do (20, p. 1872), simply divorces the judiciary from reality. Judges who persist in defining ''black'' as ''white'' disserve both themselves and the legislatures whose definitions they uncritically endorse. Second, to argue that no evidence suggests adverse impact of distribution of the films, despite the uncontested testimony of both distributors and purchasers in *Block*, renders the entire process of justification senseless. If the *Keene* Court can cite *Block* to *support* its analysis (20, p. 1873, note 18), it cannot justify *ignoring* evidence from that case which contravenes its questionable design. Third, the Court offers not a shred of hope—much less evidence—that verbal explanations will nullify the potentially disastrous effects of the government's classification. Justice Stevens' majority opinion reveals the majority's implicit double standard for proof of the efficacy of solutions. To piously propose the ''remedy'' of refutation while admitting its inefficacy (20, pp. 1868–1869) evinces a callous disregard for Keene's First Amendment rights.

The language of the statute is unquestionably perjorative, not neutral. Those who would discount the testimony of the formidable authorities to this effect, who would forsake dictionary definitions and eschew historical analysis of the meaning of ''propaganda,'' cannot but trivialize the judicial process by ignoring the demonstrable effects of the language upon those to whom it is directed. Nor can they deny that the *statutory* definition itself contains perjorative language: ''political propaganda'' includes material ''which advocates, instigates, or promotes any racial, social, political, or religious disorder, civil riot, or other conflict involving the use of force or violence'' (12, § 611[j]).

In his majority opinion in *Keene*, Justice Stevens advanced two arguments for the neutrality of the term. He noted that the ''statutory definition of 'political propaganda' has been on the books for over four decades,'' and concluded that the Court ''should *presume* that the people who have a sufficient understanding of the law . . . know that the definition is a broad, neutral one rather than a perjorative one.'' In support of this claim Justice Stevens referred to a list of films reported by foreign agents and concluded that their titles ''support the conclusion that the Act's definition of 'propaganda' is a neutrally applied one which includes allies as well as adversaries of the United States'' (20, p. 1872; emphasis supplied). This list of registrants, however, is irrelevant to the meaning of the term. Justice Stevens has established that the scope of the regulation is broad, but a broad term may not be neutral. The advocate who contends that "everyone but me is stupid" classifies others broadly, but this hardly renders the term "stupid" neutral in its meaning.

Justice Stevens offered one final argument for the neutrality of the phrase. He cited three other statutes containing the word "propaganda" and asserted that the overall frequency of usage documents neutrality (20, p. 1873, note 19). None of the statutes, however, utilized the term "*political* propaganda" employed in the regulation under consideration. This is the term that deterred exhibitors from purchasing the films and that produced the negative reactions documented in Keene's Gallup poll. In his argument Justice Stevens also fallaciously equated neutrality of meaning with frequency of usage. The fallacy is evident if we substitute "mind poisoning" for "propaganda" in every federal statute and regulation. In this way we can readily establish frequency of usage, but the term "mind poisoning" is hardly rendered neutral thereby.

Because all of the Courts' arguments to this effect are either inconsistent or defective, the assertion that the term "political propaganda" is neutral cannot survive detailed analysis. On the other hand, a suitable alternative nominee—the term "political advocacy"—is deemed acceptable to *both* parties to the suit. (Other terms, such as "political information," might also suffice.) In *Block*, Circuit Court Judge Antonin Scalia articulated three objections to the substitution of "political advocacy" for "political propaganda" (3, p. 1312). No analysis of the issue of neutrality would be complete without consideration of these concerns.

First, Justice Scalia claimed that only the term "political propaganda" accurately describes the type of political materials that Congress intended to regulate. However, he asserted what he must demonstrate: that the term is referentially unique. If the Justice Department finds the term "political advocacy" satisfactorily substitutable, this uniqueness argument must be cogently demonstrated.

Second, Justice Scalia contended that "advocacy" connotes taking a position but not its deliberate, widespread dissemination; only "propaganda" comprehends the diffusion of information. This claim is simply false, not with regard to the meaning of "advocacy," but to the meaning of "propaganda." Justice Scalia cites no definition of "propaganda" that embraces "widespread dissemination," even the statutory one. An inextricable linking of "widespread dissemination" with "propaganda" implies that a propagandist who distributed only a few copies of his materials would be exempt from the statute, which is patently erroneous. The standard for determining statutory inclusion is content-oriented, and "political advocacy" conveys that orientation precisely.

Third, Justice Scalia argued that any new term "would soon produce in the public mind the same degree of skepticism that the word 'propaganda' now evokes" (3, p. 1312). This claim is speculative and inaccurate. Once again the good Justice asserted what he is expected to demonstrate: that events prophesied will transpire. Moreover, he implied that the term "propaganda" *acquired* its perjorative meaning *after* its incorporation into the statute, a notion belied by propaganda expert Leonard Doob. Doob testified to precisely the opposite conclusion: that the term had a perjorative connotation in 1938 when FARA was initially enacted (5, pp. 12–13). Justice Harry A. Blackmun's eloquent dissent in *Keene* fastidiously documented the intent of FARA—to expose the maliciousness of foreign governments (20, pp. 1874–1875, citing 15). Thus Justice Scalia would have to link contemporary public skepticism to materials labeled "political advocacy" in order for his argument to succeed.

The point of this extensive analysis is not to demonstrate that "political advocacy" is neutral—statutorily or otherwise. Neutrality in language is but an ideal to which statute makers should aspire. The least restrictive means test aptly embodies this assumption: The term that most closely approaches neutrality should be incorporated into the statute. The fact that both parties to the suit agreed upon an alternative term should have been accepted as prima facie evidence of its superiority. Instead, the courts embarked upon a convoluted rationalization of FARA's original language. The final section of this chapter will undertake an explanation of this *tour de farce*.

More Accurate Language is Least Restrictive

The purpose of FARA is to inform the people of this nation of the identities of disseminators of "political propaganda." Even the *Keene* majority admitted that "many people assume that propaganda is a form of slanted, misleading speech that does not merit serious attention and that proceeds from a concern for advancing the narrow interests of the speaker" (20, p. 1869). Justice Blackmun's dissenting opinion in the same case noted that the clear intent of the law was to stop the "spread of pernicious propaganda," citing the 1937 Report of the House Committee on the Judiciary (20, p. 2). Blackmun argued that the films in question were obviously not "pernicious" in Congress' original sense—that they were caught in a net that was obviously cast too wide (20, p. 1384 [dissenting opinion]). Of the two possible remedies: (1) to redefine "political propaganda" in the statute to somehow include only "pernicious" stuff, or (2) to employ an alternative, more accurate designation—only the latter is practicable. The term "political advocacy" is obviously more accurate, given the class of materials embraced in the restrictive provisions of the statute.

The justification for amending the terminology employed in the statute seems apparent. It is fair to classify only the "pernicious propaganda" negatively, or to classify all of the materials neutrally, but not to classify innocuous materials negatively. Any appeal to fairness buttresses this analysis.

Amazingly, Circuit Judge Scalia admitted in *Block* that the scope of the statute overreached the intent of its creators (3, pp. 1309–1310). But he concluded that the Court was "not at liberty to eliminate . . . a legislative overbreadth" (3, p. 1310). In a single sentence this jurist, who now serves on the United States Supreme Court, denied an essential function of the courts: to assess the constitutionality of a statute. That function has been upheld consistently with regard to the determination of legislative overbreadth in First Amendment cases (2, 10, 34).

Judicial use of the overbreadth doctrine has been called "manifestly strong medicine" to be employed "sparingly and only as a last resort" (2, p. 613). Fortunately, resort to the overbreadth doctrine is entirely unnecessary in the FARA classification cases. The "least restrictive means" doctrine can be invoked to achieve the same result, on the ground that the most accurate terminology avoids miscategorization of materials. The unrebutted evidence introduced in both *Block* and *Keene* establishes that the statutory classification of materials as "political propaganda" seriously restricts their distribution. As Justice Blackmun eloquently argued in dissent, the classification system "places the power of the Federal Government, with its authority, presumed neutrality, and assumed access to all the facts, behind an appellation *designed* to reduce the effectiveness of the speech in the eyes of the public" (20, p. 1878). To classify all of these materials as "political advocacy" remedies the First Amendment problems that arise when the distribution of innocuous materials is effectively curtailed. If government officials want to explicitly condemn some particularly "pernicious" propaganda, they are free to do so. They can even call it "political propaganda." The difference between the status quo and the alternative proposed here, however, is simple: The government cannot *officially* classify innocuous materials as "political propaganda." The denigrative designation of materials thus becomes a matter of personal opinion rather than of statutory fact, a remedy unobjectionable to either Block or Keene (33, pp. 610–611).

IMPLICATIONS OF THIS ANALYSIS

Several aspects of the analysis of the courts' procedure in *Block* and *Keene* are discomforting. First, the jurists who upheld the existing system of FARA classification uniformly disregarded the most appropriate doctrine—the "least restrictive means" test—in their adjudication of the issues in these cases. Judge Scalia's cavalier treatment of overbreadth in *Block*, and the majority's sub silentio dismissal of the "least restrictive means" standard, despite the trial court's explicit reliance upon that test (3), provide no clear clues to the motives of these jurists for their questionable analysis. Second, the majority opinions in *Block* and *Keene* are fraught with erroneous characterizations of fact and obvious inconsistencies. Some of these have been developed above; others have been exposed in the emerging body of literature devoted to these cases (24, 33, 36, pp. 617–623). Third, the courts went out of their way to trivialize a solution acceptable to both of the major parties to the suit. Fourth, the courts imposed an excessively stringent standard of evidence upon those challenging the FARA classification system, while asserting the efficacy of the pseudosolutions they endorsed.

The jurists for the majority apparently have a hidden agenda which outreaches the issue of the films in question in these cases. Thus, while it is strictly correct to assert that the "government does not claim that these films endanger national security, or that they present a 'clear and present danger' to society, or . . .

indeed that there is any compelling government interest in placing any burden on the showing of the films'' (33, pp. 616–617), the precision of focus in this assertion mistakes the issues before the courts with the preoccupations of the judges. This misunderstanding will be compounded if we are convinced that these jurists need only be instructed in the error of their ways in order to secure a rehearing on the issues and a more palatable result for First Amendment concerns. In actuality, the freedom of expression we hail in the abstract appears to be in deep trouble. The crude pseudojustifications constructed by the *Block* and *Keene* majorities obscure rather than amplify the immanent value that potentially could outweigh all our rights and liberties—the maintenance of national security.

The problem these majorities face is not that the films violate national security. On the contrary, it is that the films do *not* violate national security, that they have nothing to do with national security. Strictly speaking, the majorities confront a perplexing situation: They are expected to determine the constitutionality of a regulation so broad that it is regularly applied to materials that are irrelevant to the intent of its framers. To appeal to that intent would lead the majorities hopelessly astray from the issues of the cases at bar. Yet these majorities seem to believe that the regulation is a powerful weapon in the hands of government, an instrument that can mold public opinion so readily and dramatically that the mere threat of its invocation sends would-be critics of government scurrying behind the shield of the First Amendment. Stripped of that constitutional protection, even the most accomplished propagandist could not hope to inculcate the people of this nation with political or social heresy. In the minds of the majorities, the foreign political agitator is no match for the power of the classification system, for the connotations of the label ''political propaganda.'' To put the issue in popular parlance: If you can't fight City Hall, you haven't a snowball's chance in hell against the Department of Justice.

A public confession of the unconstitutionality of the FARA classification system would deprive the Attorney General of a very potent weapon against propaganda, a weapon that may be of little use today but one that could turn the tide against some future motivator of the masses. On the other hand, respect for judicial procedure demands that the courts focus upon the actual issues brought before them. Thus these adroit judges have cleverly constructed an elaborate network of pseudojustifications for maintaining the FARA classification system. While the intensive scrutiny of cloistered scholars is likely to unmask the endemic weaknesses of their arguments, these analyses create ripples rather than waves in the pond of juridical serenity.

But only a pathetic ignorance of the technique of the propagandist could inform such convoluted political strategy. In the long run, the FARA classification system—in fact, the entire array of statutes—is impotent against a real propaganda campaign. The agents of some future political ''Prince of Darkness'' will submit no films to the Attorney General for classification, nor will they cower in obsequiousness in the face of consequent criminal sanctions. The name of the game is subversion, and it functions in an atmosphere devoid of diplomatic niceties and rules of fair play. The hope of the future is not the strong arm of government, though governments are unlikely to recognize or admit their own functional irrelevance. The only real weapon against propaganda is the skeptical attitude of the people.

A populace naive to the techniques of the propagandist and unprepared to cope with psychological warfare is far more likely to fall prey to demagogues and zealots than an informed and wizened America. Hence the irony of this political concerto: In their efforts to preserve a formidable weapon against propaganda, the Congress, the Department of Justice, and the most distinguished jurists of our time have inadvertently disabled the best defense—the lessons of experience. We are preserved in a state of pristine ignorance, buoyed by false perceptions of political and social reality, unaware that we nurture via dereliction the gnawing cancer of complacency.

The only legitimate weapon against propaganda is inoculation. Research indicates that exposure to discrepant messages permits the receiver to reformulate ideas and beliefs in order to take these discrepancies into account (e.g., 18, 19). In short, we can learn to defend our belief-systems rather than subscribe to them in a state of knee-jerk mindlessness. There is a way to achieve this goal: Open the intellectual floodgates, let the political materials flow across our ideological borders, and leave evaluation to those who check the pulse of our system—our political and social critics. Give the people a healthy dose of this evil we call propaganda. If our democracy is so fragile, our marketplace of ideas so philosophically barren that we cannot risk the intrusion of new political schemes, then we are done for already and no program of ideological protectionism will save us.

Justice William Brennan summarized the point concisely when he said that "speech concerning public affairs is more than self-expression; it is the essence of self-government" (14, pp. 74–75). When the government applies its perjorative classification system to innocuous films dealing with acid rain and nuclear war, it becomes the political propagandist it shamelessly condemns. The time has come for our own government to shed the guise of the propagandist, to restore the free flow of foreign political information, and let the political chips fall where they may. Our democracy was conceived in awareness of the risk endemic to freedom of expression. Maintenance of that liberty holds no fear for those who truly believe in the resilience of this radical experiment in self-governance.

REFERENCES

1. *Attorney General of U.S. v. Irish People, Inc.*, 684 F.2d 928 (1982).
2. *Broadrick v. Oklahoma*, 413 U.S. 601 (1973).
3. *Block v. Meese*, 793 F.2d 1303 (D.C. Cir.) (No. 84-5318); cert. denied, 106 S.Ct. 3335 (1986).

4. *Block v. Smith*, 583 F.Supp. 1288 (D.D.C. 1984).
5. Brief for Appellants, *Block v. Meese*, 793 F.2d 1303 (1986).
6. *Brown v. Glines*, 444 U.S. 348 (1979).
7. *Burstyn v. Wilson*, 343 U.S. 495 (1952).
8. *Cole v. Richardson*, 405 U.S. 676 (1972).
9. *Consolidated Edison Co. v. Public Service Commission*, 447 U.S. 530 (1980).
10. *Dombrowski v. Pfister*, 380 U.S. 479 (1965).
11. First National Bank of Boston v. Bellotti, 435 U.S. 765 (1978).
12. Foreign Agents Registration Act, CH. 327, 52 Stat. 631 (1938), codified as amended at 22 U.S.C. § § 611–21 (1982).
13. "Freedom of Speech, National Security, and Democracy: The Constitutionality of National Security Decision Directive 84." *Western State University Law Review* 12, Fall, 1984, pp. 173–204.
14. *Garrison v. Louisiana*, 379 U.S. 64 (1964).
15. H.R. Rep. No. 1381, 75th Cong., 1st Sess. (1937).
16. *Keene v. Meese*, 619 F. Supp. 1111 (D.C. Cal. 1985).
17. "Less Drastic Means and the First Amendment." *Yale Law Journal* 78, January 1969, pp. 464–714.
18. McGuire, W. J. "Resistance to Persuasion Conferred by Active and Passive Prior Refutation of the Same and Alternative Counter-Arguments." *Journal of Abnormal and Social Psychology* 63 (2), 1961, pp. 326–1332.
19. McGuire, W. J. and Papageorgis, D. "The Relative Efficacy of Various Types of Prior Belief-Defense in Producing Immunity against Persuasion." *Journal of Abnormal and Social Psychology* 62 (2), 1961, pp. 327–337.
20. Meese v. Keene, U.S , 107 S.Ct. 1862 (1987).
21. *NAACP v. Alabama*, 377, U.S. 288 (1964).
22. *NAACP v. Button*, 317 U.S. 415 (1963).
23. *New York Times Co. v. United States*, 403 U.S. 713 (1971).
24. Parker, R. A. "Assessing Judicial Opinions: Ronald Dworkin's Critical Method." In J. W. Wenzel (Eds.), *Argument and Critical Practices: Proceedings of the 1987 SCA/AFA Summer Conference on Argumentation*. Annandale, VA: Speech Communications Association, 1987, pp. 325–333.
25. *Preferred Communications, Inc. v. City of Los Angeles*, 754 F.2d 1396 (9th Cir., 1985).
26. *Procunier v. Martinez*, 416 U.S. 396 (1974).
27. *Schenck v. United States*, 249 U.S. 47 (1919).
28. Senate Report No. 913, 77th Cong., 1st Sess. (1941).
29. *Shelton v. Tucker*, 364 U.S. 479 (1960).
30. *Southeastern Promotions, Ltd. v. Conrad*, 420 U.S. 546 (1975).
31. Steinberg, P. L. *The Great "Red Menace": United States Prosecution of American Communists, 1947–1952*. Westport, CT: Greenwood Press, 1984.
32. "The Constitutionality of Expanding Prepublication Review of Government Employees Speech." *California Law Review* 72, September 1984, pp. 961–1018.
33. "The 'Political Propaganda' Label under FARA: Abridgement of Free Speech or Legitimate Regulation?" *University of Miami Law Review* 41, January 1987, pp. 591–625.
34. *Thornhill v. Alabama*, 310 U.S. 88 (1940).
35. *United States v. Robel*, 289 U.S. 258 (1967).
36. Wilson, J. G. "Constraints of Power: The Constitutional Opinions of Judges Scalia, Bork, Posner, Easterbrook and Winter." *University of Miami Law Review* 40, Spring 1986, pp. 1171–1266.
37. Yudof, M. G. *When Government Speaks: Politics, Law and Government Expression in America*. Berkeley: University of California Press, 1983.

10

The Canadian Film Market as Part of the United States Domestic Market Between the Wars

Ian Jarvie

Since the mid-1920s American film distributors have reported their Canadian box-office returns on Hollywood films as part of the domestic gross (8, p. 311). As the United States' Trade Commissioner in Ottawa put it in 1937: "For most practical purposes the Canadian film market is more a contiguous export market than a foreign export market. Even a good proportion of the overseas films shown in this territory are booked through American exchanges."[1] The Trade Commissioner's second point goes to show how closely patterned Canada was on the United States, where the country was divided into territories, and foreign as well as domestic films were distributed by American companies. Although Canada was subdivided into six territories, "Canadian rights" amounted, for U.S. distribution purposes, to one extra domestic territory. While it is true that the economies of the two contiguous countries are closely linked, to the best of my knowledge no other United States industry treat (and treats) Canada as a straightforward extension of the domestic market.

Operationally, the incorporation of Canada into the United States market meant that Canadian distribution was handled by the domestic rather than the foreign departments of the American film companies. There would seem to be two advantages to this. Perhaps the more basic was a commercial judgment that the Canadian market sufficiently resembled the United States market in that distribution strategy could and therefore should be the same in both. Implicit in

[1] NA RG 151 Department of Commerce Records, 281 Canada, Peterson to Motion Picture Section, Bureau of Foreign and Domestic Commerce, 20 August 1937. For the footnotes within this chapter, NA = National Archives, Washington, D.C.; PAC = Public Archives of Canada, Ottawa; PRO = Public Record Office, Kew, London.

such a commercial judgment was a cultural judgment: As a film-consuming culture, Canada was similar enough to the United States to require no substantial modification to the way films were handled domestically. In 1944 the Ottawa Embassy described Canadian audience reactions as practically identical to those in the United States.[2] The other reason favoring merging the two markets was that the Canadian currency was closely tied to the United States dollar, and, except for a brief period, was freely convertible. In much of the rest of the world there were many slips on the path between the turnstiles and the company bank accounts in New York. Principal among these were controls on the conversion of the local currency into dollars, and the exchange rate at which it was permitted. Since these controls were lacking in Canada, United States and Canadian box-office returns could be computed together as dollars in hand.

Tables 1–4 and Figure 1 present official statistics that give some parameters of the market, although the dire warning of Greenwald (4, p. 241) must always be borne in mind: "In virtually all cases quantitative material on the industry up to 1919 and even as recently as 1927 has to be rejected in its entirety as being unreliable." Canadian theaters constituted between 4 and 6 percent of U.S. theaters. Theatre receipts (Table 2), discounted for the value of the Canadian dollar, hovered around five percent of the U.S. figure. Per capita expenditures on film going hold no surprises. Table 2, however, discloses an interesting situation: 35 percent of theatres in 1927 were in the English-speaking Province of Ontario. Moving west from Ontario, and adding the theatres in Manitoba, Saskatchewan, Alberta, and British Columbia, all English-speaking Provinces, we find they total 78 percent of the theatres. Add the theaters of the English maritime Provinces to the east and English-speaking Canada accounts for 88 percent of theatres. Toronto, headquarters for all the American distributors, with over 100 theatres, was in the process of emerging as a city where movies had a high profile and intense use, features which led to its position as one of the handful of North American cities used for try-outs, previews, and first releases.

What about Quebec? The majority of its population was French-speaking, and Franco-Quebec society was very different from Anglo-Canada. Was the commercial and cultural assimilation of this part of Canada to the United States domestic market wise? With 11.6 percent of the theatres, and a per capita expenditure on films that was only 50–60 percent of that in Ontario, economic arguments would tell against making special provisions. Some evidence suggests that the American distributors discounted Quebec as a poor market both literally and figuratively. Censorship there was widely acknowledged to be severe.[3] For

[2] Toronto Consulate to Ottawa Embassy, November 2, 1944. NA RG 59 841.4061 Motion Pictures/11–344.

[3] Quebec was constantly singled out in official correspondence because of its strict and idiosyncratic censorship, low prices, ban on children under 16, and church opposition to Sunday opening. When the British film *Reveille* was banned and its distributors protested, the President of the Bureau de Censures Des Vues Animées, Count R. de Roussy de Sales, replied: "*comme nous ne sommes pas censeurs á Londres, mai[sic] a Montréal, nous nous inspirons dans nos décisions de la*

Table 1. Theatres in Canada and the United States*

Year	Canada (1)	U.S.A. (2)	(1) as a % of (1) + (2)
1927	1,019	21,664	4.5%
1930	910	23,000	3.8%
1933	765	18,553	4.0%
1934	799	16,885	4.5%
1935	862	15,273	5.3%
1936	959	15,858	5.7%
1937	1,047	18,192	5.4%
1938	1,133	18,192	5.8%
1939	1,186	17,829	6.2%
1940	1,232	19,042	6.0%
1941	1,244	19,750	5.9%

*Sources: Canadian figures: *Motion Picture Theatres in Canada 1942,* Ottawa, Dominion Bureau of Statistics 1944, except for 1927, U.S. Consul-General, Ottawa, to State Department, September 13, 1927, NA RG 84 840.6 Film. U.S. figures: *Film Daily Yearbook.*

Table 2. Theatre Receipts* (In millions of dollars)

Year	Canada (1)	Ontario (2)	Quebec (3)	U.S.A. (4)	(1) as a % of (1) + (4)
	CAN$	CAN$	CAN$	US$	
1930	38.4	15.9	8.3	732	4.9%*
1936	29.6	12.8	6.2	626	4.5%
1937	32.5	14.5	6.7	676	4.6%
1938	33.6	15.2	6.8	663	4.8%
1939	34.01	15.2	7.0	659	4.9%
1940	37.8	17.3	7.4	735	4.9%
1941	41.3	19.1	8.2	809	4.0%*
1942	46.44	20.7	9.3	1,022	3.96%

*Sources: Columns (1), (2), and (3), *Motion Picture Theatres in Canada 1942,* Ottawa: Dominion Bureau of Statistics 1944; Column (4) United States Department of Commerce, *Survey of Current Business.*

Canadian/US exchange rate from R.L. Bidwell, *Currency Conversion Tables,* London 1970. Between 1936 and 1940, the Canadian and U.S. dollars were at, or close to, par.

---

seule mentalité de la province de Québec'' [as we are not censors in London, but in Montreal, our decisions take their inspiration solely from the mentality of the province of Quebec], PAC RG 7 Governor General's Office, G 21, Volume 654, File 38384, Microfilm T-2520, Sales to Premier Taschereau 9 October 1925. On Sunday showings, see NA RG 151 281 Canada, North to Montreal, January 12, 1928. He refers to the censorship decisions as ''arbitrary and ridiculous'' in a letter dated July 27, 1928. Col. Cooper of the Motion Picture Distributors Association of Canada called Quebec censorship the worst in the world, see *Canadian Moving Picture Digest,* April 17, 1926.

Table 3. Canada: Film Imports from U.S.*

Year	Feet	Value (in dollars)
1913	9,000,000	71,000
1923	19,500,000	850,000
1924	19,700,000	850,000
1925	23,000,000	915,000
1926	20,985,072	731,604
1927[a]	8,432,301	302,180

*Source: C. J. North to Arthur S. Poole, F.B.O. Picture Corporation, October 27, 1927, NA RG 151 281-Canada Motion Pictures, Box 1555.

[a]Nine months only.

Table 4. Annual Per Capita Expenditure on Movies* (In Dollars and Cents)

Year	Quebec	Ontario	Canadian Average
1935	1.91	3.19	2.50
1936	2.02	3.49	2.70
1937	2.15	3.90	2.93
1938	2.17	4.07	3.02
1939	2.19	4.08	3.03
1940	2.30	4.63	3.35
1941	2.48	5.07	3.63
1942	2.76	5.44	4.01

*Source: *Motion Picture Theatres in Canada 1942*, Ottawa: Dominion Bureau of Statistics, 1944.

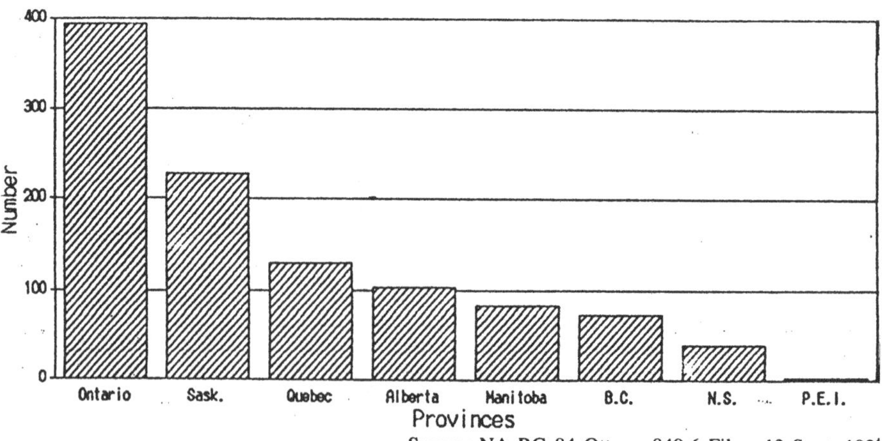

Source: NA RG 84 Ottawa 840.6 Films 13 Sept. 1921

Figure 1. Number of Theatres in Canada, 1927

much of the interwar period, children under sixteen were not eligible to go to the movies, even with their parents.[4] Also, throughout the period, Canadian movie theater prices were lowest in Quebec, and per capita expenditure on movies there was near lowest in the country.[5] We might conclude that special foreign distribution arrangements for Quebec were judged not worth the effort.

Beyond the cultural and financial reasons why the Canadian box office was classed as part of the domestic market, there was a more direct cause: From the mid-1920s, motion picture *distribution* in Canada had been dominated by the major United States companies. And distribution was the key to general domination. *Production* of commercial feature films, apart from a handful of French-Canadian films, was nonexistent in Canada; *exhibition* was a mixed bag of circuits and independents, heavily penetrated by United States and later United Kingdom interests. I do not know whether American movie moguls were the first to grasp that economic power in the motion picture industry gravitates towards distribution. What *is* fairly clear from events between the wars was that they acted swiftly and effectively as it became apparent. Even though other countries did what must have seemed like the right things, that is, made films and built theatres, Hollywood movies dominated world screens. The percentage of United States films screened in the United Kingdom by the mid-1920s was in the ninth percentile; in Canada it was the same, and, unlike in the United Kingdom, remained (and remains) so.[6]

This extraordinary world-wide success of the United States film industry is all-too-often simply taken for granted; or, worse, put down to the sinister and even imperialist machinations of a rapacious industry (or nation or system [capitalism] or some combination of the three). Such machinations, which were no doubt real, are no explanation at all. All business and businessmen seek profit and success and all, no doubt, would like to get control of the market for their products at home and abroad. Yet the machinations of some succeed; those of others do not. We need an explanation of the difference.

Sometimes the success of American films abroad is attributed to governments—not to the United Sates government so much as negatively to the inaction of foreign governments who failed to act to prevent United States

---

[4] In a letter of August 6, 1928, North noted that "it is an understood fact that children make up at least one-fourth of the admissions at motion picture theatres;" I take it that his reference is to the whole of the "domestic" market (see footnote 3.)

[5] Dominion Bureau of Statistics figures showed per capita expenditure on movies in Quebec to be near to the lowest in Canada (NA RG 151 Entry 14 Reports of Commercial Attachés, Ottawa, "Motion Picture Notes—Canada" April 23, 1935); and admission prices to be the lowest in Canada (ibid., "Motion Picture Notes—Canada" July 25, 1935).

[6] For example, as a percentage of total imports, U.S. films were: 98.2 percent in 1923, 95.3 percent in 1924, 98.7 percent in 1925, and 99.1 percent in 1926. (NA RG 59 1910–1929 800.4061 Ottawa to Department 10 March 1926.) Even after the arrival of sound and the onset of the Great Depression Commerce officials estimated that the United States held on to 65 percent of the world film market: NA RG 151 281 Motion Pictures—General, C. J. North to Arthur Eddy January 17, 1931.

domination of the local film business. For example, Canadian writers often contrast the total domination of the United States film companies in Canada with the (as they see it) "healthier" situation in the United Kingdom and France where the activities of United States companies were curbed and those of local companies fostered. An American writer, Guback (5), argued something similar for the European situation after World War II.

This explanation puts the cart before the horse. Government intervention to curb the penetration of United States firms into a foreign movie market was called for only if the United States firms were pursuing a successful policy of penetration, or if they appeared to be going to do so. The question still remains, what made that policy successful?

Within the film industry, and especially through its executives and its trade organization head for so many years, Will H. Hays, a popular explanation for the United States film industry's world-wide success was the alleged superior quality of American films; a superiority so manifest that, in fair competition with any rivals, they would emerge dominant. This explanation is one from *demand*: The Canadian audience (and indeed the world audience) demanded American films far more than it demanded any other kinds of films. Only in the absence of American films would the market not have been dominated by them. Thus, even where theatres were locally owned, they would book and show American films because those were the best generators of revenue. When a foreign government excluded American films as did the Russian revolutionary regime, or placed quotas on American films, as in Germany, France, and the U.K., one might suspect that the foreign government was implicitly accepting the *explanation from demand*. By setting a limit to the available supply of American films, the foreign government in effect managed demand, and deflected it from where it would otherwise have gone towards a goal set by the government.

The weakness of any such *explanation from demand* is well known. Supply and demand are truly measured only where market conditions are perfect: There should be many buyers, with total knowledge, and ready access; suppliers should have free entry, be numerous enough not to influence price, should not collude; and both supply and demand should be expressible in increments. None of these conditions has been present in the film market since at least World War I. The many buyers have not been well-informed, the product has been sold in quanta, and price has moved in jumps; entry to the market has been restricted; there have been very few suppliers and these have overtly and covertly colluded to extract oligopoly profit.

But perhaps the key defect of the market from the angle of deciding whether there was a genuine *strength of demand* for the American product was that the American product was aggressively sold. Hence, the potential audience was blanketed with "information" and advertising about American films, film stars, film makers, and so on, to a degree unmatched by any of the competition. Furthermore, and more questionably, the American industry was both very tough and very flexible in its pricing policy. If it had a unique product for which a good deal of demand was anticipated, such as *Gone With the Wind*, it held out for very stiff terms. In competition with other firms, however, the price might be lowered to the point where the competition went out of business trying to match it. If self-promotion is deafening and the competition is being undercut, it becomes virtually impossible to decide whether the *argument from demand* is an explanation of the dominance of American films.

Historians who come across evidence of Canadian demand (taste) for American films should interrogate it. Richards, in his study of British moviegoing in the 1930s, suggests that the taste for American films had to do with the class character of British society. American roles, settings, and accents were outside of and neutral to the British class system and hence did not arouse class antagonism in the audience the way British films utilizing stage actors playing middle- and upper-class roles did (10, pp. 29–33). John Grierson suggested that Hollywood films appealed to Britain because they had energy and optimism (7). Richards' and Grierson's work may suggest, at best, the beginnings of a *demand explanation* of American film dominance in Canada, which is also a class society. The intense ambivalence Canadians display towards the United States, perhaps stems from the tension between Canada's history as a class society and the attraction of its neighbor country's proclamation of a classless society. American films, optimistic, action-dominated, and portraying a society less hostage to class, would be more congenial than British films, which were none of these things.

One way to test the *explanation from demand* would be to explore whether some alternative explanation can be given of the success of United States films, one that stresses the *supply side* rather than the demand side of the equation. To the extent that one can be devised, we may feel free to give less weight to the allegedly superior character of the American product.

My researches have led me to the view that Hollywood's success had much more to do with the organization and management of supply than it had to do with demand. Not for a moment would I suggest the crude view that Hollywood rammed an inferior product down the throat of a reluctant public. On the contrary, for various social and cultural reasons of the sort mentioned, Hollywood did make a product with a broader appeal than any of its competition. But in business a good product is no more the royal road to market dominance than is the desire of the businessman for success, discussed earlier. Even a so-so product will suffice if only you can find the key to the market. My contention would be that Hollywood latched on to effective market-dominating strategies and pursued them more or less systematically in the foreign field. In particular, Hollywood controlled the distribution of its own product and, where it could, pursued a strategy of vertical integration abroad as well as at home.[7]

[7] On the early history of controlling its own distribution see Thompson (11, passim).

The first essential to Hollywood's market success was, as I have indicated, grasping the central economic position of distribution. This truth was not obvious. We know that for many years film was sold by the linear foot. This implies no product differentiation—one foot of film being commercially equivalent to any other. It also implies that its makers treat film as an economic good subject to outright sale. Residual copyright might demand redress against plagiarists and dupers, but the fate of the physical print was yielded to the buyer.

By a long, slow process of trial and error it was discovered that: The value of the product of the film industry could not be measured in linear feet; prints were not exploited well when sold or leased; what the public payed to see was an intangible product, with a short life in each retail outlet, but many such lives for each copy; just where, for how long, and at what price each print should be shown was a function of an anticipated demand different from film to film and between location and location.

Again, the United States industry was probably not the pioneer in figuring all this out. Perhaps the gradual accumulation of economic power by the exchanges was a surprise to all concerned. The outcome was determined by how firms acted when it became clear. Thompson's study (11) offers evidence that the American industry replaced agent selling with direct distribution before World War I. But direct control of distribution was only one part of the overall strategy. I shall run through six forms of action taken by the American industry at much the same time, all of which are important in explaining its dominance in Canada and the world.

1. *Vertical integration of production and distribution and, later, exhibition.* This is a well-known story (3). All major Hollywood companies eventually merged production and distribution, usually by the latter taking over the former. The economic logic was simple enough: Once money was tied up in a film, rapid and reliable distribution of it was imperative. This was more readily achieved if there was continuity—more product coming down the pipeline—since the exhibitor had to think of next week or the next change and beyond and did not want to deal with too many distributors. For both sides, producer and exhibitor, sure continuity of supply was the most efficient condition. The best of all possible producer-distributor links would give the distributor incentive to promote vigorously the product of a producer. The tightest guarantee of this was common ownership of the two firms.

If however, supply was already assured from another source, the distributor would be reluctant to disrupt his own schedules for less profit by taking on films made by other firms, including foreign firms. Hence, there was never any interest by Hollywood in Canadian production as long as the supply of American films was sufficient to fill the screen time available. It was not in Hollywood's direct interest to distribute foreign films in a foreign land or back in the United States. Only forcing legislation or the value of diffuse "goodwill" would make it worthwhile.

As to exhibition, clearly it saved costs if a single negotiation and contract could cover several theatres. Similarly, the more profitable theatres a firm owned the more aggregate profit. Hence the development of chains, booked and serviced from a single headquarters. Chains also constituted large and attractive outlets to distributors, hence they could demand more favorable terms. This perhaps made chains more attractive to own than to do business with. Hence from the economic power base in distribution, film companies also sought integration through ownership or control of chains.

All of this applies, *mutatis mutandis*, to Hollywood abroad. American overseas distribution handled their own product and with top priority. They bought and built theatres in commanding positions, and, where possible, acquired control of chains. Canada was so thoroughly dominated by Zukor's Famous Players that in 1930 it was subject to a federal investigation under the Combines Act.

2. *Horizontal mergers of the vertically integrated companies.* The major film companies had financial links through shareholding, personnel links through the movement of executives, and operational links through arrangements whereby they handled or favored each other's product in different regions and zones. This was inevitable since no studio produced enough films to fill the screens of its own theatres the year round if films were changed weekly. Each company was to an extent dependent on the other companies to make up whatever shortfall was left by their own production program. But this in turn meant that whereas in Canada, one company, Famous Players, had control of most of the best theaters, their sheer buying power was sufficient for them to be able to beggar their competition.

3. *Cost-push competition.* This counter-intuitive strategy derived from the theory that the more that was spent on a film in the way of lavish production values, stars, and advertising, the greater the returns. On the face of it, the contention is false: There are many expensive flops in the history of Hollywood. As a strategy against competitors, however, it was not a flop. At times of economic difficulty Hollywood on three occasions pushed costs up: the transition to sound, the adoption of wide-screen, and the almost universal use of color. Similarly, Hollywood's monopoly of stars was so complete that stars who emerged in other countries would be whisked off to the United States. Most striking of all is the attention Hollywood gave the longer-term and continuous advertising and promotion of stars and companies, and the large budgets always assigned to promote each feature film. In English-speaking foreign countries much of this material could be used with little or no modification; in English-speaking Canada none whatsoever. Whereas for British distribution, film titles were often changed where the original might be unintelligible or offensive; this was not necessary for Canada.

4. *The development of effective trade organizations to represent the industry at home and abroad.* The model here was the MPPDA, now called the MPPA,

which was formed in 1922. There have been only three heads: Will H. Hays, plucked from Harding's cabinet; Eric Johnston, once head of the U.S. Chamber of Commerce; and Jack Valenti, Chief of Staff to Lyndon Johnson. Known to film scholars mainly as the instrument of precensorship, this organization was more important in giving the industry a coherent voice in dealing with other industries and government. In the same way that Zukor set up a Canadian subsidiary, the Hays organization set up a Canadian subsidiary called the Motion Picture Distributor's Association of Canada which was wholly their creature. The Combines Investigation said it derived from the Hays Organization, on which it "was patterned and from which it originated, and from which it derived its inspiration, and with which it has kept in close touch throughout, which collects . . . the bulk of its funds, and which in fact dictates its policies and controls its activities" (2, p. 30). It was run for twenty years by one man, Col. John A. Cooper, a specialist in publicity and a Canadian patriot.

5. *Orchestration of government support for the industry, at home and abroad.*

a. *At home.* All attempts to legislate Federal or State censorship were resisted; as were any other attempts to restrict interstate commerce in films. Standard contracts and business procedures were devised. No move was made to obtain special tariff protection, quotas, or subsidies for the industry.

b. *Abroad.* The MPPDA was a contact with government for the collection of economic intelligence, through officers of the Commerce and State Departments, advising what was needed, and providing a channel for dissemination and for feedback. In foreign countries MPPDA could speak for the bulk of the industry in resisting discriminatory legislation, and could align with American diplomats and with government and Congress to back up their own lobbying.

6. *Directly buying into the foreign industry and then pursuing the same policies listed in 1 through 5.*

Canada is an ideal site to study the implementation of these policies because they were carried to their most exaggerated form there. There are several reasons for this.[8] First, none of the trade restrictions at the border applied to this new product, film, which suffered only a small tariff. Second, commercial law and practice in Canada was very similar to that of the United States, so that American firms could operate and American banks could lend with some confidence. Third, there was relatively free movement of labor for much of the period, hence American companies could send up their own personnel or hire locals more or

[8] American officials offered these ideas: "Geographical propinquity, similarity of living standards, style preferences, and social organization, plus the extensive infiltration of motion picture publicity and music via radio and magazines, serve to emphasize the similarity between the Canadian and the domestic American market for the motion picture industry." See "Required Report on Motion Pictures," February 1, 1940, NA RG 84 Foreign Service Posts of the Department of State, Ottawa. "Proximity, cultural and economic ties, and voice preference all help to account for Hollywood's predominance, which has also been strengthened and protected by financial links between the two countries." Loc. cit., "Motion Pictures in Canada—1942" August 17, 1943.

less as they saw fit. Fourth, a compliant trade organization on the lines of Motion Picture Producers and Distributors of America, known as the Cooper organization after its long-time head[9], lobbied on behalf of those Canadians whose livelihood came from American films. Fifthly, the constitutional structure of Canada made concerted action difficult to undertake on any front: Regulation of trade was divided between the Federal and Provincial levels, but amusements were a Provincial bailiwick. This explains why, before the 1960s, there was precious little one could call a Federal policy towards entertainment films.[10] Federal organs such as the Canadian Government Motion Picture Bureau and the National Film Board, for its first twenty years, concentrated on documentary. Some scholars argue there was a Federal policy but that it was negative: Grierson, first Commissioner of the NFB, because he both admired and despised Hollywood, yielded the entertainment field without a struggle (9). For all that, legislative action, such as quotas, would have been difficult to obtain federally, and, where passed provincially, as in Ontario, British Columbia, and Alberta in the earlier 1930s, was never implemented. Morris thinks this was because the legislation was mainly a threat to get voluntary compliance (8, note 1, p. 312). My own guess is that the class of persons agitating for fewer American and more British or "Empire" films was not identical with the class of moviegoers. There is box-office evidence that British films were in fact unpopular with the Canadian masses.[11] Not implementing the legislation was a way of not actually stirring up the hornet's nest, especially if those pushing the legislation were not regular moviegoers and hence sensitive to any dissatisfaction resulting from the effects of the legislation. While responding to pressure groups, politicians also have to keep an eye on how many votes their actions might lose.

There was also the fact that energies were divided: Cultural objections to the dominance of American, such as non-Empire films, were mixed up with economic objections to monopolistic American business practices. In 1930, under the Combines Investigation Act, Commissioner Peter White, K. C., went into the question of whether Famous Players Canadian Corporation, the Cooper Organization and others were engaging in practices contrary to law. He found that they were, but when the case was prosecuted in Ontario it failed. Since a

---

[9] "The liaison between our respective associations will be close" J. Homer Platten, Acting Treasurer, MPPDA to Dr. Julius Klein, Director, Bureau of Foreign and Domestic Commerce, January 12, 1925, NA RG 151 281 Motion Pictures—Canada.

[10] See Mackenzie King's remarks to the Imperial Economic Conference October 22, 1926, PAC RG 20 Trade and Industry, Vol. 31, File 16613 Part I.

[11] See Peck to O'Hara March 15, 1923, O'Hara to Skelton January 24, 1927 and Skelton to O'Hara February 1, 1927 in the PAC file note 10, above; American Consul at Winnipeg Report October 5, 1944 NA RG 84 Ottawa, says American pictures are more popular than British because prairie people "are like Americans in their taste, ideas, and mode of life, and what the Americans like they like;" also NA RG 59 1940–44 842.4061, "US Motion Pictures in Quebec" October 11, 1944: "There is an underlying prejudice in the French-Canadian against anything British which would doom to failure any attempt on the part of British producers to enter the field."

good many Canadian businessmen were making money from the import of American films, one might again conclude that the politics of the matter were for the Government to show they were willing by moving against the Americans in the courts, but not to press the matter when the moves proved unsuccessful. No effort was made to re-draft the legislation to outlaw the offending trade practices. Until the Canadian Cooperation Project episode of 1948–1955 (when Hollywood "promoted" Canada in exchange for dollar convertibility), cultural energies seem to have been channelled into the CBC and the National Film Boards, rather than policing the border against Hollywood.

Since some Canadians stood to benefit from the dominance of American films, Canada was a house divided against itself. And, pious protestations to the contrary notwithstanding, the British were not much help. When it came to film policy Canada was rather like Poland in 1939, flanked by powerful countries wanting to dismember it. The Americans established a small branch plant in Victoria, BC, in the 1930s, so the British carefully drafted their 1938 Cinematograph Films Act to prevent those "Canadian" films from counting for the British quota. Only British-based branchplants were eligible.[12] This scarcely assisted any displacement of Canada from the United States domestic film market.

In conclusion, the idea that the United States film industry thrived in Canada and elsewhere abroad, partly because it shrewdly orchestrated Federal Government support, needs exploring. By selecting former cabinet member and Republican National Chairman Will Hays as its first head, the MPPDA ensured that it had connections to Washington. Opinions are divided about Hays. Certainly he was a fluent master of applesauce. But he was also a lawyer, a politician and, if we are to believe his autobiography, a firm believer in his mission to elevate the movies and assist in their success. Though his autobiography projects him as blameless, plenty of documents in the archives of the State and Commerce Departments suggest that he counselled economic ruthlessness, as for example, the threats and boycott used to influence French treatment of American films in 1928 and 1929. The climate was propitious for his work. Secretaries of Commerce Redfield and Hoover were promoting American overseas trade by means of an expanded Department of Commerce, one with a foreign service and the collection of economic intelligence as a principal function. Hoover was very ready to use the whole weight of the American government to persuade other countries toward American demands (1, passim). Hays lobbied energetically for motion picture matters to be researched, succeeding to the extent that a separate Division was created in the Bureau of Foreign and Domestic Commerce.[13] In

[12] See Peck to O'Hara September 22, 1926, PAC loc. cit., note (10); and PRO FO 371 21530, Circular letter to the Dominions, February 17, 1938.

[13] The idea of a separate motion picture division within the Bureau of Foreign and Domestic Commerce first surfaced in the early 1920s, see Klein to Elliott (Executive Secretary, National Association of the Motion Picture Industry), August 30, 1921, NA RG 151 160.2 Specialties Division. Klein concludes this letter as follows: "I may say that Mr. Hoover and I have discussed on

1926 a special foreign-based trade commissioner for motion pictures, George Canty, was recruited by the Bureau and based in Paris, with a brief to rove Europe.[14] The Hays organization had its European office in Paris also. Its first head, Harold Smith, was none-too-successful; eventually one of the most brilliant trade commissioners in Europe, Fayette W. Allport, was recruited.[15] After the war broke out he moved headquarters to London.

While Commerce officials were eager to cooperate from the start, State officials were divided. For one thing, State was accumulating dossiers of protest from foreign countries about insults to their nationals in American movies, and about the rapacious commercial practices of American motion picture companies.[16] Concerning these they had to approach the Hays' organization, just as, when assistance was needed with French and German quota legislation, and with the negotiation of agreements about sound patents, the Hays organization needed the good offices of State. So gradually a working relationship was built up in which the Hays organization was identified with the industry for most government intents and purposes. Both the Independent MPPDA and the theatre owners—NATO—were pushed to the background, consulted only on special occasions. At times in the 1920s the Government-MPPDA relationship was so close that the State Department had to deny that they had appointed Hays, or that he ran the United States Government.[17]

Until 1929, Canada-U.S. relations were partly mediated through the British. Subsequently, with an Ottawa Embassy, and the Cooper organization based in Toronto, Canada could be pressured either by lobbying on the U.S. model, or, if that failed, with the additional weight of the Commerce and State Departments and the "interest" in the matter of the President himself.

---

several occasions the significance of motion picture exporting both as a straight commodity trade and as a powerful influence in behalf of American goods and habits of living. I hope you will assure the officials of your Association that we shall be more than pleased to have any indications from them as to how this branch of the Government might be of service either through its Washington organization or through its trade commissioners and commercial attaches abroad."

Motion picture data were actually collected within the Specialties Division for much of the time, until a separate division was created (July 1929), then abolished July 15, 1933, then re-instated (July 1937). (See NA RG 40 70801/230 Motion Picture Division, Bureau of Foreign and Domestic Commerce, Burke to Avery, March 26, 1935 and Roper to Hays July 22, 1937.) More important than this is the fact that motion picture work was consistently directed by only two men for nearly thirty years, C. J. North from 1923 to 1933, and then his former deputy, Nathan Golden, from 1933 to 1950. This continuity of top personnel, which was also true of the Hays organization, was in my view a factor of considerable value.

[14] Canty's appointment and instructions can be reconstructed at NA RG 151 Motion Pictures—General.

[15] NA RG 40 Office of the Secretary, General Correspondence, 82253/36.

[16] See the Bulky files at NA RG 59 1910–1949 811.4061.

[17] NA RG 1910–1929 851.4061 Motion Pictures (Microfilm no.M560 R 47) passim. Hays jokes about this in his *Memoirs*, p. 513.

When the Canadian government proposed to raise the tariff on positive film (1939), or to impose a special income tax on American motion picture companies (1933), the full articulations of the liaison can be seen. Direct pressure through the Legation, and lobbying by the Cooper organization, was undertaken. Although the Fordney-McCumber (1922) and Smoot-Hawley (1930) tariffs had virtually closed the U.S. market to Canadian farm products, a strength of the American motion picture industry case was always that there was free entry of films into the American market. Thus, countries considering measures against American films were on the defensive, it was they who were initiating discrimination. It was hard for them to complain that the free entry was a sham, that the controlling oligopoly in effect closed the American market off, because there were exceptional occasions when foreign films were distributed in the United States. The argument could thereby always be that films of quality were marketed in the United States whatever their source.

At all events Canada did not have those arguments. By not having a feature film industry, Canada had only revenue-raising economic arguments against American domination; not having a film culture of its own, Canada could only object to American dominance by affirming British loyalties. This created internal tensions. A section of the Canadian public was apparently very comfortable with imported American movies, which they consumed in large numbers. Canadian governing elites deplored this for they preferred British movies; but they were torn because they were also promoting a national consciousness distinct from Britain. Caught between reluctance to deprive the public of its pleasure, and faced by the disproportionate emphasis Washington placed on the movie industry, it is understandable that no policy emerged aimed at detaching the Canadian film market from the United States domestic market.

REFERENCES

1. Brandes, J. *Herbert Hoover and Economic Diplomacy, Department of Commerce Policy 1921–1928*. Pittsburgh: University of Pittsburgh Press, 1962.
2. Canada. Department of Labour. Combine Investigation Branch. *Investigation into an Alleged Combine in the Motion Picture Industry*. Ottawa: King's Printer, 1931.
3. Conant, M. *Anti-Trust in the Motion Picture Industry*. Berkeley and Los Angeles: University of California Press, 1960.
4. Greenwald, W. I. "The Motion Picture Industry: An Economic Study of the History and Practices of a Business." PhD thesis, New York University, 1950.
5. Guback, T. *The International Film Industry*. Bloomington, IN: University of Indiana Press, 1969.
6. Hays, W. H. *The Memoirs of Will H. Hays*. Garden City, NY: Doubleday and Co., 1955.
7. Jarvie, I. and Macmillan, R. "Grierson on Hollywood's Success, 1927." *Historical Journal of Film, Radio and Television*, Vol. 9, 1989, pp. 302–326.
8. Morris, P. *Embattled Shadows. A History of Canadian Cinema 1895–1939*. Montreal: McGill-Queens University Press, 1978.
9. Morris, P. "Backward to the Future: John Grierson's Film Policy for Canada." In G. Walz (Ed.), *Flashback, People and Institutions in Canadian Film History*. Montreal: Mediatexte, 1986, pp. 17–35.
10. Richards, J. *The Age of the Dream Palace*. London: Routledge and Kegan Paul, 1984.
11. Thompson, K. *Exporting Entertainment*. London: British Film Institute, 1985.

11

Imperialist Victory in Peacetime: State Functions and the British Cinema Industry

Thomas Nakayama
Lorraine A. Vachon

Films serve as a clear example of capital accumulation in the arena of international film production and distribution. The most lucrative overseas market for Hollywood is the United Kingdom which accounts for a large percentage of their foreign revenue. While our primary concern is to address the role of the State, both American and British, as an interloper in the economic structure of a private enterprise system, it is necessary to situate our study historically. Specifically, we theorize about State Imperialist functions operating in Hollywood's co-option of the British cinema industry between World War I and World War II.

We use Imperialism as a theoretical framework to locate the struggle for power between two rival nation states as the focus of our analysis. Imperialism is generally defined as the attempt of one country to dominate another in which the locus of control is established through such strategies as "a merger of bank and industrial capital into finance capital, the export of capital abroad, and militarism" (11, p. 228). Our interrogation of the U.S. actions to undercut British film production and co-opt their cinema industry are set against larger struggles for a redivision of world-wide territories (11, p. 229). Indeed, the U.S. supersedes the once superior position of the U.K. as an imperialist rival by treating Britain as a colony.

While Karl Marx recognized the importance of international circulation of capital, he did not directly discuss imperialism (3, pp. 19, 27). In Lenin's work, *Imperialism, The Highest Stage of Capitalism,* the role of the state in international capital accumulation became a Marxist concern. Lenin characterizes the imperialist structure of economic relations that engenders exploitation a " 'rentier state' (Rentnerstaat) or usurer state." Further, Lenin argues that "the world has become divided into a handful of usurer states and a vast majority of debtor states" (7, p. 121). Given this division and the power imbalances it entails, our central concern in the present study is to explore the structural relationship of imperialism as it operates in the international film industry. Since Lenin's description of rentier states focuses on rivalry relationships and ellides exploitation, we redress Lenin's portrait of imperialist structures to broaden the parameters of State functions in international cultural commodity exchange.

In an attempt to analyze both the scope and reach of this international and structured relationship, it is crucial to investigate the interplay between and across nation states to highlight points of struggle for territorial rights to a lucrative film market. This interplay is particularly relevant to the U.S. film industry which became heavily dependent upon foreign revenue. The imperialist relationship, as Lenin argued, featured a creditor–debtor structure among nations which generated parasitic rentier states. Particular international conditions laid the groundwork for the establishment and growth of an imperialist structure. Two world wars and a global depression provided the conditions for restructuring economic relations conducive for building an imperialist foundation between the U.S. and U.K. Although the role of the film industry was minor in comparison to larger economic struggles, the co-option of the British cinema must be considered within larger historical and economic conditions in order to acknowledge other state interests on the part of the U.S. and U.K.

"In any analysis of imperialism," writes Brewer, "the actions of (capitalist) *states* must play an important role" (3, p. 14). Indeed, the actions taken by the U.S. to expand its film market combined with the U.K.'s actions to protect its industry's market share construct a context for understanding the position of the film industry within imperialism. An analysis of state actions also includes the particular constellation of historical forces at work during the period of imperialist development. In drawing this latter point out further, the two world wars are obvious points affecting international economic relations and the roles of the states. Göran Therborn notes the close ties between private and public structures at this time:

> In the monopoly stage of capitalism, when the public–private distinction becomes less sharp, the upper reaches of state administration tend to merge with private corporate management. The mechanism that fuses monopoly capital with the state attained its highest degree of perfection during the two world wars. (12, p. 107)

The blurring between state (public) and private industry was not limited to the official war periods. During this time between the declared wars and signed peace treaties, the state and private industry in both the U.S. and U.K. negotiated for their respective interests. The failure on the part of the U.K. to attain its interests cannot be reduced simply to those of the film industry; however, the merger of public and private institutions played a key strategic role for establishing and solidifying the imperialist structural relationship between the U.S. and the U.K.

The various economic, social, and political relationships outlined serve as a backdrop to move into a closer inspection of the British cinema industry and points of U.S. intervention. Prior to World War I, Britain held a secure position as an Imperialist power and the cinema was a profitable area ripe for investors. In setting the tone for Britain's expected commercial future, Betts states:

> England not only prospered in the arts, she was booming commercially. There was plenty of money to launch a film industry. City men began to see that films, as Bernard Baruch the banker put it, were a "pot of gold," and they poured money into them. Indeed one of the most pleasing reflections for those engaged in the film business is that money is never far off. (2, p. 33)

Even with hefty capital investments, the British cinema industry failed to stave off the invasion of American films into this relatively young market. As Betts notes, the introduction of American film into the market coupled with the British industry's relatively nonexistent protection and organization begins to explain Britain's loss of control over its film industry. With American films already overtaking the British market by 1914, exhibitors cried for intervention on their behalf. However, exhibitors participated in their own financial demise by booking the productions they cited as disastrous for their interests (2, p. 35).

The blame for not taking some undefined action(s) falls to the British state. Prior to World War I, the British state only enacted one major piece of legislation dealing with the film industry, which was the Cinematograph Act of 1909. This act, along with minor legislation, addressed issues primarily associated with storage facilities for celluloid and fire safety. There was no substantial state intervention to protect the British cinema industry.

By 1917, Britain's economic strength was significantly weakened. Film production was severely hampered in part by financial strain, but also by a lack of human resources and an ability to find suitable filming conditions. Betts summarizes the extent of Britain's plight: "Filming was made difficult by wartime restrictions and by air raids which hit studios and homes alike. The war was bleak. Men of 45 were being called up" (2, p. 55). The conditions paralyzing Britain's ability to sustain its national cinema were not shared by the United States during the same point in time. World War I was primarily a war among rentier states, among imperialist rivals. The neutral stance taken by the U.S. early in the war helped it secure a more favorable position vis-à-vis the other imperialist powers. The tremendous exchange of capital by Allies to finance this war points to an important reversal in the inter-imperialist relation between the United States and Britain:

> World War I cost its participants $209 billion in direct expenditures. During its early years, before the United States entered the conflict, U.S. exporters sold arms to the belligerents on credit, establishing $3.5 billion in private U.S. holdings of foreign government bonds and promissory notes. In addition, the Allied powers paid for U.S. securities (railroad bonds, common stocks, and so on). U.S. private liabilities to foreigners were thereby reduced by this sum, while U.S. private and governmental financial claims on foreigners increased, for a net improvement of $7.5 billion in America's international position. While private international liabilities were being wound down, those of governments' were built up. Including

> postwar Victory loans, obligations of the Allies to the United States government grew to $12 billion by 1921, starting with a $3 billion credit granted in 1917. (5, p. 3)

By the close of World War I, the United States emerged economically stable. In part, its status as a creditor nation vis-à-vis other imperialist powers helped to structure the subsequent takeover of the British cinema industry.

The U.S. government used its economic leverage to overshadow private investment overseas. Although private investors accounted for some overseas investments, most were made by the government. According to Hudson, U.S. government investments were directed "to a Europe of then greater industrial output than the United States and visibly deficient in raw materials within its borders" (5, p. 4). Furthermore, the role of the U.S. state in capital accumulation did not end with the war; rather, its financial stature increased after the war through the use of other strategies.

More is involved than the amassing of credit against other imperialist rivals that helped the United States to structure an imperialist relation to Britain. By forcing the United Kingdom to repay its war debt on a separate financial schedule than the German war debt payments to Britain and the United States, the British were trapped in a position of having to pay a larger percentage of its war debts than Germany. The difference would have to come from the British Treasury. Further damaging the British position was the continuation of American war loans made after the war through the Victory Liberty loan program which did not end until President Harding declared war legally over as of July 2, 1921 (5, p. 12). Britain's finances were also burdened by the U.S. refusal to connect Germany's inability to repay Britain to the British-American war debts. The U.S. solidified its creditor status against Britain by calculating the German debt in commodities equivalent and the British debt was calculated in "real value" (5, p. 23). This action forced Britain into a debtor role since it could not repay its debts to the U.S. within such constraints.

At the close of this same year, 1921, the American film industry began establishing an organization to represent their interests in national and international state functions and actions. Private institutions wanting their interests represented by state interventions would fund the organization. In December 1921, Lewis J. Selznick and Saul Rogers offered William H. Hays the task of establishing and directing the Motion Picture Producers and Distributors of America (MPPDA) at $100,000 per year. Hays accepted in January 1922, and the MPPDA was established on March 6, 1922. Although the organization's role was as a spokesperson for the American film industry, it was a private organization funded by film corporations. Through careful negotiations with the U.S. government, the MPPDA acted as a conduit to align private corporate interests with the U.S. State to enhance the American film industry's position in the British market.

On a national level, the MPPDA focused primarily on creating a system for Hollywood's self-regulation of films to block any state interference, such as developing censorship guidelines. The MPPDA was also responsible for developing a Foreign Department to oversee the exportation of American films and keep foreign markets open. Hays hired Frederick L. Herron to head the Foreign Department and create the "proper" state connections for further use. Herron essentially acted as a liaison between the Hays office and various foreign representatives and officials within the government and abroad (9, p. 171). The Hays Office (MPPDA) is an example of the direct involvement of private industry in state functions. More importantly, however, it represents the unification of private interests into one organization. The MPPDA represented the interests of the American film industry in negotiations with Washington and overseas. Whereas the MPPDA functioned to minimize conflicts and divergent interests within the film industry, the state functioned as the negotiating arm of the film industry with other nation states. The MPPDA did not have this ability on its own, despite the many contacts made by Hays and Herron.

The film industry worked to balance its interests both internally and with the state. Although the industry tried to avoid interference from the state, one of the first episodes of state intervention occurred with the passage of the Cinematograph Films Act of 1927. The Act was intended to serve as protectionist legislation to encourage the development and maintenance of the British film industry over a period of 10 years beginning in 1928. Through a system of quotas, the state tried to guarantee a market for British films within Britain.

The passage of this legislation was not without its opponents. Although some criticism originated in Britain, the strongest reaction came from the United States, the nation with the most to lose. While the MPPDA protested strongly against such protectionist measures, the Act remained in effect for 10 years. In order to avoid losing capital during this time, many American companies established "British companies," not "British-controlled companies," to make inexpensive films to fulfill the quotas outlined in the 1927 Act. With a large number of "British" films produced, this created space for a significant number of American films to enter the British market as stipulated by the quota. These films, named "quota quickies" (9, p. 178), offered little to the public in either quality or entertainment value. The effect of this circumvention, which was led primarily by American film corporations, further undercut the British film industry. Because the films were of such poor technical quality and so short in length, they had no commercial value. Britain's reputation as a competitor in film production and distribution sharply declined.

In 1936, the British government established the Moyne committee to evaluate the 1927 Act and to propose recommendations after its expiration in 1938. The Moyne Report *recognized the circumvention that was occurring*. Under the Act, it was clear that renters focused on cost-effectiveness and meeting quotas with little regard for film quality. The result was a stable of films that were "worthless" and remained "largely unsold and unused" (*Moyne Report*, quoted in 8, pp. 103–104). Because of these abuses, the 1927 Act was useless in assisting either the commercial or aesthetic development of the British cinema industry.

Yet, the attempt to develop a national cinema industry must be framed against a backdrop of the United States' economic power during this time.

The end of British imperialism vis-à-vis the United States occurred quickly during the 1930s. Britain lost its footing as an imperialist rival with the U.S. through a series of economic problems in conjunction with World War II. By 1931, Britain was forced off the gold standard, yet the United States still refused to tie German war debts to the Allies' war debts:

> The United States Government refused to acknowledge the connection between the inter-Ally debts and German reparations. Europe insisted upon this connection at the Lausanne Conference in 1932, when Premier Herriot of France demanded that "cancellation of reparations without corresponding readjustment of allied war debts would place Germany in a privileged position." (5, p. 26)

By refusing to acknowledge this economic relationship and readjust war debts, the United States was able to strengthen its advantageous position. As such, by the end of 1932, the United Kingdom was grossly in debt. British attempts to repay war debts resulted in an unfavorable fall in value of the British pound against the American dollar. This inequity of exchange rates exposes Britain's weakened economic position:

> With the pound sterling at par, the British Treasury needed £20,000,000 to purchase the dollars required to pay principal and interest falling due in December, 1932, with the pound sterling at $3.22, it needed nearly £30,000,000. (United States Council on Foreign Relations, quoted in 5, p. 26)

Britain could not escape its debtor status; the more the debt was paid, the more it increased. Hudson explains this dynamic in light of currency difference: "In sterling, Britain's debt to the United States increased the more of this dollar debt she paid, forcing down the value of sterling against the dollar accordingly. This made her debt transfer an infinite function" (5, p. 26).

In 1934, the devaluation of the American dollar raised gold prices and brought an increase in foreign capital from abroad. This was the result of both the increased value of the stated American gold stock and the influx of foreign capital due to rumors of war. Thus, the gold stocks of the U.S. rose to $7.4 billion which represented about one-third of the world gold reserves at the time. "By the end of 1937, as war loomed in Europe, U.S. holdings had increased from $11.3 billion, more than half the world monetary reserves" (5, p. 35). After 1938, the flow of gold into the United States increased astronomically and reached "panic proportions" after the Four Powers Agreement (5, p. 36). The gold stock soared to $22.7 billion by the time the United States entered the war in 1941.

Britain's decision to renew the 1927 Act by passing the Cinematograph Film Act of 1938 was not uncontested nor unchallenged by the MPPDA. From the inception of the Moyne Commission in 1936 through World War II, the provisions of the 1938 Act were negotiated by both the MPPDA and U.S. government to open the British market given the foreign-exchange situation. From January 1937 to March 1938, the U.S. government and the MPPDA tried to determine the best possible conditions under the new Act. Moley underscores this private–public cooperation by pointing out sympathetic ties operating between the Hays Office and two U.S. ambassadors—the late Robert W. Bingham and his successor, Joseph P. Kennedy. The industry garnered further support from the State Department in Washington (9, pp. 180–181).

The interests of the U.S. state resided with maintaining and expanding the capital transfer from the United Kingdom to the United States. The American state functioned as an official arbiter with the British state in order to advance the interests of the American film industry. Because the film industry's interests were represented by the MPPDA, it was much easier for the state to collaborate officially with private industry interests. While certainly fulfilling the negotiating role, these state actions have to be read against the background of the larger balance of trade issues between the United Kingdom and the United States.

As World War II approached, the British need for capital increased. At this point, the pressures from the larger economic exchange relationship between Britain and the United States directly affected the American accumulation of British capital through the film industry. Britain needed to mobilize and transfer dollar exchanges for the purchase of war materials. Capital transferred for American films was blocked by the British Treasury (9, p. 181). That is, once Britain entered the war in 1939, "all foreign-exchange transactions in Great Britain were placed under rigid control" (9, p. 181). Once again, the U.S. government and the MPPDA negotiated with the British government to allow larger amounts of capital for transfer to the United States from film revenue. Three trade agreements were negotiated. The first agreement extended one year from October 30, 1939 and allowed American film corporations to take out half of their previous remittances from British showings. The second agreement in 1940 and the third agreement in 1941 further stipulated that "if the dollar-exchange position of Great Britain should materially improve during the life of the agreement, the British government would, upon application by the industry, consider the possibility of increased transfers" (9, p. 183). At this time, Britain was in a desperate trade position with the United States. Since Britain was at war, it was forced to divert as much capital as possible to the purchase of war materials. The need for capital forced Britain to draw capital from virtually all potential sources, including film revenues. As we will see shortly, the war placed Britain in a position where there were few choices in negotiations with the United States.

Of particular note here is the final fall of the United Kingdom to the United States. The advent of World War II forced Britain into the imperialist structure with the United States by financially breaking the British Treasury. As such, the economic relationship shaped during the war foreshadowed postwar conditions. Britain tried to sustain some economic leverage during the war by nationalizing private overseas investment holdings of its citizens and offering these for sales overseas. Although this substantially increased war monies, much of the revenue was used to purchase arms from the U.S. However, Britain's need for war materials outweighed purchase power and by December 1940, the country was virtually bankrupt and dependent on the U.S. in order to continue in the war (5, p. 37).

Since the United States did not enter the war until 1941, it was officially neutral and would not give arms to Britain; arms had to be bought. Hence, in December 1940, the U.S. Treasury Department recommended passing the Lend-Lease Act. Yet, "when Congress signed the Lend-Lease Act into law on March 11, 1941, a financially exhausted Britain was left with only $12 million in uncommitted revenues" (5, p. 39).

The Lend-Lease Act further solidified the debtor status of the United Kingdom. The stipulations on this loan program were such that Keynes called them "lunatic proposals of Mr. Hull" who was at the time U.S. Secretary of State. Yet, Britain was not in a position to negotiate the terms of the loans. While the British wanted to avoid increasing their debt to the U.S., they finally agreed to the terms of the loan after their loss of Singapore to Japan in February 1942 (5, p. 40).

Britain's acceptance of the Lend-Lease Act "opened the door of hope for the [American film] companies" (9, p. 183). Once again the U.S. government and the MPPDA believed they could renegotiate with Britain for more capital. The MPPDA "took the position that inasmuch as Lend-Lease greatly reduced the amount of dollar exchange that Great Britain had to find for the purchase of war materials, it should be possible for the British Treasury to divert some of its exchange holdings to the transfer of the accumulating film revenues" (9, p. 183). Under these conditions, the British government "officially agreed to release half the funds that had already accumulated and to increase the authorized remittance for the third agreement year" (9, p. 183). After the war ended, however, the U.S. demands on the British state would increase and effectively destroy opportunities for the establishment of a vital British cinema industry in the foreseeable future.

At the end of the war, the United States was able to negotiate from its creditor position and gained a number of concessions from the British, especially the opening of British colonial markets to the U.S. In the arena of the film industry, the transfer of capital was again opened. Near the end of the war, the Chancellor to the Exchequer advised that: "all special restrictions on the transfer of the film companies' revenues in Great Britain would be removed and transfers would thenceforth be dealt with in the same manner as those of other American industries and businesses operating in Great Britain. Shortly thereafter similar arrangements were completed with the Dominions, and the funds impounded elsewhere in the 'sterling area' were released" (9, pp. 183–184). Thus, Hudson notes that "the financial effects of World War I between Europe and America repeated themselves" (5, p. 36). This repeated performance of increasing British debts to the United States forced Britain into an imperialist structure.

Bereft with economic difficulties, Britain's film industry was a clear target for an invasion by Hollywood. The British state's attempts to protect its film industry failed. England was economically trapped by debts incurred to the U.S. and had to relinquish "Empire preference" by opening its markets to the U.S. at a point when Britain needed full market control to fund its sterling debt. The loss of market power crippled Britain and "what Germany as foe had been unable to accomplish in two World Wars against England, the United States accomplished with ease as an ally" (5, p. 48).

THEORETICAL IMPLICATIONS

In any macroscopic study of these proportions there are generalizations that are made at the expense of more specific microscopic analyses. This case study represents but one instance of international state intervention. Yet, over this more than 25-year period, there are some important trends and points that need to be examined and theorized. The role of the American state in the co-option of the British cinema industry during this time period points toward some underlying theoretical questions that need to be articulated.

Unfortunately, imperialism and international economic exchange has been of little interest to contemporary Marxist theorists until quite recently. Gold, Lo, and Wright suggest that: "It is especially important that future theoretical and empirical work on the capitalist state should attempt to understand the relationship of the internationalization of capital to the dynamics of state involvement in accumulation (4, p. 49). Since the emergence of the United States as the undisputed leader in the capitalist world, little substantive work has been done with imperialism. It was only after the position of the United States began to be questioned that interest was renewed. Since the United States emerged from World War II as the strongest and most powerful capitalist country, it was virtually uncontested that the U.S. was dominant and free from "inter-imperialist rivalry" (3, p. 281). However, several shifts in the United States' political and economic agendas, such as "the rapid recovery of the European and Japanese economies, the weakness of the US dollar and the defeat in Vietnam," have renewed debate about the United States' imperialist position (3, p. 281).

NATIONALISM AND IMPERIALIST STRUCTURE

This case study demonstrates that the displacement of Britain's economic position was accomplished through a combination of state intervention into economic exchange and exploitation of particular historical forces during the two world wars set within a worldwide economic depression. Because the imperialist relationship is structural, rather than essential, the imperialist structure must be viewed as dynamic. Thus, interest in studying imperialism need not and should not assume that the United States will continue to dominate the imperialist structure.

The larger structural relationship among capitalist nation states also needs further study. While Lenin dichotomizes states into usurer states and debtor states, this extremely binary system needs to be further problematized. As we have seen, the inter-imperialist rivalry between the U.K. and U.S. cannot be adequately explained by a binary opposition. Baran and Sweezy offer an alternative structure that positions nation states into exploitative relations with each other:

> The hierarchy of nations which make up the capitalist system is characterized by a complex set of exploitative relations. Those at the top exploit in varying degrees all the lower layers, and similarly those at any given level exploit those below them until we reach the very lowest layer which has no one to exploit. At the same time, each unit at a given level strives to be the sole exploiter of as large a number as possible of the units beneath it. Thus we have a network of antagonistic relations pitting exploiters against exploited and rival exploiters against each other. (1, p. 179)

The specific modes of exploitation have yet to be fully articulated which entails how exploiter nations are able to alter their positions within the hierarchy of exploitation. Thus, the inter-imperialist rivalry between the United States and the United Kingdom, combined with the negotiations and agreements between these two states, formed the basis upon which further exploitation was made possible.

In specific regard to the film industry, the national aspect of the industry cannot be separated from its production and cultural functions. Even today, the Common Market film industries are unable to cooperate effectively beyond the national, linguistic, and cultural boundaries (see 6, pp. 361–372). The film industry, as well as other industries, is centered around a particular nation state. The consolidation of the American film industry under the umbrella group, the MPPDA, further points to the national status of the film industry. Recognizing the cinema industry's nationalism is imperative in tracing the boundaries of international trade, as Brewer notes:

> The essential point here is that capital that operates internationally needs the support of a home state to protect its interests. The whole range of needs that are met internally by the state (protection of property, enforcement of contracts, etc.) are met internationally by interstate negotiations and agreements. A large part of the diplomatic apparatus through which the nation states deal with each other (in the time of peace) has grown up precisely to negotiate the regulation of commercial activities. (3, p. 280)

The American film industry is heavily dependent upon international revenue and, therefore, needs the negotiation function of the American state. The U.S. government assisted the MPPDA in securing favorable conditions in the negotiations with the British government. The interests of the American state were recognized as being with the American film industry, a collection of private capitalists.

The nationalism played out by the role of the state is recognized by Therborn who argues that: "the capitalist state is a representative of the national public, and strictly nationalistic factors play a role in the formation of foreign policy alongside the dominant contradiction between different national capitals'' (12, p. 98). In this case study, the American government worked with the MPPDA in order to secure, through negotiation, a favorable position for the American film industry in the British market. The MPPDA represents the interests of a group of capitalists that produce films; their interests were viewed as the interests of the nation. The role of the American state was to provide both protection to the film industry, as well as the apparatus for negotiating with the British government. Without the American state, many of the negotiations and agreements, particularly near the beginning of World War II, might not have been possible. The state, in this instance, was serving the interests of private industry. In this sense, then, we may view the role of the State as an extended structure of the capitalists for their use internationally.

THE QUALITY ISSUE

''We know that an announcement 'British Film' outside a movie theatre will chill the hardiest away from its door,'' *Close Up* declared in 1927 (quoted in 8, p. 298). The quality of British films has long been held responsible for the American takeover of the British cinema industry. Betts' explanation of the fall of the British film industry is typical of this type of analysis:

> Their films were better than ours. . . . We lacked the expertise, the imagination and the money to compete on equal terms. A Betty Balfour or an Ivor Novello might arise and prove immensely popular, but British stars, it became evident, were made in Hollywood and Hollywood stars made British films. (2, p. 46)

The quality of British films continued to explain the inability of the British film industry to compete with the American film industry. Such arguments were frequently repeated. In July 1927, *Close Ups* argued that ''really good art is commercial, and the mob has a curious nose for what is good'' (quoted in 8, p. 306). The relationship between ''good art'' and financial success is clearly linked here. Underlying this analysis of the failure of the British film industry is a naive belief in the Free Market System in which the ''mob'' is able to identify ''good art'' and rewards such art financially. This assumes, of course, that the public had the opportunity to choose which films to watch.

Two points need to be addressed further to explain the failure of the British film industry. First, notions of ''quality'' are quite difficult to define and almost impossible to connect to the success of films in the Free Market System. Does the financial success of *Bachelor Party* or *Porky's* attest to their ''quality''? Quality leaves us with an ideological construction that inadequately explains the demise of the British film industry. The problems involved in making judgments about quality are clearer when Rachael Low notes: ''Many of the American films they praised so whimsically have stood the test of time no better than the British ones, and to later tastes appear naive in conception and boring in execution'' (8, p. 306).

Second, our case study points to a more complex explanation for the rejection of British films by the "mob." The tremendous flood of "quota quickies" by "British companies," which were American subsidiaries, only further set back the development of the British film industry. British talent was wasted on the production of films that would not be shown or would be hastily put together to fulfill the quotas established by the Cinematograph Acts.

While the imperialist interaction here is occurring between two rentier states, the destruction of the British film industry is crucial in developing theories of imperialism. The ability of imperialism to retard the development of the British film industry should consistently be brought to bear upon theories of imperialist development. Thus, Warren's claim that imperialism does not retard development nor encourage underdevelopment of the debtor nations must be carefully scrutinized. Warren writes:

> There is no evidence that any *process* of underdevelopment has occurred in modern times, and particularly in the period since the West made its impact on other continents. The evidence rather supports a contrary thesis: that a process of *development* has been taking place at least since the English industrial revolution, much accelerated in comparison with any earlier period; and that this has been the direct result of the impact of the West, of imperialism. (13, p. 113)

Warren's interest is in the relationship between the First and Third World; however, the ability of American imperialism to undermine, to this day, the British film industry throws such analysis into question. The "development" in Britain has been a development of an independent film industry that could compete with Hollywood for the British market.

Here, then, the contradiction of the quality explanation must be clarified: The "quality" of the British films was blamed for the demise of the British film industry when a large number of these films were produced by American-owned, British subsidiaries with the express intent of fulfilling the legal requirements only. Thus, British films of "poor quality" were not necessarily "British." This contradiction is pointed out in the *Moyne Report*:

> Production of cheap British films, made at the lowest cost, irrespective of quality, by or at the order of foreign-controlled (American) renters solely to enable them to show formal compliance with those provisions of the Act which relate to the renters' quota. Such films, known as "quota quickies" from the speed at which they were made, have tended to bring British films into disrepute. (quoted in 8, p. 105)

Such disrepute hurt the marketing of British films, both in Britain and internationally, which forced the British to accept Hollywood films.

CONCLUSION

In the opening speech at the British Film Institute's 1943 conference, "The Film in National Life," John Murray declared that the British cinema is foreign; it is American. He went even further by stating:

> I am free to confess that if I could not be a Britisher, I should be very well content to be American. Every time I have been in America I have felt that I could settle down easier and easier in America. Nevertheless, I complain that the cinema is American. Nations usually have got the colleges and the education systems they deserve. They usually have the cinema that they deserve. And if the cinema is blameworthy, so are the people. It is a measure of their merit, their need, their taste. But I object to having a cinema that some other nation deserves. (10, p. 4)

Whatever Britain "deserves" is left unstated, but illuminated here are the lateral and vertical alliances between the American film industry, the American government working through the State Department, and the MPPDA to secure the British film market for Hollywood. By destroying the ability of the British film industry to compete with Hollywood, the American film industry was able to open the British market to its monopolization.

However, the ability of the United States to secure this market was part of a larger effort to undermine the British position in the capitalist hierarchy. In taking advantage of both war situations and Britain's desperate need for capital and war materials, the United States gained a large number of concessions from the British State.

The possibility of another shift in the imperialist hierarchy is clear; structures are dynamic, not static. While this shift will not be an easy one to make, the U.S. may be seeing the onset of such a shift in the increasingly important trade deficit with Japan. Given the negotiating and agreements that are made within peacetime constraints, however, there is little chance of any major shifts in the hierarchy. Yet, major economic demands brought about by two world wars allowed the United States to take advantage of the British position. The paralyzing of the British cinema industry is but one of the imperialist state actions taken within this larger structural movement.

REFERENCES

1. Baran, P. A. and Sweezy, P. M. *Monopoly Capital: An Essay on the Economic and Social Order*. New York: Modern Reader, 1966.
2. Betts, E. *The Film Business: A History of British Cinema, 1896–1972*. London: George Allen and Unwin, 1973.
3. Brewer, A. *Marxist Theories of Imperialism: A Critical Survey*. Boston: Routledge & Kegan Paul, 1980.
4. Gold, D., Lo, C. Y. H., and Wright, E. O. "Recent Developments in Marxist Theories of the State." *Monthly Review*, October 1975, p. 49.
5. Hudson, M. *Super Imperialism: The Economic Strategy of The American Empire*. New York: Holt, Rinehart, and Winston, 1972.
6. Le Duc, D. R. "The Common Market Film Industry: Beyond Law and Economics." In G. Kinden (Ed.), *The American Film Industry: The Business of Motion Pictures*. Carbondale: IL: Southern Illinois University Press, 1982, pp. 361–372.
7. Lenin, V. I. *Imperialism, The Highest Stage of Capitalism*. Beijing: Foreign Languages Press, 1973.
8. Low, R. *The History of the British Film, 1918–1929*. London: George Allen & Unwin, 1971.
9. Moley, R. *The Hays Office*. Indianapolis: Bobbs-Merrill, 1945.

10. Murray, J. "Opening Session." *The Film in National Life. April 1943*. London: British Film Institute, 1943.
11. Sherman, H. *Foundations of Radical Political Economy*. Armonk, NY: M. E. Sharpe, Inc., 1987.
12. Therborn, G. *What Does The Ruling Class Do When It Rules?: State Apparatuses and State Power Under Feudalism, Capitalism and Socialism*. London: Verso, 1980.
13. Warren, B. *Imperialism: Pioneer of Capitalism*. London: NLB, 1980.

12

Fighting With Film: 16mm Amateur Film, World War II, and Participatory Realism 1941–1950*

Patricia R. Zimmermann

INTRODUCTION

> Motion picture cameramen, many from Hollywood, are marching and flying side by side with fighting men, shooting film instead of bullets (31, p. 324)

America fought World War II with both cameras and guns. If the guns downed Japanese or German planes, 16mm cameras not only raised morale in the shooting of propaganda films for the home front, but instilled a new conception of stylistic realism to Hollywood films. World War II did more to advertise and legitimate 16mm amateur equipment than Kodak or Bell and Howell, the major American manufacturers of amateur gear, could ever have predicted. Besides spurring technological progress and innovation in this smaller, cheaper gauge, World War II brought amateurs and Hollywood professionals together on the battlefields, and this intersection altered both technique and technology in the postwar period.

This period from 1941 to 1950 is extremely significant for film history. It illustrates how the social relations of production between amateurs and professionals, amateur technology, political context, and visual codes of realism combined, and through their coordination for the war effort, eventually transformed. By focusing on World War II combat and training cinematography by the United States, this study examines the interrelationship between amateurs, technology, stylistic codes, and political practice to trace their historical influence on Hollywood filmmaking. Rather than concentrating solely on 16mm technology as a causal explanation for this shift from studio realism to a more

*Archival research at George Eastman House for this project was partially funded by a summer research grant from Ithaca College.

immediate, hand-held shooting style, this study instead analyzes how three interdependent levels of discourse reformulated the definitions of both amateur and professional film: The social relations between Hollywood-trained professional cinematographers and a marginal subgroup like amateur hobbyists; the incorporation of ideologies of standardization and observability to systematize both personnel and equipment for political efficacy; and the level of aesthetic norms in film style. These three levels of discourse delineate the social, political, and aesthetic organization of 16mm technology during World War II. While each level is distinct, they are all nonetheless structured by an assumption of scientism rather than art. Observability, empirical analysis, prediction, reproduction, standardization, interchangeability, and a reliance on technology rather than a subjective, aesthetic response underpin all of their practices. This ideological contradiction between the empirical capacities of the camera and its more subjectively formulated uses for aesthetics and narrative expanded graphically during World War II: 16mm cameras were used for reconnaissance and engineering tests as well as for "artistic" documentation of the American war effort.

Although the relationship between the Hollywood film industry and the military suggests a broad range of historical questions, their connection is significant for this discussion of how amateur film equipment was utilized because it explains three important transformations. First, by World War II, the discussion of 16mm equipment and use begins to change from an emphasis on aesthetics in mass market and speciality amateur cinematography magazines like *Movie Maker* to an emphasis on how to use this equipment for the war in professional cinematography magazines like *American Cinematographer,* which began to consider the utilization of 16mm in order to fully exploit its flexibility and lightness, rather than forcing it into a more narrative mold. Second, this relationship demonstrated how Hollywood had gained cultural power as the standard setter for motion pictures, even to the point of training combat cameramen. And third, the intermingling between Hollywood and the military during the war provided an avenue for newly developed combat hand-held camera techniques to infiltrate Hollywood visual codes during the postwar period. The impact of this conjunction between Hollywood and combat photographic work was to exert a new visual standard based on audience participation rather than on the codes of pictorial harmony and composition based on natural lines. These changes between technology, social groups, standardization of procedures, equipment and personnel, and style demonstrate how historical transformation occurs both within each level and between each separate discourse.

First, on the level of technology, World War II precipitated some major changes in amateur film because of its massive incorporation of 16mm amateur film equipment for military work. Although substandard film technology and Hollywood narrative style had functioned as powerful constituents of the cultural definition of amateur film during the 1920s and 1930s in amateur movie-making magazines and columns, by 1942 the war had dramatically repositioned amateur film technology as a more standard medium and modified aesthetic norms toward more documentary-like techniques.

Through the military's use of 16mm film, this amateur gauge gradually shifted its social and cultural position from a hobbyist's medium to a semi-professional one. It would emerge from the war as a more legitimate, standardized, and utilitarian technology. This merger of empiricism and realism—the ideology of the eye and direct observation as the extreme exaggeration of the scientific application of the camera—depended on a notion of the camera as an infallible instrument of measurement, as a tool. This cinematic style anticipated the development of cinema verite in the 1950s. "Equipment now in use by the Army and Navy, developed from the necessities of war expediency, cannot help contributing to the motion picture industry a new and much needed mechanical flexibility and simplicity," James Wong Howe (38, p. 10), the famous Hollywood cinematographer, predicted, but cautioned that the construction of the story would always remain the primary objective of the cinematographer. While these technological and aesthetic changes forged a new technical legitimacy for 16mm and new standards of realism for Hollywood films, military uses of amateur film technology demonstrated how massive alterations in the orientation of 16mm could occur as a result of its enlistment into the war effort, the dominant ideology, and the state. With Hollywood and the military coordinating the filming of the war, the military directed and dominated the use of amateur film equipment.

Secondly, on the level of social relations, the relationship between Hollywood professionals and the United States military during World War II has been well-documented. For example, in 1945 the editors of *Look* magazine published an account heralding Hollywood's patriotism in cooperating with the motion picture needs of the military called *From Movie Lot to Beachhead.* This book described how Hollywood actors entertained the troops, how directors made training films, how actors enlisted, and how Hollywood professionals contributed to the training of cameramen fin the Army Signal Corps. According to this account, one-sixth of all people involved in the production, distribution, and exhibition of motion pictures were in the armed services. This figure represented 40,000 out of a total number of 240,000 industry workers and included 132 members of the Screen Directors' Guild, 230 members of the Screen Writers' Guild, 40 cameramen, 75 electricians and sound technicians, 453 film technicians, and 80 machinists (49). The military, in particular the Army Signal Corps, recruited not only amateur equipment but amateur filmmakers as well.

Thirdly, despite the new fluidity between amateurs and professionals in the Army Signal Corps, an ideology of scientism directed their relationship to 16mm technology in two ways. Not only was equipment standardized and interchangeable, but so were its operators, trained in the rationalized procedures of combat photography to excise subjectivity. In addition, the reception of these films was oriented to mass producing standardized responses in spectators. For example, the training of bomber pilots through repeated viewings and the utilization of film as empirical evidence for observation, analysis, and prediction. The principles of scientific management, which had sought to instill industry with higher productivity through efficiency, were transferred to the war.

Fourth, on the level of aesthetics, the more compact and flexible 16mm technology was deployed because of the uncertainties of combat photography, inducing a major reversal to the edicts of control and pre-planning of traditional Hollywood narrative style through a reinsertion of spontaneous shooting on the battlefield. Skewing more and more away from the professional norm of pictorialist compositional harmony because of the unpredictability of the war, this filming technique established a new sort of untampered, visceral, photographic realism as a professional standard. This hand-held shooting style, adamantly discouraged in the 1920s and 1930s by amateur advice writers, was considered by professional cinematographers a good technique to stimulate increased audience participation. This shift in the discourse on aesthetic codes constituted an example of amateur film use, or more specifically, in this case technology, contributing to a change in professional film aesthetics.

For example, in a 1944 *American Cinematographer* piece, James Wong Howe asserted that the proliferation of documentary films during World War II trained audiences to better ascertain cinematic realism. He wrote "the audience cannot help comparing them (newsreels from the front and narrative films) and can draw only one conclusion: that the Hollywood concept is artificial and therefore unbelievable," but cautioned that this documentary "perfection" had its own rules: "Perfect, that is, in realistic terms, certainly not perfect in Hollywood terms" (38, p. 10).

To map these complex changes more specifically, this chapter analyzes the discourse on World War II shooting in professional and amateur cinematography magazines, U.S. government sources, engineering journals, and general circulation publications according to these three levels of the social relations of production, the inscription of an ideology of scientism, and the transformation of aesthetic norms.

HISTORICAL CONTEXT OF DOCUMENTARY CONVENTIONS

To fully understand the significance of this dramatic shift towards a more participatory and less controlled standard of realism, it is first necessary to elaborate the historical context of what were popularly held documentary visual conventions to situate the unique and important impact of the use of amateur film technology by the Army Signal Corps. These pre-planned, controlled norms, which evoked the aesthetics of pictorialism by invoking subjectivity, spread over a wide range of media from documentary filmmaking, propaganda films, newsreels, broadcasting, commercial still photography, and government directives, illustrating the expanse and grip of this soon-to-be dislodged ideology.

Documentary historians have expounded on the contributions of feature film directors like William Wyler, John Huston, and Frank Capra, during World War II, who shot combat footage and directed training films. Perhaps the most celebrated of all was Hollywood director Frank Capra's *Why We Fight* series—compilation documentaries whose footage was culled from captured enemy combat footage. Capra pulled footage from such diverse documentary filmmakers as Humphrey Jennings, Joris Ivens, Leni Riefenstahl, and Ian Watt. Erik Barnouw, in his *Documentary: A History of the Non-Fiction Film*, has noted that the *Why We Fight* series relied on fictionalized recreations to "fill in" when actuality footage was not available (9). Joris Ivens, an independent filmmaker who later joined the Capra unit, had photographed the Spanish Civil War extensively, and was one of the few independent documentary filmmakers to even photograph wars on the front. Most documentary filmmakers up to that time selected more romantic, stylized topics that conformed to the tenets of pictorialism, typified in films like Pare Lorentz's *The River* (U.S. Dept. of Agriculture, 1937). In fact, the documentary explosion of the 1930s—in journalism, film, photography, and eyewitness accounts—was characterized by a social commitment elaborated with a highly stylized and above all personalized method. Feeling and experience were elevated above accuracy or intimacy. With their emphasis on composition and sorrowful faces and pity, Margaret Bourke-White's photographs of migrant workers stand as consummate examples of this emotional aesthetic (68). Thus, documentary film did not extinguish narrative control and emotional states.

If we analyze the discourse on documentary camera technique as displayed in *American Cinematographer*, a magazine geared to professional film technicians, its aesthetic directives also emulated Hollywood style. Interest in documentary form escalated with World War II, with John Grierson and Joris Ivens writing essays for *American Cinematographer* on documentary form. In 1937, in an article called "Amateur Film Patterned from Prizewinners" in *American Cinematographer*, Barry Staley encouraged amateurs to produce documentaries, but hastened to add that the form required more thought and planning than a haphazard "celluloid scrapbook of events" (66). By 1942, both *American Cinematographer* and *Movie Makers* encouraged amateurs who owned 16mm equipment to produce Civil Defense Films, since the Army used 16mm projection equipment.[1] The often repeated axiom "make your films authentic" was offered as an incentive to use narrative techniques to upgrade the credibility of the topic. Mobilizing public opinion through dramatization of fact—documentary, as described by many of these professional cinematographers in the pages of *American Cinematographer*—expressed ideas but still told sequential stories. Again, pre-planning to work out visual ideas became crucial and

[1] For examples of the arguments *American Cinematographer* made to encourage amateurs to produce defense films rather than home movies see (13, 25, 32, 69).

curtailed more spontaneous on-the-spot shooting.[2] According to their view, the main difference between Hollywood narrative films and documentaries was in the relation of their story to technique: They assumed that everything in Hollywood narratives propped up the story or contributed to its exposition, while every technique and story in documentaries supposedly supported an abstract, social idea.

These attitudes about the function of compositional harmony were not limited to Hollywood cinematographers. John Grierson, the British documentary producer, writing in *American Cinematographer*, continued, for instance, to advance the idea of dramatic elements beyond the actuality footage. He was less concerned with documentary style—how images were composed on the screen—than with their effects. In an article called "Documentary Films in War Time," published in *American Cinematographer* in 1942, he wrote:

> We have more difficult duty—the most difficult of all from a mental point of view—of shaping from our war observations on every front—both military and civilian—the strategic pattern of highly complex events . . . *in simple dramatic patterns of thought and feeling*. (my emphasis, 30, p. 10)

Even Joris Ivens, who had pioneered some forms of combat shooting in his *The Spanish Earth* (Contemporary Historians, Inc., 1937) concurred, as illustrated in this 1942 *American Cinematographer* piece: "Only as long as your subject is firmly connected with dramatic reality, can the film you are making develop you and your co-workers artistically." Although Ivens felt that the on-the-spot filming of documentary constituted its visual force, he advanced that he had no qualms about re-enactments in order to deliver "an emotional presentation of fact" (42).

Richard Meran Barsam, describing World War II documentary films in his *Non-Fiction Film: A Critical History,* observed that Hollywood professional and independent documentary filmmakers worked on combat films, but did not mention the infusion of amateurs. He further explained that these combat films were shaped into propaganda films for military and domestic use. Barsam praised the realistic shock value of the war scenes but also noted their gradual improvement in technique, organization, and narrative largely as a result of the influx of Hollywood theatrical film technicians (10). According to the official history of the Signal Corps, called *The Signal Corps: The Test,* the training of combat motion picture cameramen reiterated the need for "story coverage" on assignments, with trainees getting news assignments to plan out as part of their instruction. In addition, Darryl F. Zanuck, vice-president of Twentieth Century-Fox and an officer of the Research Council of the Academy of Motion Picture Arts and Sciences, helped to reorganize the training film division of the Corps along Hollywood lines, commenting in a report that these training films needed

[2] For further discussion of how Hollywood cinematographers emphasized dramatization and narrative techniques for documentary film see (11, 44, 63, 64).

humor and professional actors. For the invasion of North Africa in 1942, Zanuck organized special photographic detachments to document assault landings and land action. They shot over 5,000 feet of film. As an example of this influence of Hollywood style, Zanuck's response to the invasion footage was "I don't suppose our war scenes will look as savage and realistic as those we usually make on the backlot, but then you can't have everything" (74, p. 396). The official military history of the Signal Corps recounts, for instance, that combat cinematographers in the early stages of the war envied the Germans, whose staged battle scenes they thought provided a more authentic screen image than their documentary footage, often shot, they complained, from the worst angle because the enemy occupied the better angle.[3] Rather than trying to mirror "reality," it appeared that military documentary and even some combat films in the early stages of the war conversely strove for Hollywood narrative style, similar to the discourse on amateur films of the 1920s and 1930s.

This government-produced combat footage was supplied to newsreel companies. The relationship between newsreel companies and the military was particularly close. In 1941 at the Fort Monmouth Training Film Production Laboratory of the Signal Corps School, *The March of Time* began a course in movie filming and editing. Many professional cinematographers and newsreelers were eliminated from the draft due to age, making it difficult for the Signal Corps to find inductees with previous professional photographic experience to meet the increased demands for war coverage by the military (71, p. 224; 74, p. 394–396). Although some of the cameramen in the Army Signal Corps and the Navy received their initial training from companies such as *The March of Time* and *Fox Movietone*, in the first year of the war, the newsreels themselves did not survive autonomously during World War II. The government provided a majority of combat footage, newsreels from different companies resembled each other and often utilized the same footage, film was censored in Washington, reel length was reduced due to raw stock shortages, and controversial issues disappeared.

These documentary norms established a context for not only formal aesthetic rules, but for the social relations between the amateur and the professional to be characterized by pictorial and Hollywood domination of amateur practice. However, during the war, the structure of their relationship was altered towards a more reciprocal exchange due to constraints on technology and personnel.

TECHNOLOGY

Within this aesthetic context of narrative, the influence of the use of amateur film technology in combat on notions of realism was enormous. Ironically, this postwar discursive and aesthetic trend towards a less controlled, more sponta-

[3] For the Signal Corps point of view concerning the difficulties of obtaining good angles in combat shooting see (71, 74).

neous form of shooting was not generated from the aesthetic level, but from procedures that invoked the scientific standards of industrial capitalism. In this environment, 16mm technology went to war with B-17s and was used as a scientific tool for experimental purposes, for training, and for reconnaissance. Small, portable cameras were as necessary as radar to analyze enemy equipment and to record battles. Through these scientific procedures a discourse on realism was appended to camera technology.

Indeed, the employment of lighter weight, hand-held equipment, like Bell and Howell's 35mm Eyemos and 16mm Filmos, was encouraged by combat cinematographers, who (according to military sources) found them easier to operate under adverse conditions, more durable under changing climates than most other cameras, and more portable. Because Bell and Howell and Eastman Kodak, whose Cine-Kodak Special was also used for combat, had converted to war production, these cameras were in short supply. Along with other manufacturers, Eastman Kodak had discontinued amateur camera production for 1941 and 1942, due to shortages in metal and optics. Consequently, the Signal Corps and the War Activities Committee asked hobbyists to sell their equipment, especially 16mm projectors to be used for training purposes. The official military history of the Signal Corps reasoned that the Signal Corps had lacked a plan for pre-war procurement of photographic equipment, and, consequently, aluminum shortages forced it to purchase cameras of substandard design.[4]

This military control of amateur film technology was also evidenced with amateur stock. By August of 1942, the War Production Board froze all motion picture film, requiring producers to apply for authority to acquire unexposed film because the chemicals in film stock were also required for munitions production. By October, commercial producers saw a 24 percent reduction in stock availability. While Eastman Kodak began rationing film supplies to dealers in October of 1942, by early 1943, the War Production Board cut the production of amateur film for consumers by 50 percent. This reduction, according to photographic dealers, precipitated a corresponding 50 percent decline in the amateur hobbyist market. By 1945, only one million feet of amateur film stock was shot by hobbyists, compared to an average of 65 million feet in the years before the war. In addition, the U.S. government issued calls for amateur film and photographs shot outside the United States to be registered and catalogued.[5] Responding to this directive, *Movie Makers*, an amateur filmmaking magazine, proclaimed in an April 1942 editorial: "Our government recognizes our hobby as a national

---

[4] For discussion about how shortages of standard cameras forced the military into purchasing substandard amateur equipment see (18, 24, 57, 61, 74 [pp. 402–411], 78).

[5] For discussion of raw stock shortages and their impact on amateur film see (5, 18, 22, 26, 53, 56, 58, 77, 81). By January of 1943, *Movie Makers*, the magazine for amateur filmmakers, ran a monthly column that spanned the war years called "Washington Film News." This column discussed government 16mm film activity and its impact on amateurs.

weapon, and it calls upon us to use that weapon intelligently and actively, under its direction to win the war'' (72, p. 143). The relationship between amateurs and professionals was reconfigured. 16mm camera and film stock was directed almost entirely towards the military. The amateur hobbyist market declined significantly, and those who did not sell their cameras to the government were urged by amateur magazines to make civil defense films. Because the substandard and standard gauges were employed by the military, and because the category of amateur diminished, the boundaries between amateur and professional diffused. The combination of the rapidly multiplying needs of the military for still and motion picture coverage of the war for reconnaissance, training information, and public relations, and the resulting shortages in raw stock and cameras, explained why amateur cinema magazines and professional magazines shifted their public discourse from aesthetics to combat and the war. Of course, the larger context of the national mobilization towards the war effort set the tone for this shift in orientation as well.

THE SOCIAL RELATIONSHIP BETWEEN AMATEURS AND PROFESSIONALS

With personnel, Hollywood and amateurs intermingled. Many A.S.C. members served in the Signal Corps.[6] Indeed, many wartime covers of *American Cinematographer* showed battle scenes being shot by Hollywood-like crews (76). Consequently, this new form of realism may have been more of a consequence of lack of training, equipment, and war contingency than anything else: ''We tried to obtain as much realism as possible, which required the fastest available film. Shooting army locations in wartime prevents the use of lights with the freedom associated with Hollywood,'' a Hollywood cinematographer named Ray Fernstrom serving in the Army Signal Corps explained in *American Cinematographer* (23, p. 406).

Despite their grand claims, newsreel companies were not the major organizations to train the Army Signal Corps, although some of the former younger employees may have joined it during the war. Hollywood mass-produced military cameramen, thus increasing its domination as it temporarily created more mobility between amateurs and professionals. The Research Council of the Academy of Motion Picture Arts and Sciences, the American Society of Cinematographers, the International Photographers Local 659 of I.A.T.S.E., and technical experts from film manufacturing companies provided intensive six-week cinematography courses to amateurs enlisted in the Army Signal Corps. Ironically, trainees learned how to shoot in the field from studio exterior experts. Perhaps, more significantly, the course was the first time that the A.S.C. offered

[6] For example, *American Cinematographer* listed A.S.C. members serving in the Army Signal Corps (8). Military sources also discuss Hollywood personnel serving in the Signal Corps (71, 73).

camera training of any kind. They claimed in a June 1942 *American Cinematographer* article called "A.S.C. and Academy to Train Cameramen for Military Service" that:

> Today, a motion picture section is an integral part of every military unit . . . unfortunately, this country has a great untapped reserve of capable cinematographic talent among *amateurs and semi-professionals—men who thought they may not have made a career out of photography, have yet attained great skill with their 16mm and 8mm cameras.* (my emphasis, 7)

This military, assembly-line production of cinematographers was perhaps best exemplified in a 1943 picture of Marine cameramen lined up in uniform on a studio back lot in formation, holding their tripods like guns, facing their Hollywood instructors. These trainees learned only exterior techniques; the instructors bypassed lighting and interior shooting, not required for shooting in combat (51).

The military needed as many competent camerapersons as possible to collect reconnaissance and combat footage and to maintain an effective organization. Skills not only had to be interchangeable, but standardized. In a June 1942 article called "Navy's Use of Motion Picture Films for Training Purposes" in the *Journal of the Society of Motion Picture Engineers,* Walter Exton saw the training of military recruits and the training of Signal Corps cinematographers as fulfilling identical functions: "The interchangeability of men is of importance to the efficiency of the fleet" (20, p. 504). It was paramount for the coordination of photography units that camera skills be interchangeable, standardized, and homogenized, just like industrial machinery. This standardization of producers, a form of professionalism, also temporarily instigated a fluidity between amateurs and professionals, although the military and Hollywood controlled and commandeered it.

THE IDEOLOGY OF SCIENTISM

However, this training of camerapersons on the social level was permeated with scientism on the ideological level. Rather than a subjective response to the subject matter as promoted by pictorialism, this scientism erected standards of technological and empirical proficiency, efficient production, and the reproduction of sensory experience.

Of course, it is important to note that this relationship between scientific pursuits and photographic reproduction was not a new development, but was a primary use of photography since its inception. It was only with the rise of the pictorialist movement in the late 19th century that scientific and industrial uses of photography were distinguished from more subjective, high art expressions. During the period of World War II, this scientism promoting observation and analysis temporarily dislodged individual artistic notions of cinematography. Instead of positioning cameras as a means to extract inner truths, the military elevated the camera into a necessary observational tool, more critical to the war than its fallible, human operators. This orientation towards empiricism had a particular ideological effect on amateur technology. The military reorganized the discursive framework of amateur technology away from subjectivity, leisure, art, and the idylls of family life and towards rationality, objectivity, observation, and science. In this movement, the political needs of the war dissolved amateur film's position as a consumer commodity and instead identified it with the scientific axioms of corporate capitalism. Rather than a chronicler of human interaction, amateur cameras became a technology to implement scientism. Thus, the military discursively and practically legitimated substandard and smaller 16mm equipment by endowing it with a crucial goal: victory through technology.

These scientific principles of observation and analysis were also articulated in the military's use of amateur cameras as empirical instruments: "We make movies of tests when the action involved is too fast, too complicated, or too remote for accurate observation with the human eye," explained a writer in the June 1942 issue of the *Journal of Motion Picture Engineers* (20, p. 504). 16mm Filmos and 35mm Eyemos measured airplane takeoffs and landings, deciphered propeller problems, followed bombs, did structural tests on planes, and, after the war, even studied the atomic blasts at Bikini Island with the largest film crew in history. A 1943 piece by a major in the Army Air Force First Motion Picture Unit in *American Photographer* explained this empirical function of cinematography could save "months of training and a plane worth hundreds of thousands of dollars (6, p. 363).[7]

By connecting 16mm technology to guns, technological and scientific capacities were emphasized over proper aesthetic execution and control. The analogy between cameras and guns was perhaps most explicitly revealed in a 1938 *American Cinematographer* article demonstrating how a gun lock could replace a tripod. Leica's were mounted on rifle stocks, enabling the amateur to obtain rock steady shots. Military use also influenced amateur articles. An amateur motion picture aficionado in a 1942 *American Cinematographer* story called "Shooting Action Movies With a Gunstock Mount" even suggested that amateurs attach their Eyemos and Filmos to guns in order to pan more smoothly—like combat "sharpshooters" filming from foxholes. These anecdotes evidenced a discursive shift from an artistic cinematic consciousness located in the filmmaker to an infatuation with technology as the center of filmmaking activity. However, these metaphorical connections were duplicated in the training of combat photographers and cinematographers, where Signal Corps training schools taught them to carry and shoot both weapons and guns simultaneously, a task most Hollywood cinematographers did not need to master.[8]

Another facet of this scientific positioning of amateur film that dispelled

[7] For further, more detailed examples of the military's use of cameras as empirical instruments see (12, 27, 46, 50, 59, 79).

[8] For examples of this conflation of cameras and guns see (34, 48, 73, 74).

individual, emotional artistry and facilitated its move into less controlled aesthetic technique was its use in the production of interactive training films. For example, with over 300 theaters, three distribution exchanges, and 1,000 feature programs in circulation in both 16mm and 35mm as early as 1932, the Navy was equipped to show a vast amount of training films. Some ships were even dubbed "floating studios," with not only production facilities, but processing as well. Films of target practices trained gunners and spotters, substituting film for experience and reenacting battles with actuality footage. These simulations created an odd mixture of audience participation, realism, and recreation, much like computer war games currently in vogue. In the 1930s, the military screened historical war footage to analyze tactics and advocated the creation of a continuous record of all divisions in future confrontations. According to the official military history of the Signal Corps, film production did not become a high priority until World War II, when most footage shot by cameramen was slated for use in the making of films for public screenings to provide updates on the war. By 1943, an article in *International Projectionist* called "16mm vs 35mm Projection in Army Training Camps" reflected that the military had already contemplated the effects of its wide usage of 16mm technology on civilian industry, given a surplus of camerapersons and equipment.[9]

16mm technology was not only aligned with scientism, but with the efficiency requirements of industrial production. Military training films relied on tried and true Hollywood style production methods—full crews, pre-production planning, scripts, emotional appeal—which were analyzed in the pages of the *Journal of the Society of Motion Picture Engineers*.[10] However, the smaller gauge equipment permitted more efficiency in these productions according to Carl Preyer, A.S.C., in his article "Movie Report on Defense Programs" in a 1943 *American Cinematographer*:

> The technical requirements of such a small production unit is rather confusing to those accustomed to Hollywood standards. The first requirement is absolute mobility, to travel cheaply and quickly under any conditions—plane, auto, boat . . . Equipment must be reduced to a minimum both as to camera equipment and lighting equipment for interiors. (60, p. 445)

TRANSFORMATION OF AESTHETIC NORMS

What was the mechanism, then, that associated shaky, moving camerawork with realism during World War II? As the third level of analysis, this transformation of the aesthetic norms of realism resulted from technological innovation displac-

---

[9] For further examples of the military's use of 16mm film for training see (19, 37, 54, 65, 71, 73, 75).

[10] Discussion of the relationship between industrial efficiency, military needs, and Hollywood style production can be found in (14, 15, 21, 29, 35, 47).

ing camera operators, the responses of lightweight cameras to war conditions, and combat photography's unique priorities. Subject to the uncontrolled conditions of war, field cinematography reconstituted realist codes towards a more visceral, participatory, and sensory model.

The combat film unit performed three military tasks: to aid in saving the lives of men, to expose any technological weakness of the enemy, and to reveal the enemy's war machines. The goal was primarily tactical and operational. Using 16mm cameras on B-17s, cameramen, ironically enough, were also trained as gunners so that they could "drop their cameras for a gun" if the time came when they did not have to "shoot to preserve the war" (43, p. 147; 52, p. 104).

War-time needs for obtaining footage to replicate experience for simulation gunnery training, for remote-control mechanisms, and for efficiency altered 16mm technology, and effected a change in visual style. Because the camera operator was either nonexistent, inconsequential in relation to content, or subservient to mobility and speed, the images produced reflected documentation and replication of experience rather than compositional elegance. Subject matter replaced subjectivity. The association between cameras and guns strengthened when cameras were inserted on machine gun mounts in bomber planes and operated by pilots. The war also propelled Hollywood camera designers to create 35mm and 16mm hand-held cameras in gunstock forms with pistol grips—the Cunningham Combat camera with studio-type pilot pin registering movement is an outstanding example. Other technologies also were developed for combat photography: the continuous step printer that could churn out 1,000 prints per hour, and camera remote controls first developed by an amateur were improved. Remote-control mechanisms for cameras emphasized this scientific application of World War II film activity; the connection between thought and narrative was displaced by more efficient technological designs. In fact, by May of 1942, an A.S.C. cinematographer writing in *American Cinematographer* recommended 16mm Filmos over Akeley, DeBrie, or studio Mitchells, simply because they did not require any set-up time. These suggested changes were clearly the result of experience in the field. For example, after Darryl Zanuck realized that the massive motion picture crew mounted for the North African invasion was not efficient, crews were reduced to one motion picture and one still photographer to increase their mobility.[11]

These light, hand-held 16mm and 35mm cameras, more flexible than tripod-mounted 35mm DeVry cameras, bounded and shook during turbulence, anti-aircraft fire, or combat. James Wong Howe's photography in Hollywood military dramas imitated this style in interior shots of airplanes by shaking the camera to simulate turbulence. This "camera rattling," once regarded as an amateur transgression against Hollywood conventions of unified composition and organi-

---

[11] Assessments of the technological limitations and advantages of 16mm for combat field cinematography can be found in (2, 17, 33, 67, 70, 74).

zation, was reinterpreted as experiential, audience-directed, participatory realism when employed in commercial film. For example, in a 1944 *Journal of the Society of Motion Picture Engineers* article entitled "Cinematography Goes to War," W. R. McGee lamented:

> I might add that flak (anti-aircraft explosions) is the cameraman's nemesis. Its concussions bounce the ship sot hat the resulting films are jerky. It's difficult enough to shoot good films from a flying ship with a hand held camera, but when flak enters the picture the hazards are multiplied.
>
> Sometimes these concussions result in a "jump." An excellent example of this appeared in *The Battle of Midway* film. You may recall one scene in which the film jumped an entire frame. This was probably caused by FLAK. (52, p. 105)

The Battle of Midway (1942), shot and directed by John Ford and his crew with 16mm cameras, won the Documentary Short Subject Oscar in 1942. An Eastman Kodak Cine-Kodak Ad in 1943 exploited the turbulent images as evidence for their superior cameras, further emphasizing technology over operator and image instability for experience over composition: "You may have noticed that the movie was rough and jerky in spots—that was because the cameramen were reeling under the concussions" (16, p. 260, 62).

The compactness of Eyemos and Filmos allowed cameramen to get into filmic action almost instantly. Due to its small size and lightness, 16mm equipment was easier to hand-hold and to carry anywhere under the most severe conditions, compared to larger, 35mm professional cameras. Thus, the cinematic preconsciousness demanded of amateurs in aesthetic discourse before the war appeared to collapse with combat expediency. The camera, the battle, and the operator were unified in a relationship that lacked time to execute shots with planning or control. In fact, some Hollywood technicians wondered how to achieve these stupendous "special effects." Lieutenant Arthur Arling, U.S.N.R., A.S.C., in his October 1943 piece, "Cameramen in Uniform," which appeared in *American Cinematographer*, justified the use of less than perfect camerawork:

> The first screening of the 16mm film revealed a very disturbing fault: the violent concussion of the exploding bombs had caused the film to jump out of frame in the camera aperture, but fortunately it regained its normal frame after a few feet. At first the film didn't seem usable, but since no other film of the explosions were to be had we put them in just as they were and the result, as seen in the public release of *The Battle of Midway*, caused considerable comment by several Hollywood technicians who thought we had done this optically just to produce this effect. (6, p. 363)

Personal accounts of combat cameramen in *American Cinematographer* underlined how this chaotic composition came about. Cameramen were constantly reacting to the battle and the enemy to save their own lives, and justified "cinematic mistakes," omissions, and less than stable camerawork with explanations of their daring and courage. All the accounts heralded the cameramen's speed in reacting cinematically to the enemy's advances, with little regard for studio technique. No story or preplanning to achieve pictorial harmony could be performed here; the point was to "capture the enemy on film," to make a record, not a narrative film with emotional appeal. As one writer in *Theater Arts* reasoned in 1944, "in combat, facts are incapable of rearrangement to suit a plot, nor can actors be set arbitrarily for the most satisfactory camera angle. There is no screenplay written in advance. The combat photographer is forced by the circumstances of his profession to speak his piece in pictures" (41, p. 344).

The advertising and marketing departments of Bell and Howell exploited this influx of amateur and professional filmmaking equipment into the war effort to garner increased legitimacy for their products, particularly 16mm substandard equipment. In corporate ads placed in *American Cinematographer*, *Personal Movies*, newspapers, and other more national magazines, the Filmo and Eyemo were placed against an ideal backdrop to underline their superior manufacturing—World War II combat. These ads also exhibited a shift from an aesthetic discourse that linked amateur cameras with the leisure time of nuclear families to a primarily male technological discourse associated with war. In this strategy, the camera's use replaced preplanning for narrative. Instead, it transformed into an aggressive recording instrument that directly experienced the war, foreshadowing the participatory realism that surfaced in actual documentary and feature film imagery.

According to corporate ads, Eyemos had "versatility and stamina on the front," "matched the war's lightning pace," were "the camera for men of action," "the aircorps super snooper," and ignored "falls, mud, jars, shocks and vibration." In another ad, H. S. "Newsreel" Wong attested that he preferred an Eyemo because it was "rugged and always ready for action." Amateur cameras also were presented as possessing memories during World War II: "This Eyemo remembers Pearl Harbor," "Eyemos are shooting Japanese," "Eyemo's War Began Years Ago." Cine-Kodaks, once passively recording family history, now were dubbed "the fighting cine-kodaks" (36).

Corporate advertisements for 16mm cameras suggested that technology, rather than operators, actually experienced the war. An ideology of technological infallibility replaced a pervasive ideology that the amateur should use the technology to imitate Hollywood studio style. Just as early writers on amateur film debated whether professionalism and capitalism would mechanize people and stultify them with a technocratic consciousness, the context of World War II anthropomorphised cameras. These ads asserted the superiority of cameras over people; they could secure images beyond the reaches of normal human capacities like bombing, technical information, and combat recording. Cameras, rather than operators, possessed cognitive abilities to decipher the war. The camera directly experienced the war and recorded these realistic images. This advertising naturalized camera technology by implicitly arguing it could both improve upon and replace human attributes. In effect, with camera operators removed or rendered insignificant, an image was created that there was an unmediated connection between cameras and subject. Because they appeared to lack human interference, the images of war could be coded as more accurately realistic.

The combination of scientific use, smallness, and lack of trained camera people shooting in combat situations contributed to a change in codes of realism towards a more spontaneous, less controlled style reserved exclusively for professionals. Although the war increased the possibilities for fluidity between amateur and professional film, in terms of both technology, style, and producers, the basic structure of this movement was dominated by Hollywood and the military. However, the war did significantly alter 16mm practice on the level of standardization for both technology and this hand-held shooting style, one of the major changes in the discourse on amateur film in its history.

> When you pan or tilt a camera on a tripod, as we do today with the 35mm, it is quite different from panning to tilting by hand. Hand tilting and panning is more sensitive. Such movements are often very important to the story and they should never be obvious as they often are . . . The more we keep artificial and obvious movements out of the camera in telling a story, the less disturbing it is to the audience. The spectator should never be conscious of the mechanics of a movie . . . *Jimmy's arguments in favor of the 16mm camera's more natural and realistic documentation of its subject matter is borned out by the vivid combat photography that slashes across the nation's newsreel screens everyday.* (my emphasis, 38, p. 32)

As this quotation from James Wong Howe in a 1944 *American Cinematographer* postwar article shows, following World War II narrative concerns submerged the more reflexive element of "realistic" camera technique. Reviewers of these films employing this shaky camerawork noted how the lack of planning in the execution of shots contributed to their immediacy and realism. *Movie Makers* explained in 1943 that these realistic, unsteady pans were done without a tripod, as the cameramen happened upon them, while a writer in the *Nation* in 1945 argued that these films brought the war home because they could substitute visual experience for actual experience. James Agee, writing in the *Nation* in 1944 and 1945, responded to these combat films by reflecting on their "petrifying immediacy." Unlike most writers reviewing war footage who saluted this advance in realistic, participatory shooting simulating the war, Agee questioned its ethics. Likening this footage to pornography, he queried the morality of using images of men killing each other to nurture patriotism (3, 4, 45, 55). Within this discursive and practical framework, the codes of realism changed from lighting and composition to unplanned shooting, immediacy, camera jolts to events, and a simulation of experience promoting a more participatory spectatorship.

CONCLUSION

The social relations of production between amateurs and professionals, the inscription of an ideology of scientism, and the transformation of aesthetic norms cultivated important shifts in the discourse and practice of amateur and professional film. The cultural position and discourse of amateur film technology and amateur filmmaking was altered by World War II. The definition of amateur shifted from an aesthetic base to a technological identity. Amateur film technology was reframed within the attributes of science—observation, analysis, recording, efficiency—serving to expel any lingering notions of composition, artistry, or individualism. Because of its flexibility, compactness, and lightness, amateur technology was easily adapted to the efficiency demands of combat cinematography. The widespread usage of this amateur gauge during the war legitimated 16mm through increased standardization and led to attempts to further "professionalize" amateur equipment by adding more technological control to cameras. For Hollywood filmmaking, the war-time use of amateur gear and nonprofessional shooting styles pushed studios towards location shooting rather than sets, established a war archive for Hollywood studios to check their footage for accuracy, and instituted a sort of realistic simulation narrative style that co-opted combat technique into an invisible, mechanically induced viewing experience.

This postwar period demonstrated an inversion of the previous, almost continuous 20-year trend of Hollywood's downward domination and hierarchicalization of amateur films: It incorporated technologies and styles precipitated through the employment of amateur film technology and the public exhibition of combat films by the military during World War II. Although this co-optation and adaptation of smaller technologies and hand-held style slightly shifted Hollywood style away from compositional standards derived from photographic pictorialism, it did not represent an increased legitimation of amateur filmmaking. Rather, it ransacked combat cinematography shot with more mobile equipment for technical and stylistic innovations, but then "professionalized" these forms by encircling them within the dominant structures of Hollywood narrative and technical expertise. This rendered the assumed indigenous, hand-held, spontaneous style one might assume would become a new aesthetic for amateurs beyond the reach of amateurs themselves. Hollywood professionals could "perfect" the execution of this more realistic and intimate technique by studying, duplicating, and even improving upon combat footage. In this sense, professionals now controlled naturalism through a legitimation of technology and style, thus metamorphising its spontaneous efficient shooting style into an example of professional technical manipulation and control.

One of the initial mechanisms of this co-optation of amateur film practice was its standardization, which hypothetically could increase access to commercial filmmaking because of its interchangeability. Before the war, 16mm equipment was only standardized in relation to film gauge perforations. Confronted by the military's enormous photographic needs, 16mm manufacturing capacity increased and accelerated, just as in the radio and electronics industries. To facilitate equipment production and to further standardize filmmaking training, the equipment needed to be as interchangeable as the combat photographers who operated it. In addition, equipment broke down more easily in wartime situations, and so standardization of parts was crucial. On December 15, 1943, the

Society of Motion Picture Engineers, together with the Signal Corps, the Army Air Force, Army Engineer Corps, and the Navy and Marine Corps, created the War Standards Committee. Experienced motion picture engineers who formerly solved Hollywood technical problems now answered the needs of the military.[12] 16mm was now on its way out of amateur ranks and into the realm of professionalism.

The Signal Corps' use of 16mm also influenced Hollywood sets to lean towards a more realistic construction. With wartime restrictions of $5,000 worth of new material per picture, many studios moved to shooting in actual locations and used more documentary rear-screen projection. This change from elaborate sets to pared down productions was hailed as more "realistic" by both set designers and directors. This trend also maximized the camera's ability to "suggest" and elevated cinematography to a vital narrative service. Directors wanted camera work to be "down-to-earth." According to a 1945 *American Cinematographer* assessment of postwar films, shooting in actual towns, factories, or battlefields, time constraints, and an impulse to employ documentary style forced cinematographers to eliminate complicated lighting schemes and to light in a flatter style (28).

This tendency toward more realism and authenticity in Hollywood films reached its apex with the formation of the Academy War Film Library in 1945. This library, a collection of 16mm and 35mm battle films culled from various governmental, military, and international sources, loaned its films to studios to aid them in checking the accuracy of their war presentations. If the studios desired actual footage for their projects, they had to contact the military unit that had initially produced it in order to obtain rights. This collection of combat footage functioned as a touchstone for this new standard of realism (1).

While many Hollywood features during the war were shot on destroyers or in military camps in cooperation with the government, the most convincing evidence of this 16mm induced realistic surge into Hollywood films seems on the surface the most trivial: the shaking camera in studio shots. *Air Force* (1943, directed by Howard Hawks) stands as but one example of a film produced by Hollywood that exhibits this technique to create a more intimate and sensory viewing experience by the spectator. Virtually all the interior scenes inside the plane in this film, shot by James Wong Howe, demonstrate this shifting of the camera to simulate the bumpiness inside a B-17 bomber. When antiaircraft flak escalates, so do the slight camera rattles. This "realistic" technique exhibits how 16mm amateur technology and war contingency shooting moved into dominant Hollywood films. Rather than advancing the narrative, these movements induced the emotional side of cinematography through audience participation, according to Howe:

---

[12] For a discussion of the work of the Society of Motion Picture Engineers War Standards Committee (see 39, 40, 80).

For only one example: in some of the most spectacular explosion shots, say, in bombed ships at sea (in *Air Force*), I directed an operator to shake his camera as if from concussion, let the actors blur out of focus, and tip the camera sharply as the decks tipped high in the air. *This gave the audience a sense of real participation—an effect, difficult, even impossible to get with a big camera.* (my emphasis, 38, p. 32)

Postwar Hollywood film transposed the empirical link between camera and subject established in and on the battlefields of World War II with 16mm equipment into the creation of a participatory connection between spectators and the narrative, whose professional means of production remained even more naturalized, more invisible, and therefore more inaccessible to the amateur.

While the standardization of 16mm as a gauge for public exhibition would eventually allow independent filmmakers in the 1950s limited access to art house distribution, Hollywood's control over these new, hand-held, aesthetic codes of realism cornered a technique that was within the resources of the amateur by positioning it as advanced, complicated, technical simulations.

Major transformations in the actual use of 16mm were located in its military use during World War II. With camera designs fairly standardized and very flexible for war use, their employment for combat cinematography broke with the norms of aesthetic, narrative control through an augmentation of their capacity for scientific, recording functions. This utilization created a standard of audience participation reserved for professionals. Although the war propelled the further standardization of 16mm as a medium for public exhibition, in actuality it merely translated these innovations into more diffuse and inaccessible professional standards.

World War II increased the fluidity between amateurs and professionals through its dependence on hand-held combat cinematography, but this coordination was controlled by the Army Signal Corps and by Hollywood. After the war, 16mm was positioned as a more standard professional medium with increased possibilities for public exhibition, particularly for educational and training purposes, but these were quickly dominated by industry, advertising, and Hollywood. While the hand-held spontaneous shooting style of combat cinematography instigated a new standard of realism shot by a one-person crew, Hollywood co-opted it as yet another demonstration of its technical prowess and cultural power.

REFERENCES

1. "Academy War Film Library." *American Cinematographer*, April 1945, p. 46.
2. "Aerial Photography First Step to Battle." *American Cinematographer*, December 1943, p. 435.
3. Agee, J. "Films." *Nation* 160, March 24, 1945, p. 342.
4. Agee, J. "Films." *Nation* 158, June 24, 1944, p. 743.
5. "Area Pricing Plan Initiated by GPA." *New York Times*, December 16, 1942, p. 33.

6. Arling, Lt. A., U.S.N.R., A.S.C. "Cameramen in Uniform." *American Cinematographer*, October 1943, p. 363.
7. "A.S.C. and the Academy to Train Cameramen for Army Service." *American Cinematographer*, June 1942, p. 255.
8. "A.S.C. on Parade." *American Cinematographer*, July 1942, p. 306.
9. Barnouw, E. *Documentary: A History of the Non-Fiction Film*. London: Oxford University Press, 1974, p. 155.
10. Barsam, R. M. *Non-Fiction: A Critical History*. New York: E. P. Dutton, 1973, p. 180–181.
11. Blaisdell, G. "Documentary No. 1." *American Cinematographer*, August 1939, p. 342.
12. Boon, J. L. "Some Unusual Adaptions of 16mm Equipment for Special Purposes." *Journal of the Society of Motion Picture Engineers*, October 1938, p. 386–392.
13. Bosco, W. G. C. "Amateur Movies and War Effort." *American Cinematographer*, February 1943, p. 62, 68.
14. Bradley, J. G. "Motion Pictures and the War Effort." *Journal of the Society of Motion Picture Engineers*, May 1943, p. 281–290.
15. Carr, L. "Motion Picture in Service of Army Air Forces." *Journal of the Society of Motion Picture Engineers*, October 1943, p. 329–331.
16. Cine Kodak Advertisement. *Movie Makers* 18(7), July 1943, p. 260–261.
17. Devinna, C. "Field Hints for Military Cinematographers." *American Cinematographer*, May 1942, p. 198.
18. "Eastman Kodak Rations Film Supplies for Public." *New York Times*, October 19, 1942, p. 27.
19. Eraser, C. E. "Motion Pictures in United States Navy." *Journal of the Society of Motion Picture Engineers*, December 1932, p. 546–552.
20. Exton, W. "Navy's Use of Motion Picture Films for Training Purposes." *Journal of the Society of Motion Picture Engineers*, June 1942, p. 504.
21. Exton, W. "Development in Use of Motion Pictures by Navy." *Journal of the Society of Motion Picture Engineers*, August 1943, p. 141–145.
22. "Fashions of Films May WPB Poser." *New York Times*, December 6, 1942, p. 7.
23. Fernstrom, R., A.S.C. "Solving Army Photo Problems." *American Cinematographer*, December 1944, p. 406.
24. "Film Conservation: An Editorial." *Movie Makers* 17(11), November 1942, p. 443.
25. Fosholdt, L. "Diary of a Defense Film." *American Cinematographer*, April 1942, p. 162, 176.
26. "Freezes Movie Film to Assure War Needs." *New York Times*, August 20, 1942, p. 34.
27. Gayhardt, E. L. "Mode/Basin High Speed Camera for Propellor Research." *American Society of Naval Engineers* 49(2), May 1937, p. 174–183.
28. Goodman, E. "Post War Motion Pictures." *American Cinematographer*, May 1943, p. 160, 176.
29. Gouldner, O. "Problems in Production of U.S. Navy Training Films." *Journal of the Society of Motion Picture Engineers*, August 1943, p. 146–156.
30. Grierson, J. "Documentary Films in War Time.' *American Cinematographer*, March 1942, p. 10.
31. Hall, H. "Fighting with Film." *American Cinematographer*, September 1943, p. 324.
32. Haskin, B. "Miniatures for 16mm Defense Films."*American Cinematographer*, March 1942, p. 116–117, 145.
33. Haythorne, R., A.S.C. "The Air Corps' Newest Camera Gun." *American Cinematographer*, January 1942, p. 11.
34. Hazzlewood, K. O. "Shooting Action Movies from a Gunstock Mount." *American Cinematographer*, October 1942, p. 444.
35. Heron, F. "U.S. Naval Photographic Services Depot." *Journal of the Society of Motion Picture Engineers*, October 1945, p. 294–296.

36. Historical File on Bell and Howell Equipment Advertisements (1940–1945), Bell and Howell Corporate Archive, Chicago, IL.
37. Horn, F. W. "Military Training and Historical Films." *Journal of the Society of Motion Picture Engineers*, October 1933, p. 337–342.
38. Howe, J. W., A.S.C. "The Documentary Technique and Hollywood." *American Cinematographer*, September 1944, p. 10, 32.
39. Hundman, D. E. "War Standards for Motion Picture Equipment and Processes." *Journal of the Society of Motion Picture Engineers*, April 1944, p. 211–229.
40. Hyndham, P. "Report of Engineering V.P. on Standardization." *Journal of the Society of Motion Picture Engineers*, July 1944, p. 1–4.
41. Isaacs, H. R. "War Fronts and Film Fronts." *Theatre Arts*, June 28, 1944, p. 343–349.
42. Ivens, J. "Making Documentary Films to Meet Today's Need." *American Cinematographer*, July 1942, p. 298–299.
43. Jester, R. "Operation of Army Air Force Combat Units in Theatres of War." *Journal of the Society of Motion Picture Engineers*, August 1943, p. 136–140.
44. "John Grierson: Maker of Documentary." *American Cinematographer*, October 1939, p. 442.
45. Jones, D. B. "Hollywood Goes to War." *Nation* 160, January 27, 1945, p. 93–95.
46. Knechter, L. W., A.S.C. "Photographing the Underwater Atomic Bomb Text at Bikini." *American Cinematographer*, September 1946, p. 315.
47. Konikow, R. B. "Motion Pictures in the Army." *American Cinematographer*, February 1942, p. 59, 84.
48. "Leica Gets Away from Tripod by Employing Gunstock for Platform." *American Cinematographer*, March 1938, p. 117.
49. Look. (Ed.). *Movie Lot to Beachhead: The Motion Picture Goes to War and Prepares for the Future*. Garden City, NJ: Double Day, Doran and Company, 1945.
50. Manning, Maj. C. K. "Fighters With Film." *American Photographer* 37, August 1943, p. 20–21.
51. "Marines Learn Photography in Hollywood." *American Cinematographer*, October 1943, p. 364.
52. McGee, W. R. "Cinematography Goes to War." *Journal of the Society of Motion Picture Engineers*, February 1944, p. 104.
53. "Movie Savings Reported." *New York Times*, June 24, 1942, p. 24.
54. Nadell, A. "16mm vs. 35mm Projection in Army Training Camps." *International Projectionist*, June 1943, p. 7–8, 18–19.
55. Nelson, W. M. "Washington Film News." *Movie Makers* 18(5), May 1943, p. 164.
56. Nelson, W. M. "Washington Film News." *Movie Makers* 18(1), January 1943, p. 23.
57. Nelson, W. M. "Washington Film News." *Movie Makers* 18(6), June 1943, p. 204.
58. Nelson, W. M. "Washington Film News: Film Shortage." *Movie Makers* 20(2), February 1945, p. 46.
59. Newhard, G. G. "Motion Picture Camera in Army Air Forces." *Journal of the Society of Motion Picture Engineers*, June 1942, p. 510.
60. Pryer, C., A.S.C. "Movies Report on Defense Programs." *American Cinematographer*, August 1943, p. 445.
61. Pryor, T. M. "Random Notes on the Film Scene." *New York Times*, December 20, 1942, VIII, p. 3.
62. Sebring, L. B. "The Marines Record Their Fights." *Movie Makers* 19(4), April 1944, p. 141, 169.
63. Sherlock, J. A. "Documentary for the Amateur." *American Cinematographer*, September 1939, p. 414.
64. Shustack, E. H. "Documentary Film in America." *American Cinematographer*, March 1939, p. 130.
65. "Spotting by Film." *Aeroplane* 25, October 1940, p. 460–461.

66. Staley, B. "Documentary Film Patterned from Prizewinners." *American Cinematographer*, February 1937, p. 69.
67. Stott, W. "Amateur Movie Gadget Contributes to War Effort." *American Cinematographer*, April 1942, p. 142.
68. Stott, W. *Documentary Expression and Thirties America*. London: Oxford University Press, 1973.
69. Stull, W., A.S.C. "Amateurs Make Defense Films." *American Cinematographer*, February 1942, p. 68.
70. Stull, W., A.S.C. "The First Real Combat Camera." *American Cinematographer*, November 1942, p. 474.
71. Terret, D. *United States Army in World War II, The Technical Services, The Signal Corps: The Emergency (to December 1941)*. Washington, DC: Office of the Chief of Military History, Department of the Army, 1956, p. 224–230.
72. "The First Call." *Movie Makers 17*(4), April 1942, p. 143.
73. Thompson, G. R. and Harris, D. R. *United States Army in World War II, The Technical Services, The Signal Corps: The Outcome (Mid-1943 through 1945)*. Washington, DC: Office of the Chief of Military History, United States Army, 1966, p. 565–569, 569–572.
74. Thompson, G. R., Harris, D. R., Oakes, P. M., and Terret, D. *United States Army in World War II, The Technical Services, The Signal Corps: The Test (December 1941 to July 1943)*. Washington, DC: Office of the Chief of Military History, Department of the Army, 1957, p. 104, 394–396, 401–411.
75. "Training Apparatus for Air Gunners." *Engineering 158*(4112), November 3, 1944, p. 347.
76. "Uncle Sam's Cameramen are Coming." *American Cinematographer*, September 1942, p. 418.
77. "Urgent: Where Have You Filmed." *Movie Makers 17*(4), April 1942, p. 150.
78. "U.S. to Buy Movie Projectors." *New York Times*, March 11, 1942, p. 2.
79. Warrenton, Maj. G., A.S.C., U.S.A.A.F. "Greatest Photographic Organization in History Shot Bikini Blast." *American Cinematographer*, October 1946, p. 352.
80. Whittenton, J. M. "Report of Subcommittee G on Exposure Meters." *Journal of the Society of Motion Picture Engineers*, July 1944, p. 250–259.
81. "WPB Limits Movies on Amount of Film." *New York Times*, September 18, 1942, p. 26.

Author Index

Subject Index

Lightning Source UK Ltd.
Milton Keynes UK
UKOW06n2237291015

261681UK00001B/13/P

9 780893 915520